Better regulation in the European Union:
Lost in Translation or Full Steam Ahead?

The transposition of EU transport directives across member states

Leiden University Press

The dissertation was made possible by the financial support of the Netherlands Organization for Scientific Research under grant NWO-403-01-505.

Editing: Ann and Maureen Weller, Chicago
Lay-out: AlphaZet prepress, Waddinxveen

Leiden University Press is an imprint of Amsterdam University Press

ISBN 978 90 8728 026 0

Better regulation in the European Union: Lost in Translation or Full Steam Ahead?

The transposition of EU transport directives across member states

PROEFSCHRIFT

ter verkrijging van
de graad van Doctor aan de Universiteit Leiden,
op gezag van de Rector Magnificus, prof. dr. P.F. van der Heijden,
volgens besluit van het College voor Promoties
te verdedigen op donderdag 25 oktober 2007
klokke 15 uur

door

Michael Kaeding

geboren te Wuppertal (Duitsland) in 1977

Promotiecommissie:

Promotor:	Prof. Dr. Bernard Steunenberg
Referent:	Dr. Fabio Franchino (University College London)
Overige leden:	Prof. Dr. Adrienne Héritier (European University Institute)
	Prof. Dr. David Lowery
	Prof. Dr. B. Frans van Waarden (Universiteit Utrecht)
	Dr. Antoaneta Dimitrova

Preface

This Ph.D. research was a privileged time of learning due to many circumstances. First, I would like to thank the *Fachbereich der Politik- und Verwaltungswissenschaften* of the University of Konstanz for its excellent preparatory academic formation; the Department of Public Administration of Leiden University for its generously admitted academic freedom and its first-class research facilities; and colleagues for their support, their interest shown in my research and their constructive criticism. My special thanks here go to Frank Häge, Dimiter Toshkov, Caspar v. d. Berg, Mark Rhinard, Andreas Mom, Ingo Rohlfing, Karen Anderson, Coen van der Giessen, Martijn Groenleer, Rutger Hagen, Markus Haverland, Sanneke Kuipers, Michael Lewis-Beck, Brooke Luetgert, Ellen Mastenbroek, Alexandro Martínez-Godin, Wim van Noort, Fred Pampel, Gerald Schneider, Torsten Selck, Semin Suvarierol and Amy Verdun.

Furthermore, I am thankful to the Centre for European Policy Studies (CEPS) team and the Transport Unit at the General Secretariat of the Council of the European Union, with special attention to Louise van Schaik, Christian Egenhofer, Elisabeth Alteköster, Aris Tekelenburg, Nicholas Platten, Peter Asanger and Luc Lapère. In addition, I enjoyed the four-year company of the research group associated with the 'Analyzing EU Policies: The Transposition of Directives' program. Obviously, I owe a huge debt of gratitude to all of the European and national administrators, politicians and their assistants who took time to answer all my questions about the perfidies of EU legislation and national domestic arenas from the very first moment.

From a logistical point of view, I would like to mention Ann and Maureen Weller who edited the entire manuscript skillfully and creatively. Financial assistance is gratefully acknowledged from a number of institutions: the Netherlands Organization for Scientific Research (NWO), the Leiden University Fund (LUF), the Netherlands Institute for Government (NIG), the Meijers Instituut of Leiden University, the European Consortium for Political Research (ECPR), the University Association for Contemporary European Studies (UACES), the European Union Studies Association (EUSA), the French-German Talks in Law and Economics, the LSE Hellenic Observatory PhD Symposia, the European Research Colloquium of the Netherlands Institute of Government and CONNEX, the UVic EU Initiative at the University of Victoria, the Dutch Political Science Association (NKWP), the Dutch Ministry of Justice, the UK Department of International Development (DFID) and the European Commission.

Last but not least, I would like to thank my family, partner and close friends who have always supported me in every way possible. I dedicate this book to my grandmother.

Danke, bedankt, grazie, thanks, mersi and *merci*.
These have been the best years of my life so far.

Contents in brief

Contents in detail

List of figures:

List of tables:

List of abbreviations:

Acquis	*Acquis communautaire*
ADIF	*Administrador de Infraestructuras Ferroviarias*
AIS	Automatic Vessel Identification System
AU	Austria
BE	Belgium
BIC	Bayesian Information Criterion
BOE	*Boletín Oficial del Estado*
BV	*Bureau Veritas*
CARE	Community database on road accidents
CCAA	Communidades Autónomas
Celex	*Communitatis Europeae Lex*
Commission	European Commission
COSS	Committee on Safe Seas and the Prevention of Pollution from Ships
Court	European Court of Justice
CP	Comparative politics
CTP	Common transport policy
DDAC	Omnibus bill (*Diverses dispositions d'adaptation au droit communautaire*)
DE	Germany
DK	Denmark
DM	Deutsche Mark
EC	European Communities
EEC	European Economic Community
ECAC	Eurocontrol Organization
ECJ	European Court of Justice
EdF	*Electricité de France*
EDI	Electronic Data Interchanges
EFTA	European Free Trade Agreement
EL	Greece
ELDR	European Liberal Democrat Reform
EP	European Parliament
ES	Spain
EU	European Union
EUR	Euro
Eurlex	The portal to European Union law
FR	France
FI	Finland
FS/QCA	Fuzzy Set/ Qualitative Comparative Analysis
FT	Financial Times
GdF	*Gaz de France*
GDP	Gross Domestic Product
ICAO	International Civil Aviation Organization

ICE	InterCityExpress
IE	Ireland
IMF	International Monetary Fund
IMO	International Maritime Organization
INF	International code for the Safe Carriage of packaged irradiated nuclear fuel, plutonium and high-level radioactive wastes on board ships
IPX	Interview partner X
IT	Italy
LU	Luxembourg
MARPOL	International Convention for the Prevention of Pollution from Ships
MED	Marine Equipment Directive
MEP	Member of European Parliament
NL	The Netherlands
n.r.	No reference
OMC	Open method of coordination
PCF	*Parti communiste français*
Prelex	Monitoring of the decision-making process between institutions
PS	*Parti socialiste*
PSE	*Parti socialiste européen*
PSOE	*Partido sociolista obrero espanol*
PT	Portugal
QMV	Qualified majority voting
Radicals	European Radical Alliance
RAM	Radioactive materials
RENFE	*Red Nacional de los Ferrocarriles Espanoles*
RIS	River Information Systems
SE	Sweden
SEA	Single European Act
SEMAF	*Sindicado de Maquinistas y Ayudantes Ferroviarios*
SGCI	*Secrétariat Général du Comité Interministériel pour les questions de coopération économique européenne*
SGG	*Secrétariat Général du Gouvernement*
SOLAS	International Convention for the Safety of Life at Sea
SQ	Status quo
STCW	International Convention on Standard of Training, Certiciation and Watchkeeping
TEU	Treaty on European Union ('Maastricht Treaty')
TERFN	Trans-European Rail Freight Network
UJT	Transistors Uniunión
UK	United Kingdom
UMP	Union for a Popular Movement
UNECE	United National Economic Committee for Europe
UV	Unanimity voting
VDR	Voyage Data Recorder

Part I

Introduction and background

Chapter 1: Introduction

'What's the point of having new legislation if it remains dead in the water?' Frits Bolkestein, April 2003, Internal Market Commissioner.

The European Union (EU) consists of member states. Over the last 50 years it has developed a complex and highly developed system of law that directly influences the legal systems of its member states (Snyder, 1993). There are three types of EU law. Primary law includes treaties. Secondary law includes interinstitutional agreements, such as regulations, directives, decisions, recommendations, and opinions. Tertiary law includes the decisions of the European Court of Justice (ECJ). These three types of EU law, otherwise known, cumulatively, as the *acquis communautaire* represent the full set of distributive, constituent and regulatory European policies.

Each of these policies has a 'life cycle'. The EU policy cycle is composed of three phases (Zeff and Pirro, 2001), namely: development, decision-making, and implementation. In the policy development phase, the European Commission discusses, develops, and compiles new programs; it also drafts legislation, and, finally delivers a proposal to the decision-making bodies. These bodies are the Council of Ministers (Council) and the European Parliament (EP). In the decision-making phase, the Council and the EP co-decide in most policy fields that fall under the Community method (Hix, 2005). The third phase, implementation, is defined as 'the process by which national law is modified in accordance with Community law' (Eijlander and Voermans, 2000: 257). Member states involved in making EU legislation must implement Community legislation that induces policy change including the legal transposition, application and evaluation process (Prechal, 1995: 5-6; Kassim, Peters and Wright, 2000: 15; Dimitrakopoulos, 2005).

The first step, transposition, is defined as the process whereby European directives are incorporated into national law in order to make their objectives, requirements, and deadlines applicable in the member states. Application is defined as the process whereby full compliance with EU law is monitored and secured, and the effect posterior evaluated; in this step, non-compliance is systematically evaluated by national and supranational courts. Figure 1.1 presents the different stages and sub-stages of the EU policy-cycle.

As displayed in Figure 1.1, 'adapting and implementing legal rules are two of the most important mechanisms through which European integration influences member states' (Sverdrup, 2005: 6). Transposition, in particular, is the first step in the implementation phase because it is here that 'the goals and the objectives of the EU result or fail to result in real change for European states'

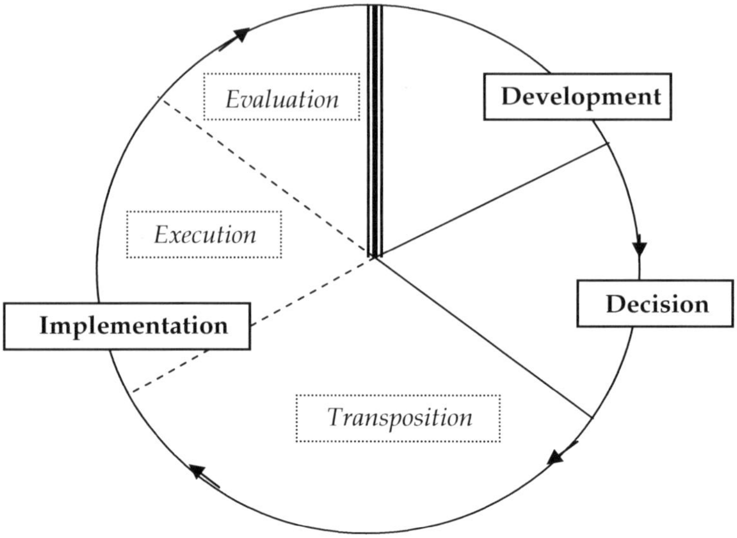

Figure 1.1: European policy cycle: Three policy phases – development, decision and implementation.

(Zeff and Pirro, 2001: 16-19). More general, a swift coordination of the transposition process across member states appears to be a necessary condition for the functioning of the EU policy-cycle and especially of the internal market. Note, however, that transposition does not apply to the actual working practices, but only represent a change in formal law inducing policy change.

Implementation of European law – positive and negative legal obligation for full compliance:
Member states are obliged to comply with EC law, as dictated by Article 10 (formerly Article 5). In the spirit of this article, states must adopt necessary legislative and regulatory measures, apply or execute them, and supervise and enforce their proper application in their respective territories. Article 10 imposes the mandatory duties on member states, which have, however, some discretion in the carrying out of such actions. Failure to fulfill the duties of Article 10 can lead to infringement proceedings under Article 226 (formerly Article 169). Article 10 (2) also includes prohibitions for member states, who must to refrain from keeping or introducing any measure that might render ineffective the application of Community legislation. The ECJ has confirmed in numerous decisions that both the obligations and the prohibitions stated in Article 10 apply to all the authorities of member states, including the national courts for matters within their jurisdiction (de Búrca, 1992; Plata Martin, 1994). The European Commission's (Commission) primary role is to propose and monitor the implementation of EU legislation. It also acts as 'guardian of the treaties', taking responsibility for initiating infringement proceedings at the ECJ against non-compliant member states, i.e. when national legislation breaches EU law.

1.1 Two big pieces of a puzzle

As a matter of fact, EU member states breach EU law – perpetuately. For 2005, the Commission's scoreboard recorded a 1.3 percent deficit (European Commission, 2006). The question, however, is whether this is a self-defeating figure. Should we bother? Why would the EU bother in the first place?

Indeed, this record appears vanishing small – at first sight. A closer look at the figures and the so-called fragmentation factor indicate, however, that the presence of an EU implementation problem seems clear and worth the research– the forest just in front. On the other hand, scholars have responded to the challenges of European law; have developed unique concepts and approaches in their studies of the EU. But despite the fact that the translation of EU legislation into national law has been a burgeoning area of interest over the last years there is still plenty of room for improvement. A closer look at the paperwork, hence, unveils mainly two puzzling elements of empirical and theoretical natures. While the recorded implementation deficit across EU member states becomes even more troublesome when contextually assessing it in more detail, it is the dissatisfactory state-of-art of the implementation literature that puzzles the interested scholar.

1.1.1 *The empirical puzzle: 'Cannot see the forest for the numbers'*

Since 1989, the Commission as EU's supervisor of policy implementation has regularly published figures and tables, so-called scoreboards, to point to member states that do not comply with Article 10, or to find benevolent rhetoric for those that do. These scoreboards, by both name and content, call to mind sport events rather than EU politics. Yet they have displayed recent figures that tell of the awe-inspiring and steady improvement of member state's implementation records. Figure 1.2 presents aggregate data from 1989 to 2005, and shows that the average implementation rate has not only tremendously increased, but that 'laggards' including Greece and Italy, have caught up in implementing EU legislation. Differences between the best and the worst performing member states have decreased over the years from 25 percent to around 3 percent.[1]

In 2005, the average transposition rate of internal market directives reached 98.7 percent, showing that the share of implemented directives is at a comforting high. At first sight, the trend over the last 16 years is good news, and the 1.3 per cent deficit appears vanishingly small.

---

1 Note that the slump in 1995 is due to the enlargement with Austria, Finland, and Sweden.

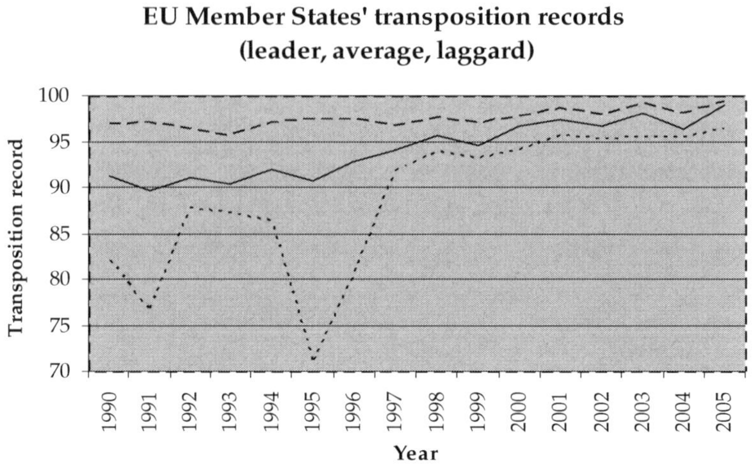

The dashed line displays the best record, the middle line the average record of all member states, and the dotted line the worst performing member state record. Source: Information gathered from all Commission Internal market scoreboards published from 1989 to 2005.

Figure 1.2: Member States' transposition record (1989 –2005).

At second sight, however, one begins 'to discern the trees'. Figure 1.2 reveals some interesting findings and irregularities about the 2005 implementation figures. Accounting for the legal obligations in numbers and performances, it displays the results for the total number of directives in each member state of the EU 25.

First, the Commission's figures are based on the total amount of directives that have accrued over the last 50 years, which forms a rather conservative measure for the actual implementation performance across member states (Börzel, 2001; Mastenbroek, 2003). To put it differently, the enumerator varies little year by year. But the denominator increases steadily, which makes a deficit of 30 directives in 2005 with a denominator of 2570 (1.2 per cent) appear very small compared to the same amount of directives still requiring notification in early 1980s, with an average number of directives to be transposed of 1280 (2.3 per cent). Although the actual deficit of 30 non-implemented directives remains constant, the denominator has *doubled* since the early 1980s, which decreases the percentage for non-implemented legislation by 100 per cent.

Table 1.1, furthermore, shows that an EU-wide implementation backlog of 1.3 per cent means that, in 2005, each member state, on average, had 34 directives left to be implemented. Actually, this is a considerable number in a union where on average only 100 directives are adopted each year.[2]

2 Number of adopted directives in 2000 (78), 2001 (104), 2002 (96), 2003 (122), 2004 (123), 2005 (90) (Eurlex).

Table 1.1: Transposition of EU directives in the member states on 18 July 2005.

	Total number of directives	Delayed transposition	Percentage of non-transposed directives
Lithuania	2601	4	0.15
Poland	2577	13	0.50
Denmark	2549	13	0.51
Finland	2548	18	0.71
Spain	2570	20	0.78
Germany	2553	20	0.78
Slovenia	2585	21	0.81
Hungary	2579	22	0.85
Malta	2582	25	0.97
Austria	2556	26	1.02
United Kingdom	2547	28	1.10
Netherlands	2552	29	1.14
Belgium	2607	30	1.15
France	2552	30	1.18
Ireland	2565	31	1.21
Estonia	2561	35	1.37
Cyprus	2582	37	1.43
Latvia	2602	39	1.50
Sweden	2535	39	1.54
Czech Republic	2584	40	1.55
Slovakia	2594	48	1.85
Portugal	2592	56	2.16
Greece	2556	67	2.62
Luxembourg	2557	70	2.74
Italy	2561	80	3.12
EU 25 average	*2570*	*34*	*1.31*

Source: European Commission 2005 (Asmodee II)

At last, the total number of directives to be transposed (denominator) varies across member states, namely between 2547 in the United Kingdom and 2607 in Belgium – a difference of precisely 60 directives, which may have a warping effect on the results. In addition, table 1.1 shows that the numbers of delayed notification differ respectively, namely between 4 in Lithuania and 80 in Italy, which compounds the distorting effects of this scoreboard. It appears that with every closer look, the data tell a very different story than that of ultimate success. Do we begin 'to see the forest for the trees'? Are the original appearances, then, deceiving?

Fragmentation factor – Nine per cent deficit in the EU or 772 notifications awaiting
A final look at EU data, however, may even exceed our earlier concern about an implementation deficit in the EU. Next to the chronological overview of the Commission scoreboards, and the recent figures for 2005, the so-called 'fragmentation factor' (European Commission, 2006: 15) has found its way to the implementation debate. It exemplifies the percentage of the overall outstanding directives that have not been implemented in at least one member state.

The fragmentation level for 2006 is 9 percent. This means that 9 percent of the internal market directives have not achieved their full effect. In absolute terms, this means that 144 Internal Market directives were not implemented in at least one member state. In 2006, hence, the Commission was still waiting for 772 notifications of national transposition measures. This fact is quite a bit more worrying than the 1.3 figure of success referred to in the scoreboards. The presence of an EU implementation problem seems clear – the forest directly in front of us. The problem has been noted by a considerable number of scholars in the field (Curtin, 1990; Mendriou, 1996; Sverdrup, 2004; Versluis, 2004; Börzel, Hoffmann and Dudziak, 2005; König, Luetgert and Mäder, 2005; Falkner, Hartlapp, Leiber and Treib, 2005; Steunenberg and Rhinard, 2005; Borghetto, Franchino and Giannetti, 2006; Giuliani, 2006), seems clear – the forest just in front of us.

Image marring and costly

Regardless of which statistics the Commission goes by, the member states' non-compliant behaviour is punished. Every year the Commission initiates hundreds of infringement proceedings against member states before the ECJ in an effort to induce them to comply with their legal obligations, which, in the end, may become both image damaging and pricy for the denunciated.

Some member states have proclaimed to take implementation very seriously, because poor performance in this stage can stain one's image. For example, French Prime Minister Raffarin (2004) declared implementation to be high on the political agenda, and set out to take care of France's backlog, so as not to loose face in Europe. Nonetheless, despite such efforts by some member states, the latest available annual report of the ECJ (2004) tells that the Commission initiated 193 proceedings against member states. During the same year, Nicolaides and Oberg (2006) report that the ECJ found in 144 out of 155 cases that a member state had failed to fulfil its obligations. This means that in more than 90% of cases the Commission was right to take action against one or more member states. Failing to fulfil obligations, however, does not necessarily indicate that states are guilty of non-compliance with EU legislation. Few of those infringement proceedings culminated in an ECJ judgment, against a member state, of 'guilty.' But, fines will be imposed as a punishment for failure to fulfil obligations. The amount owed by member states in fines, in the meantime, has reached astronomical dimensions. It seems unlikely that most member states will be able to pay up in times of constraint budgets. Yet the Commission just recently announced an even tougher policy on the determination of fines for non-compliance.[3]

3 The ECJ has imposed fines on Greece, Spain, and France. In 2000, Greece became the first member state to adjudged a daily fine of 20,000 EUR. It took Greece six months to comply and ended up paying a total of 4.7 million EUR. In November 2003, Spain became the first member state to be fined twice for the same infringement. Its penalty was modest, only 625,000 EUR per year (Nicolaides and Oberg, 2006). In July 2005, France harvested the largest penalty in EU history, which was both a lump-sum of 20 million EUR and an additional biannual sum of 57.7 million EUR if it continued to ignore EU legislation relating to fishing - amounting to a daily fine of 321,000 EUR.

Legal uncertainty
Non-compliant behaviour implies legal uncertainty; this hampers the European regulatory framework in which businesses operate. Late and incorrect transposition can have reverberating effects on the EU legal *zeitgeist*. It frustrates further European integration, including the free movement of goods, persons, services and capital (Article 3(1)c). It jeopardizes market competitiveness, national growth, and employment performances in Europe and beyond.

To understand the importance of legal certainty, consider the case of France's dealings with Directive 96/92/EC. In December, 1996, the energy ministers of the 15 member states adopted the directive, which concerns common rules for the internal market in electricity. However, France caused major irritations among its neighbouring countries. The French were heavily criticized for being very slow in opening their natural gas and power markets to competition. In December 2000, almost two years after the first transposition deadline, France passed legislation to only *begin* the electricity sector's liberalization. The last transposing measure was adopted in February 2003. In total, it took France six years (four years after the deadline) to adopt the European directive on natural gas deregulation into French law.

These four years transposition delay has injured the internal market, in general, and the common electricity market, in particular. Critics claim that, in the meantime, France has benefited from European privatizations while keeping a protected share of its home market. *Electricité de France* (EdF), the French utility manager, in particular, has used the proceeds from its unchallenged market position in France to buy major assets across Europe.[4] This behaviour has sparked hostility among member states, and in the Commission, too. The Commission ruled, lately that EdF had been charged unjustifiably low corporate income taxes, therefore EdF had an unfair competitive edge in the European energy market. EdF was condemned to repay a record sum of 889 million euros (Sprongenberg, 2006), plus interest.

Renewed Lisbon strategy 2005: Better regulation for competitiveness, growth and employment
Finally, non-compliant behaviour impairs day-to-day operations of the internal market which precludes the successful achievement of the so-called Lisbon strategy and of which the EU and member states plead guilty. On the European level, after successive summits (Lisbon, March 2000); Stockholm, March 2001: Gothenburg, June 2001; Laeken, December 2001; and Barcelona,

4 EdF acquired major stakes in Germany's EnBW, (*Energie Baden-Württemberg*), in Spain's Hidrocantabrico, in Italy's Edison, and in a number of eastern European companies. It also owns the UK's London Electricity Group, and other partnerships or acquisitions are currently being explored. Similarly, in 2001, *Gaz de France's* (GdF) gas foreign sales rose 43 percent. More recently, GdF has bought a 24.5 percent stake in the Slovak company SPP for 1.4 billion euros and German assets of *Preussag Energie*, a subsidiary of the TUI group, for 859 million euros.

March 2002) and the devastating mid-term evaluation of the Lisbon strategy by the Kok report (2004), the Commission laid down an improved strategy, entitled *Better regulation for Growth and Jobs in the European Union.* One key objective of the renewed Lisbon Strategy, launched in 2005, is to focus exclusively on ensuring a simple and high quality regulatory environment, which is subsumed under the buzz word: *better regulation* (Radaelli, 2007).[5] Simplification within EU competitiveness policy entails legislation (Barrosso, 2006) which carefully strikes the right balance between the cost and benefits of legislation. Since effective, timely transposition of internal market legislation affects the costs and benefits of the new policy, timely and correct transposition is the *first action point* falling under the Lisbon action plan (European Commission, 2005) adopted by the member states in February 2005. In line with Allio and Fandel (2006:7), I argue that better regulation cannot be achieved without serious attention to transposition, enforcement and evaluation.

In parallel, on the national level, most of the member states are seriously concerned about the persistent transposition deficit in the European Union, as well as its causes and consequences. This concern makes the transposition issue an interesting field of research. In the UK, the *Bellis report* (2003) lays out guidelines to improve the implementation of EU legislation in the United Kingdom. In Germany, a federal government modernising committee has made a lot of noise in its discussions about reforming German federal constitution; in particular, the committee has been pushing for expedited processes of implementing EC directives. In the Netherlands, in November 2004, the secretary of state of Foreign Affairs and the minister of Justice announced six recommendations on how to improve the speed of transposition on short notice. Even better performing member states, like Sweden, have reconsidered their coordination system (Kaeding, 2007) and moved the EU co-ordination secretariat from the ministry of Foreign Affairs to the Prime Minister's office to better coordinate the policies towards the EU in general and to improve their transposition records in particular.

Obviously, from an empirical point of view, EU implementation is a puzzling phenomenon. On one hand, compliance with EU legislation stands reputedly high on governments' agendas, which alone is crucial for the achievement of the Lisbon goals set for 2010. Furthermore, full implementation of EU legislation is a legal obligation enshrined in the treaties. Nevertheless, on the other hand, it is yet not followed by most member states. Demystifying the Commission's implementation deficit figure of 1.3 per cent, the fragmentation factor uncovers that 9 percent of the internal market directives have not achieved their full affect in 2006, with more than 770 notifications still pending. At the

5 The current EU initiative on 'better regulation' has its origins in the Edinburgh European summit of December 1992. EU heads of state decided to make the task of simplifying and improving the EU regulatory environment one of the Community's main priorities.

same time, the ECJ recently set record fines for non-implementation, penalties that have the damaging effect on a 'laggard's image. 'What's the point of having new legislation if it remains dead in the water?', Why do some member states refuse to comply with EU law, despite the image-marring effect and costly consequences?

1.1.2 *The theoretical puzzle: 'Plenty of room for improvement'*

Interestingly, in EU studies, each component of the policy cycle has garnered different degrees of attention. For a long time, studies about European integration focused mainly on the coming about of European integration (Haas, 1958; Spinelli, 1972; Mitrany, 1966; Moravcsik, 1991; Sandholtz and Stone Sweet, 1997).[6] In the mid-1990s, there was an upsurge in Europeanization studies dealing with the effects of European integration on the member states in general (for an overview see Olsen, 2002; Featherstone and Radaelli, 2003; Mair, 2004). However, it was not until a few years later that studies on the implementation phase became a burgeoning field of scholarly interest that they are today. Over the last couple of years, the field has grown out of childhood and entered adolescence.

Some puzzling features, however, indicate that additional scholarly efforts in the field are compulsory in order for it to finally reach maturity. Five areas of improvement are eligible. Each will be executed successively here, and in the literature review chapter in more detail. The improvements are: increases in empirical and conceptual strength; a lesson from the 1970s implementation literature; a straightforward combined methodological approach; a contribution to existing cumulative data; a theoretical motivated selection of cases.

Indeed, the first 'two waves' (Mastenbroek, 2005) of the implementation literature were either eclectic in nature or failed to facilitate the ex-post formulation of clear predictions. Only recent efforts of the so-called third wave (ibid) have started to engage in a more analytical research (Haverland, 2000; Héritier, Kerwer, Knill, Lehmkuhl, Teutsch and Dourillet, 2001; Giuliani, 2003; Treib, 2003; Falkner et al., 2005) by bringing in 'political' variables that may capture the overriding power of substantive positions of domestic policy makers. They have set in to leave aside the foremost ad-hoc legal and public administration explanations (Krislov et al., 1986; Siedentopf and Ziller, 1988; Pappas, 1995) and the spurious and deterministic goodness-of-fit argument (Duina, 1997; Börzel, 2003) which have been critically assessed in Mastenbroek and Kaeding (2006).

---

6 For a detailed overview see Rosamond (2000).

When theorizing policy outcomes of the subsequent implementation phase, most existing EU implementation studies give no attention to the adoption phase of the EU policy-cycle. In other words, scholars have not taken on board Pressman and Wildawsky's (1973) notion that 'implementation should be part of design,' suggesting that policy theory is formulated 'with a view toward its execution' (ibid: 189). Since we should consider 'the EU as a laboratory [even] for testing and advancing theories and models of implementation in general' (Sverdrup, 2005: 5), scholars may follow recent efforts (Mastenbroek, 2003; Kaeding, 2006) to include policy design-related and policy implementation-related factors in the theoretical models. Features of the European legislation adopted by the Council of Ministers in the decision-making phase may have considerable influence on the outcome of the subsequent national implementation process, such as national transposing instruments.

In terms of methodology, scholarly work in the field has been dominated by the use of monostrand research designs (Gabel, Hix and Schneider, 2002; Nyikos and Pollack, 2003; Jupille, 2005). The scholarly work on EU implementation has especially been been driven by case study oriented research (Versluis, 2004; Beach, 2005; among others). Some recent contributions have added quantitative research designs (Lampinen and Uusikyla, 1998; Börzel, 2001; Mbaye, 2001; Bursens, 2002; Sverdrup, 2002; Giuliani, 2003; Linos, 2007; Perkins and Neumayer, 2007). Nevertheless, these two methodologically divided groups often stand apart. In line with recent developments in other academic fields (Tashakkori and Teddlie, 2003) the implementation literature may improve its empirical and conceptual strengths using combined approaches. An integrated strategy may improve the prospects of making valid causal inferences in cross-national research by drawing on the distinct strengths of a so-called mixed-method approach. Lieberman's article (2005) in the *American Political Science Review* may prove a helpful guide for carrying out such work.

In addition, more attention should be given to the improvement of the data quality of large-n studies. The limited number of scholars consists of two generations. Whereas the first generation relies exclusively on existing Commission scoreboards and infringement data, the second generation (Mastenbroek, 2003; Steunenberg and Rhinard, 2005; Berglund, Gange and van Waarden, 2006; Haverland and Romeijn, 2007; Kaeding, 2006) has started to improve the data quality by cross-checking; as a result, these studies have and replenished existing EU data with national sources.

Last but not least, implementation research may further profit from selecting untended but theoretically relevant member states and policy areas. Why is it that despite its importance for European integration and its theoretical relevance in terms of its centralist politico-administrative structure in Europe, France is rarely covered in comparative implementation projects? Even smaller member states, such as Austria, Finland, Greece, Luxembourg,

Portugal and Sweden, have not attracted much scholarly attention (Mastenbroek, 2005). An additional look at the policy areas corroborates the selection bias found in the literature. As in the case for EU studies in general and the implementation literature in particular environmental and social policy are clearly the most-researched policy areas (Ostner and Lewis, 1995; Eichener, 1995; Knill and Lenschow, 1998; Haverland, 2000; Falkner et al., 2005; Haverland and Romeijn, 2007). For a better understanding of the EU policy outcomes, and in line with Franchino (2005), scholars may invest more time in older policies that are at the core of the Union and still follow the theoretically relevant regulatory style, such as transport (Alesina, Angeloni and Schuknecht, 2005).

All in all, the EU implementation phenomenon is puzzling in two ways. Although full implementation of EU legislation is a legal obligation enshrined in the treaties, and also a necessary step in meeting the Lisbon goals in 2010, it is yet not followed by most member states. More than 770 notifications still pending and coincide with ever new ECJ record fines. Why do some member states refuse to comply with EU law, despite the image-marring effect in posterior EU negotiations and costly consequences in times of tight budgelines and swooning domestic confidence with the EU (Anderson and Kaeding, 2006)? Even more bewildering, existing EU implementation studies have left the research community with some additional inconsistencies. While a considerable number of studies lack empirical and conceptual strengths and do not draw from earlier findings such as the implementation literature of the 1970s or recent scholarly efforts to improve quantitative data. Moreover, this area of research yet has not attempted combined research designs that draw on the distinct strengths of the important approaches which at present divide the scholarly contributions along the artificial lines of rivalling quantitative and qualitative camps.

1.2 Research question

Until now, this paper applied the terms compliance, implementation and transposition interchangeably. However, in line with Giuliani (2005), I argue that the concept of compliance 'goes well beyond the process of transposition of legal provisions'(ibid: 1).[7] In the remaining chapters, this current study will only refer to transposition as the term action that denotes the 'process of transforming directives into provisions of national law by the competent national legislative body or bodies' (Prechal, 1995: 5).

7 It includes the implicit recognition of firmly-established 'ways of doing things', the observance of loosely-established pacts, rational compliance with self-interested agreements, the observance of appropriate conduct with the EU 'club', the fulfillment of rather severely controlled and sanctioned obligations and duties' (Giuliani, 2005: 1).

Two transposition aspects, according to Articles 10 and 249 EC, are important, namely: timeliness and correctness. First, transposition of EU legislation entails that member states transpose legislation *on time*. Second, member states must adopt national legislation that is in line with the contents of the original EU law. Also, with regard to timely and correct transposition, directives are of particular interest. 'A directive shall be binding, as to the result to be achieved, upon each Member State to which it is addressed, but shall leave to the national authorities the choice of form and methods.' (Article 249 EC). Hence, directives are not directly applicable at the national level, but have to be incorporated into national law first.

This study focuses on the time aspect of national transposition processes of European directives across member states. Posed to unravel the implementation puzzles, the main and subsequent research questions are as follows:

> **Main question:**
> Why do member states miss deadlines when transposing EU internal market directives?
>
> **Subsequent questions:**
> What factors determine delays when transposing EU directives?
> How do these factors influence the timeliness of the national transposition processes?
> Under what conditions are transpositions of directives delayed?

To give a satisfactory answer to the main research question *'Why member states miss deadlines when transposing EU internal market directives'* and its sub-questions, this study opts for a combined research design. To review, the first research sub- question (*'What factors determine delayed national transposition processes?'*) calls for an investigation of the underlying correlations between the dependent and independent variables. The second research sub- question (*'How these determinants influence the timeliness of the national transposition processes?'*) addresses the underlying causal effects. The third research sub- question (*'Under what conditions these national transposition processes are delayed?'*) assesses the relative importance of the causal mechanisms identified by the second research sub- question and lying underneath the correlations specified with the first research sub- question.

1.3 The Theoretical argument

To address the abovementioned research question and in line with some recent burgeoning rationalist explanations for EU policy implementation outcomes (Dimitrova and Steunenberg, 2000; Franchino, 2005; Steunenberg, 2006; 2007) this study presents an actor-centred theoretical framework. The argument will be developed in subsequent chapters, at length, but can be succinctly summarized as follows:

To start, this study argues that a transposition process normally induces policy change at the member state level. Decisions on policy change are, quite often, fundamental bargaining problems about *who* gets *what* and *when*. Drawing from the war of attrition games in economics literature this study refers to the transposition outcome as a bargaining game between groups of actors who must agree, within an allotted timeframe, on a new national policy. National transposition actors, such as administrators and politicians, must, within a set deadline, agree on how to implement the policy in a manner complying with EU law. They are able to weigh every choice against its alternatives and they invariably choose the most preferred option. Assuming that the demands are incompatible, the actors can either reiterate the previous demand and wait for the opponent to lower his demand or actors can change their demand. Waiting (i.e. delaying national transposition processes) can be costly. Who ends the game and when, depends on the player's expected payoff. There exist payoffs to certain actors that choose to wait for a particular waiting time. The expected flows of payoffs to an actor equals to the difference between benefits and costs, while both elements are affected by particular factors. Whereas both include the time component that determines the flow of benefits and costs, respectively, they vary in terms of additional elements: rent proportion, rent-seeking costs and discount factor.

Indulged by the new policy and the total amount of waiting time expected during the encounter, each player must choose a moment of agreement at which he plans to concede in the event that the other payer has not already conceded. The first player to quit the contest cedes the reward to the other side. Increasing the rent proportion decreases the benefits and increases the risk of waiting. Furthermore, it is the rent-seeking costs, i.e. the cost of the battle in the pursuit of these benefits that determine the flow of payoff. Increasing the cost determinant increases the cost-side of the difference and decreases the likelihood of a complicated and time-consuming negotiation process. In addition, increasing an actor's waiting time increases the waiting costs with every additional unit per time. Therefore, payoffs decrease over time. Last but not least, players discount future payoffs. The higher the discount rate (the less players discount future payoffs), future cost/benefit payoffs are perceived as almost similar to the current ones.

In sum, three sets of explanatory factors for the timeliness of national transposition processes that influence the cost/benefit structure of the actors can be identified combining legal, administrative as well as political factors: EU-level, national-level and crises-related multipliers. While the European level indicators are policy-design related, national are policy-implementation related and crises-related factors stand on their own.

Policy-design related:
This study acknowledges that transposition actors cannot modify the policy in ways that are substantially different from the draft adopted by the Council. If already existing national measures lie within the margins of discretion controlled by the Commission, then no new national transposing instrument has to be agreed upon. If the national status quo lies outside the discretionary margins set by the directive, then, new legislation has to be adopted (Steunenberg, 2006). *The higher the amount of discretion, ceteris paribus, the more difficult to settle an agreement on time.*

Furthermore, delays can be minimized if sufficient time is allotted, that is, if the deadline gives member states ample time to act. A comfortable transposition timeframe extends the time-horizon and discounts future payoffs considerably which increases the likelihood of a swift transposition. *The more time a member state has to transpose a directive, ceteris paribus, the swifter the national transposition process.*

In addition, the fixed transposition deadline affects the rent-seeking costs per unit of time which are constant until the deadline. Only with its expiry the potential threat of a likely cumbersome, time-consuming and image damaging infringement procedure becomes real and adds an additional cost function to the payoff equation. Therefore, this study argues that there is a positive, unidirectional probability of a compromise at the transposition deadline- *deadline effect* (Carré, 2000). *Actors come to an agreement around the date of expiry.*

Policy-implementation-related:
Depending on the form of the national implementing instrument, the number of actors varies and affects the timeliness of transposition (Steunenberg and Voermans, 2005). The more actors that are involved, the more difficult it is to coordinate and to reach a settlement of the conflict (Shepsle and Boncheck, 1997). N- games are more complicated to resolve due to problems common to group interaction (Raiffa, Richardson and Metcalfe, 2002). Since delay is costly, this study suggests that countries with a good deal of political fragmentation commonly adopted policy change later (Haverland, 2000; Giuliani, 2003; Steunenberg, 2006). *The fewer actors involved in the making of a legal instrument, ceteris paribus, the less likely a delayed transposition process.*

Member states often use one national transposing measure to transpose a handful of EU directives at the same time, in what is known as a national transposition package approach. Depending on the position of the EU directive within the transposition package, which is determined by the package's size and range of deadlines, the rent-seeking costs may remain low; however, they are raised tremendously after the expiry of the deadline of the first EU directives in the package. Due to actors' cost function, *a national transposition package increases the probability of delayed settlement of the first directive in the national transposition package, whereas, in turn, it accelerates a settlement of the last European directive.*

Depending on its timing, a national general election can have either a retarding or accelerating effect. Its affect hinges on the value of the discount factor of the future. While general elections that fall at the end of a national transposition process increases the costs of waiting dramatically (threat of withdrawal or new introduction due to 'legislative deadline'), the actor discounting future payoffs very marginally. If transposition is not concluded before the start of the next legislative term, a general election will shelf it, along with all other unfinished legislative projects. Hence, all non-adopted legislation in the concluding legislative term would have to be re-introduced in the forthcoming term, which would increase the discount rate unbearably, making transposition before the end of the legislative period more likely. *Whereas a national general election falling at the beginning of the transposition procedure decreases the probability of a problem-free settlement, a general election at the end of a transposition process accelerates the adoption of new national legislation.*

Crisis-related:
Exogenous shocks that aggravate economic conditions increase the cost of not adopting reforms and thus prompt a solution to the bargaining problem (Drazen and Grilli, 1993; Alesina and Drazen, 1991). Analogically, situational changes in member states also affect the progress of transposition. Such changes, for the purposes of this study, include accidents which occur relatively often in the transport sector – the later focus of this study. These accidents add additional costs to the constant rent-seeking costs additional costs, unbalancing the payoff equation and thereby increasing the probability of a fast settlement. *An accident increases the probability of a timely settlement.*

1.4 The research design

In order to answer the main research question and its three subsequent questions and to test the hypotheses derived from the study's theoretical framework, different methods are required. Following Lieberman's systematic guide (2005) for carrying out a combined design, I first test the correlations of explanatory variables with a large-n data set applying an ordered multinomial logistic regression analysis. This large-n analyses will guide case selection and provide direction for more focused case studies and comparisons. Then, four case studies are presented; they corroborate existing findings by the earlier technique, but also, uncover the causal mechanisms that lay beneath the correlations between the timeliness of the national transposition processes and the individual components of the theoretical framework. In particular these case studies are used to generate theoretical insights from off-liner cases. Finally, I end with a concluding test of the hypotheses (that is generated from the large-n and small-n research) by running an intermediate research technique: the fuzzy set technique. Next to its test for generalizability of the case studies' findings, the fuzzy set technique develops better measurement strategies to bring the relative significance of single and combinations of conditions forward.

Generally speaking, this study will show that a 'triangulation' of research techniques can eventually result in a rich and well-rounded understanding of the national transposition processes. Quantitative analysis can offer overall trends in deceptively similar national transposition records that based upon coded national transposition instruments. Qualitative analysis can potentially explain ambivalent statistical results produced by those data. Special attention here is paid to the added value given by the diversity-oriented fuzzy set technique which has not found its way yet in EU studies, in general, or EU implementation, in particular.

More specifically, the population of cases to which the theory is meant to apply are all national transposition instruments. The dependent variable is *timeliness of a national transposition process of a EU directive* operationalized as transposition delay. In order to test the hypotheses, a selection of observations from this population is required. This study, therefore, will focus on the *transport acquis communautaire adopted between 1995 and 2004*. The largely ignored transport sector is selected because it represents, among other things, the predominantly regulatory character of EU policies with a comparatively high number of directives –the focus of this study. Since social science cannot be explained without comparison, this study opted to compare nine member states, namely: *Germany, France, the United Kingdom, Italy, Spain, the Netherlands, Greece, Sweden, and Ireland*. All dimensions of the explanatory variables are covered through these nine states.

Drawing from recent scholarly efforts the collected data on the dependent and independent variables are of second generation. First, I have tried to rely, as far as possible, on what Moravcsik (1998: 80) calls 'hard primary sources', with a strong preference for contemporary official European and national data bases available for citation and replication by other scholars. I supplement and cross-check these official data through additional political data provided by the *European Journal of Political Research* and newspapers. In addition, I carefully used insider publications, such as *Agence Europe*, and conducted interviews with key officials from EU, who are rich sources of behind-the-scenes information about the national transposition processes. Interviews with experts provide the possibility of obtaining the information required for the theoretical framework, and also provide deep and accurate information that cannot be expected from surveys or from data content analysis. The policy experts interviewed were selected according to their knowledge of the EU directives and the national transposition instruments, respectively. Generally, since they were active participants of the negotiation and the national transposition process, they had first-hand knowledge of the situations investigated.

1.5 Outline of the book

The book is divided into four parts. The first part is devoted to acquainting the reader with the several potholes in the existing EU implementation literature, and with the main characteristics of EU transport policy. A look at the inner-workings of the transport sector will support the application of an actor-centred theoretical framework to explain the timeliness of national transposition processes. This framework forms the second part of the study. The third part of the study is devoted to the analysis of the research. Some time will be devoted to present the ways in which one can improve the quality of existing EU data, which then will accurately assess the EU's problematic implementation deficit. What follows is a broad array of quantitative and qualitative evidence aimed at testing the expectations derived in the theoretical chapter, measuring the timeliness of national transposition processes. A large-n analysis is succeeded by four case studies fleshing out existing findings and pinpointing an important missing factor. Then, the fuzzy set technique tests the hypotheses generated from the large-n and small-n research. Furthermore, it develops better measurement strategies to bring the relative significance of single and combinations of conditions forward. The fourth part of this study summarizes the findings and elaborates on their contributions and broader implications.

Part I – Introduction and background:
Chapter two: Literature review
This chapter provides a critical assessment of the existing body of literature that is most relevant to the theoretical, methodological, and empirical focus of this study. It announces major problematic characteristics that plague the literature on EU implementation: *ad-hoc, little explanatory power, deterministic, myopic and biased*. This chapter especially embraces the recent efforts of the so-called 'third wave' implementation studies by researching the role of domestic politics on processes of implementation, in order to generate clearer predictions that can be empirically tested. In the subsequent chapters, this study attempts to add to these recent improvement efforts and to address the theoretical, empirical, and methodological weaknesses of EU implementation studies.

Chapter three: Development of EU transport policy (1957-2006)
This chapter examines the historical development of the EU transport policy field. A look into this field will later inform the theoretical framework by explaining why member states miss the EU directive transposition deadlines. After reviewing the scarce political science literature on EU transport policy, the chapter presents the European institutional setting in terms of transport policy. Subsequently, it is put forth that the integration process can be characterized as *recent, gradual, uneven, complex, and crises-driven*. The EU's subsequent rounds of enlargement, as well as the shifting of the Commission's approach toward transport, have shaped the development of EU transport policy. Yet, it is reasoned that transport policy is particularly shaped by subsector specific crises.

Part II – The timing of transposition:
Chapter four: Theoretical framework
Chapter four develops an actor-centred theoretical bargaining framework for the timeliness of national transposition processes. It offers a series of testable hypothesis tailored to the transport sector, but which can be generalised to any EU policy area. Drawing from the war of attrition logic, *first, this chapter walks through the ways in which policy change occurs; a look at the effects of change follows. Next to European directive specific and national forms and methods of implementation, which form the first two parts of the theoretical framework, this chapter also identifies the particular role of transport-related accidents in the transposition phase.* All these factors affect timeliness of national transposition processes. Who ends the bargain and when, depends on the players' expected payoff, i.e. the cost/benefit structures of the actors for waiting a particular time. Whereas the flow of benefits to actors is positively related to the rent proportion and negatively related to time, the flow of costs is determined by the players' cost determinant and time. Furthermore, discounting the future benefits shadows on the players' decisions on whether to delay, wait and hold out for the reward in question, i.e. waiting in the hope that the other will make some significant concession.

Part III – Analysis within a combined research design:
Chapter five: EU 1995-2004 transport transposition data set
This chapter presents a high quality data set of basic variables that helps us make a deductive, systematic, empirical, and analytical study of the EU transposition performance of member states. *This new, more reliable data set covers almost two-third of the full population of the EU transport acquis from 1995 to 2004.* It includes EU directive specific features, and the characteristics of the national implementing instruments of nine member states, namely: *France, Germany, the UK, the Netherlands, Greece, Spain, Ireland, Sweden, and Italy.* First, this chapter addresses the choices on selection of, among others, the policy field, the member states, and the time period of investigation. Subsequently, it presents the sources of information and assesses the completeness of the data set, devoting some attention to missing values. It then conducts first descriptive analyses of the national implementing instruments.

Chapter six: Transposition deficit – Statistical illusion or reality?
This chapter offers a more advanced assessment of the new data set. *It shows that especially the Netherlands, France, Italy, Ireland, Greece, and Germany have serious transposition problems in their transport sectors.* Based on the information of 367 national implementing measures, this chapter shows that EU transposition deficit is more than just a statistical illusion. *Almost 50 per cent of the national transposition instruments are not transposed on time, and in fact are delayed up to almost five years.* Cross-country variance is respectable, the difference between the laggard the Netherlands and the champion Sweden, remarkable. Furthermore, differences in median and mean values of delay uncover that 70 percent of delayed directives are more than six months tardy (mean value).

Consequently, this chapter identifies three groups of outcome: on time, delayed by less than six months, and delayed by more than six months.

Chapter seven: Determinants of transposition delay
In this chapter, the independent variables are operationalised and the following research methods presented. With a dependent variable coded trichotomously (no delay, short and long delay) this study runs an ordered multinomial logistic regression and discusses its results. By these, existing arguments in the current literature are confirmed and challenged. Comparing three groups of transposition outcomes it shows that EU directive specific characteristics explain short delays, but national level explanatory variables explain long delays. *The statistical results strongly support the central argument that European level, national level, and crises-related factors together account for transposition delays* and that an actor-centred model has some explanatory power.

Chapter eight: Case selection
There are clear benefits of using large-n and case study research designs concomitantly in EU implementation studies in particular. As an example of how to undertake such a challenge, this chapter deals with case selection for the subsequent case study chapter which will help to further fine-tune the findings and address some remaining limitations of the prior results. First, it presents the criteria for case selection. A case is eligible if the fit of the statistical model is relatively satisfying or not, depending on the calculated deviant residuals. *This study opts for carrying out a model-testing and -improving approach.* A most-similar/most-different design, then, guides the selection of four national implementing measures: two well-explained (on-the-line) cases and two outlying (off-the-line) cases. The four cases include three countries and two transport sub-sectors.

Chapter nine: Four case studies – Two on- and two off-liners
This chapter carries out the case study analysis. The structures of the four case studies, which are traced back, are outlined. They include: the French implementing process of Directive 1998/55/EC of July 1998 *on minimum requirements for vessels*, the Spanish transposition process of Directive 2001/14/EC *on the allocation of railway infrastructure capacity*, the German transposition process for Directive 2002/59/EC *on Community vessels traffic monitoring and information system*, and the French implementing process of Directive 2001/53/EC *on marine equipment*. The evidence from these cases shows that the process-tracing method is a helpful research tool and contributing to the underlying mixed-method research design of this book. *It strongly confirms overall expectations about the conditions under which member states miss transposition deadlines. It also pinpoints a missing explanatory variable: political priority assigned to the specific transposition process.*

Chapter ten: Necessary and sufficient conditions for timely transposition
Since it would be problematic to account for political priority in 365 cases a third method is presented. Completing the combined design, chapter ten provides an additional test of the extended list of hypotheses generated from the small-n research for a 'middle range' set of data. Futhermore, in addressing some limitations of the earlier analyses, it is the so-called fuzzy set technique, which, eventually, identifies usually necessary and sufficient set of conditions for timely transposition. Its 'calibrated data' of the outcome and the causal factors, individually, can show that logic of partial membership conveys the diversity of the real world, rather than the artificial research dichotomies of yes/no assignments. *The results of four usually necessary conditions, which exert their effect independent of all other factors and are present in all instances of an outcome, are discussed.*

PART IV: CONCLUSIONS:
Chapter eleven: Discussion, conclusion and outlook
In this chapter, the findings of the empirical examination are synthesised. The evidence bearing on the hypotheses of the transposition framework is assessed. The findings of this study are mainly twofold, namely: empirical, and methodological. It is argued that the EU has a multifaceted implementation problem. *Seven driving factors crucial to the timeliness of national transposition processes of EU legislation are identified.* They are subsumed under three broader groups: policy design-related (EU level), policy implementation related (national level), crisis-related factors. Potential generalisations, from the empirical data to the broader range of EU legislation, are suggested. From a methodological point of view, it is suggested that, despite epistemological inconsistencies, one can employ the correlational, case study and the fuzzy set techniques, which is not yet used in EU studies, to enrich knowledge on the implementation of EU legislation. Whereas regression analysis is concerned more with the effects of a cause and case studies on the causes of the effect, the diversity-oriented fuzzy set method allows asking under which assumptions given causal factors might be necessary or sufficient for an outcome. *Hence, the mixed-method approaches, in general and the fuzzy set technique, in particular, are, in EU implementation studies, heralded as 'diamonds in the rough'.*

Chapter 2: Literature review

'Lost in translation? Responding to the challenges of European Law' (Title of twenty-seventh report of UK House of Commons Committee of Public Accounts (2005-2006), 1 February 2006).

Responding to the challenges of European law, scholars have developed unique concepts and approaches in their studies of the EU. Both the EU's effects on member states (Europeanization), in general, and the EU's effects on the translation of EU legislation into national law, in particular, have been areas of interest.

2.1 Introduction

This particular body of literature will be screened to assess its potential to answer the research question: 'Why do member states miss deadlines when transposing EU internal market directives?' Reviewing this implementation literature accordingly, I identify five puzzling main features. First, while all three neo-institutionalisms have offered 'potential' explanations for policy change, the sociological has clearly attracted the most scholarly attention. Absorbed in the so-called goodness-of-fit literature, however, this perspective has limits. A clear problem is its overly deterministic nature: it presupposes that national governments and parliaments want to maintain the status quo (Duina, 1997). Second, the methodological approach is biased toward mono-method designs (small-n qualitative case studies), with an exclusive focus on a handful of member states and very few policy areas. In addition, most studies are recent and isolated from the decision making process on the European level in Brussels. This study, however, argues that we must engage in the carry-over of the development and decision-making phases to the implementation phase. This amalgamation of ideas is important in the sense that states may be more or less likely to transpose depending on the extent to which the European directive agreed upon at the European level conforms with national forms and methods of implementation, capacity, and interests.

The chapter is structured as follows. First, it sketches the bottom-up European integration literature and then the top-down Europeanization literature, which closes the loop of the three-step EU policy cycle by bringing back the domestic level to EU studies. Then, I review the comparative politics implementation literature [8] in light of the research question. In particular, I assess

8 Note that I do not address the IR compliance literature, which has been reviewed extensively elsewhere (Haas, 2000; Tallberg, 2002; Mbaye, 2001; Börzel, Hoffman and Dudziak, 2005, Linos, 2007). For an assessment of potential theoretical approaches to compliance see Giuliani (2005).

the main contributions to the rich scholarly field, and identify five puzzling main characteristics. To conclude, the study summarizes the findings that will further guide the current study's line of argumentation.

2.2 European integration and Europeanization

For the past several years, the main focus of comparative politics has been on the bottom-up process of institution-building and political integration at the European level. There exist two inter-related processes at the European level. First, policy competences are delegated to the supranational level to achieve particular policy outcomes. Second, a new set of political institutions are established, with executive, legislative, and judicial powers (Goetz and Hix, 2000). Different integration theories have emerged over the last decades (Rosamond, 2000), namely: neo-functionalism (Haas, 1958; Lindberg, 1963), intergovernmentalism (Hofmann, 1966; Taylor, 1982), federalism (Spinelli, 1972), liberal-intergouvernmentalism (Moravcsik, 1993; 1998), multi-level governance (Marks, Hooghe and Blank, 1996), historical institutionalism (Sandholtz and Stone Sweet, 1997), and sociological constructivism (Risse in Diez and Wiener, 2003). Scholars who have systematically applied one, two, or all three new institutionalisms to European integration have been reviewed extensively elsewhere (Pollack, 2001; Jupille and Caporaso, 1999; Aspinwall and Schneider, 2000; Dowding, 2000).

Less attention, however, has been paid to the reverse top-down relationship, namely how European integration might impact EU member states. However, with the re-launch of the integration process in the mid-1980s, the European Community (EC) had become a polity – a political system that can be analyzed with the tools of most domestic systems. In the end, the term 'Europeanization' was coined to mean the effects of integration. Europeanization represents a response to the challenge to bring the domestic level back to European studies and, consequently, 'closes the loop' (see Figure 2.3).

Generally speaking, Europeanization is a recently expanding field of research as well as a 'highly contested concept' (Kassim, Peters and Wright, 2000: 235). Europeanization, like globalization, is *not one thing*. The impact of Europeanization varies across countries, sectors, and regions (Börzel, 2003). Furthermore, Europeanization is *not* political integration, which belongs rather to the ontological stage of research. Instead, Europeanization is concerned with what happens once EU institutions are in place and produce their effects (Caporaso and Wittenbrinck, 2006; Featherstone and Radaelli, 2003: 35). Europeanization is not tantamount with convergence (Ladrech, 1994), which can be a consequence of Europeanization; nor, in fact, is it synonymous to harmonization, which reduces regulatory diversity.

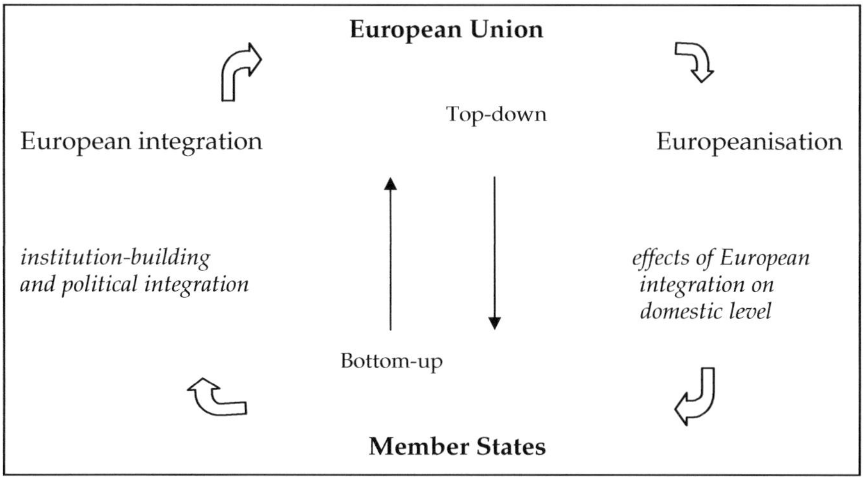

Figure 2.3: European integration and Europeanization.

But, then, what is Europeanization? Recent studies (Olsen, 2002; Featherstone and Radaelli, 2003; Buller and Gamble, 2002; Green Cowles, Caporaso and Risse, 2001; Knill and Lehmkuhl, 2000; Vink, 2003; Giuliani, 2004) identify a number of understandings, as follows. First, Europeanization is the development of institutions of governance at the European level (Green Cowles et al, 2001). Whereas Sbragia (2001) focuses on policy changes, Risse (2001) on normative changes, and Checkel (2003) on constitutional changes, Cowles focuses on state-society relations. Much of this literature, hence, deals with both direct and binding pressures of EU legislation more specifically for national adaptation and the implementation of EU legislation in particular. Second, it is the end goal of political unification in Europe. Third, Europeanization is the European form of organization and governance that is being exported from Europe. Fourth, it is a process in which domestic politics becomes increasingly subjected to European policy-making. Finally, Europeanization is a 'smokescreen for domestic policy manoeuvres' (Buller and Gamble, 2002).

Later, a considerable part of the Europeanization literature review that follows deals with the implementation of EU legislation, which is defined as the processes through which European norms are transposed, enforced, and evaluated. In this context, scholars have turned their attention to the institutional patterns of adjustment to European policies, and in particular to the national implementation of EU law, the latter of which is central in this book and will be the focus of the remaining literature review.

2.3 LITERATURE ON EU IMPLEMENTATION: *RELATIVELY RECENT, WITH LITTLE EXPLANATORY POWER, MYOPIC AND BIASED*

Some scholars put the impact of European integration, understood here as the impact of the EU on national legal output, in perspective (Bovens and Yesilkagit, 2004; van Kersbergen and Lauwers, 2005). Testing the '80% thesis' [9] figures for the Netherlands uncover that only about 12.5 per cent of Dutch legal measures were influenced by EU law. UK figures reveal that, for example, in 2002/2003, 41 per cent of regulations originated in the EU. Irrespective of the broader debate about whether implementation is an interesting and important field of research in political science, the literature in the area has flourished since the late 1980s. The literature on EU implementation is comprised of a mixture of studies that offer 'potential' theoretical explanations of the extent to which Europeanization occurs. Mastenbroek (2005) identifies three waves of scholarship on EU implementation which inherently have the following characteristics (see also Treib, 2006).

2.3.1 Recent and ad-hoc explanations with little explanatory power:

The *first wave* (Mastenbroek, 2005) was rather eclectic in nature, proposing numerous *legal and politico-administrative explanations* about the implementation deficit in member states (Krislov, Ehlermann and Weiler, 1986; Siedentop and Ziller, 1988; Metcalfe, 1994; Pappas and Arpino, 1995; Ciavarini Azzi, 2000; Demmke, 2001; Lampinen and Uusikylä, 1998; Mastenbroek, 2003). Pappas (1995) examines the implementation of Commission decisions by national administrations and identifies the role of national parliaments, the seniority and level of centralization of coordination units across the national ministries crucial. Siedentop and Ziller (1988) study the implementation of 17 European directives in various member states look for 'national patterns of enforcement of EC law' (ibid: 57). More particularly, the variables that these studies invoke to explain regulatory dynamics are usually located at the national level. For example, national legislation and legal framework (Peacock, 1988), national policy-making processes and such as the consultation of national representatives of workers and employers (Richardson, Gustafsson and Jordan, 1982: 1-26), national business cultures (Vogel, 1986), national regulatory agencies (Kelman, 1988), the national civil service (Vogel, 1986), national public (Vogel, 1986).

The *second wave* has focused on the *goodness-of-fit hypothesis* and has resulted in contradictory findings. The goodness-of-fit can be usefully presented as a historically institutionalist argument (Mahoney, 2000; Pierson, 2004). The cen-

9 According to several scholars in the field (Hix, 1999: 3), at least 80% of member states' legislation is derived from EU legislation, suggesting a very high impact of the EU on national legislation and administration.

tral claim is that existing institutional paths are resistant to change. If European policy demands can be accommodated within the confines of the path already taken, adaptation will be smooth. Conversely, if a directive requires profound changes of the existing institutions, EU adaptation will be time-consuming and initially incorrect. Underpinning this relationship are one of two mechanisms depending on whether the, rational choice or sociological institutionalism perspective is ascribed to. Some focus on the cost-awareness of national actors (Duina, 1997; Börzel, 2003; Knill and Lenschow, 1998). Others suggest normative notions, bringing the logic of appropriateness to the forefront (see Héritier et al., 2001; Börzel and Risse, 2003; Knill, 2001).

Although a handful of scholars have argued that successful implementation depends on the fit between European policy requirements and existing institutions at the national level (Duina, 1997; Duina and Blithe, 1999; Green Cowles et al, 2001; Börzel, 2003; Börzel and Risse, 2003), studies have shown that a 'good fit' is neither a necessary nor a sufficient condition for problem-free implementation (Knill and Lenschow, 1998; Haverland, 2000; Héritier et al., 2001; Falkner et al. 2005; Mastenbroek and Van Keulen, 2006). Focusing on national administrative traditions, Knill and Lenschow (1998), for example, hypothesize that implementers' responses to EU requirements are institutionally framed. Striking a more critical note, Haverland (2000) finds that the goodness-of-fit is not pivotal in explaining the implementation of a directive on packaging waste. Despite a high misfit, the UK, for example, implemented the directive relatively on time and correctly. Germany, on the other hand, only faced moderate adaptation pressure, but implemented the directive two years late. The key to these puzzling results, according to Haverland, are the institutional veto points.

Despite these examples most of the second wave models of the implementation literature, however, do not facilitate the formulation of clear predictions, but formulate any *ex-post* explanations of virtually every implementation pattern, which often jeopardizes their necessary explanatory power (Mastenbroek and Kaeding, 2006). The connections between the research and the theoretical, substantive, and political concerns that motivate such research have little meaningful connection to the actual empirical process (unit of analysis and unit of observation problematic). In addition, the second wave models are very often overdetermined by adding more and more variables to the initial hypothesis. This clearly is not helpful because it leads to overly complex models, which do not allow for ex ante hypothesizing on implementation outcomes lacking parsimony (Mastenbroek and Kaeding, 2006).

All in all, the goodness-of-fit models lack empirical and conceptual strength. Often the relationship between the status quo and the response to the EU is spurious, as both variables are contingent upon the preferences of domestic political and administrative actors. This shortcoming in strength has been recognized by advocates of the thesis, who have crafted more dynamic frameworks revolving around the goodness-of-fit by bringing in 'political' variables that may capture the overriding power of substantive positions of domestic policy makers.

The *third wave* of the implementation literature is characterized by its attempts to theorize and research the *role of domestic politics on the process of implementation* (Mastenbroek, 2005) paving the way for future research in the field. Héritier et al. (2001) identify a country's stage of liberalization, its reform capacity, and its dominant belief system as explanatory factors. Haverland (2000) argues that the presence or absence of institutional veto positions allow domestic actors to hamper implementation. Along these lines, Mbaye (2001) and Giuliani (2003) investigate the effects of the number of veto players; Treib (2003) argues that a party's political preferences of national governments shape transposition records of member states. Falkner et al. (2004) posit that the effect of domestic opposition on timely transposition is mediated by a member state's culture of implementation.

More general, rationalist explanations are only recently burgeoning, and are still very limited. An insightful example of an institution-based model, that focuses on the role of domestic politics on processes of implementation, is a model of implementation developed by Dimitrova and Steunenberg (2000) based on insights from game theory and analytical politics. A second promising application is Franchino's (2005) work on formal models of delegation in the European Union, which are closely linked to the issue of implementation. Last but not least, Steunenberg (2006; 2007) analyses the transposition problematic by focusing on an actor-oriented approach of transposition coordination in the domestic policy arena. Domestic actors are taken as policy-specific veto players, which is illustrated by two cases of decision-making on EU directives in the Netherlands, namely: the cocoa and chocolate products directive, and the laying hens directive. These studies provide empirical and conceptional strong research in the field.

2.3.2 *Myopic:*

Another investigative look at the existing literature on EU implementation unveils that scholars have not been inspired by the 1970s public policy implementation studies (Pressman and Wildavsky, 1973; Bardach, 1977; Berman, 1978; Mazamanian and Sabatier, 1981). 'This field of research gradually lost academic prominence' (Giuliani, 2005: 5). However, its rich contributions include an interesting finding that may prove helpful for theoretical approaches that model national implementation processes: the link between the adoption phase and the subsequent implementation phase. Pressman and Wildavsky (1973: 189) argue that 'implementation should be part of design,' suggesting that policy theory is formulated 'with a view toward its execution' (ibid: 189). So far, only few recent contributions (Jonsson and Tallberg, 1998; Mastenbroek, 2003; Kaeding, 2006 among others) explicitly refer to policy design-related and policy implementation-related factors in their explanatory statistical models.

2.3.3 *Methodological divide:*

Another characteristic of the EU implementation literature is a clear methodological divide, namely: qualitative work and quantitative contributions. This study shows that the implementation literature has not used a so-called mixed-method approach, such as, for example, the welfare state literature, but primarily uses monostrand designs.[10] The scholarly work on EU implementation, which aims at developing and testing explanatory factors for the implementation deficit in member states and in particular policy sectors, has been dominated by case study oriented research (for example, Knill and Lenschow, 1998; Haverland, 2000; Héritier et al., 2001; Falkner et al., 2005). Here, the thorough selection of cases is crucial. Poorly applied, one of the greatest pitfalls in the exploratory study involves premature conclusions: the findings may seem convincing enough for their inappropriate title of 'conclusions'. Another hazard of case study analysis is the tendency to extend the exploratory phase, and to inadequately represent diversity. Only recently contributions have added quantitative research designs to the implementation debate,with the aim of drawing more generalizable findings.

2.3.4 *Statistical data of first and second rounds:*

Nevertheless, quantitative research on the implementation of EU law is still 'wet behind the ears'. The group of scholars consists of *two rounds*. Whereas the first generation relies exclusively on existing EU data, the second generation has further improved the quality of the data.

First generation: (a) Commission scoreboards and infringement proceedings
Commission scoreboards: The first proxy for non-implementation of EU law is the Commission's records that monitor the application of Community laws that are implemented[11]. Relying on scoreboards published by the EC, Lampinen and Uusikyla (1998) show that critical mass opinion towards the EU does not influence implementation behaviour. On the other hand, member states traditionally labelled as corporatist succeed better than non-corporatist

10 'These design use a single research method or data collection technique and corresponding data analysis procedures to answer research questions. They are also known as single-phase designs ' (Tashakkori and Teddlie, 2003: 711).

11 Since the late 1970s, under the Jenkins' Presidency, the Commission started pursuing a rigorous policy of enforcement by gradually establishing CELEX, which grew into an indispensable interinstitutional information source for non-implementation.

ones. In line with Bursens (2002), Giuliani (2003) and Sverdrup (2004), who tested implementation performance in different countries, Borgehetto et al. (2006) assess the causes of noncompliance with the transposition deadlines of 2179 EU directives, using the Commission data adopted by the Italian authorities. In the same vein, but for all EU 15 member states, König, Luetgert and Mäder (2005) gathered procedural information on all directives initiated by the Commission between 1984 and 2002. In total, they piled up 21,227 cases. Their findings reveal that the larger the level of EU conflict, the more EU legislative actors involved: moreover, the findings suggest that the more qualified majority voting is applied in the Council, the higher the probability is for compliance. The more controversial a directive is, the more likely the Commission and other member states will demand compliance: but meeting the prescribed deadline may be slightly eased in these cases if the member states government welcome EU legislation as an opportunity to circumvent the domestic legislative arena by means of secondary instruments.

Commission data, however, have serious shortcomings. The data are very unreliable because the scoreboards depend entirely on the notification of the national implementing measures by the member states to the Commission (Börzel, 2001). Moreover, the validity of the Commission's data, in light of the alleged transposition deficit, is deceptive. By the end of 2003, 2553 directives were part of the *acquis communeautaire* (Commission, 2003). Most of the directives are in force for many years leading to considerable 'upward bias' (Mastenbroek, 2003).

First round: (b) Infringement proceedings
The number of infringements within the different stages is usually taken as the second indicator of member state performance when implementing Community law. Scholars and policy-makers alike base their assessments on statistics published in the Annual Reports on Monitoring the Application of Community Law. Focusing on the determinants of the opening up of infringement proceedings (Börzel, 2001; Tallberg, 2002; Sverdrup, 2004; Beach, 2005; Perkins and Neumayer, 2007; Linos, 2007), Mbaye (2001) gathered infringement data from 1972 to 1993. She broadens the horizon by systematically drawing from the implementation literature in IR, EU studies, and American federalism. She argues that cases of non-implementation in the EU rise with bargaining power in the Council, length of membership, and regional autonomy. Börzel et al. (2005) and Tallberg (2002) have also collected data on infringement proceedings, resulting in large-n data sets, with the goal of garnering more reliable data on implementation. Sverdrup (2002) takes the Nordic countries as a focus and points at a 'Nordic model' of good implementation culture. However, these scholars focus solely on explaining infringements, which implies a different empirical focus, and is only a crude proxy for timely and correct implementation.

Again, there are a few reasons to question whether infringement proceedings are valid and reliable indicators of implementation deficit. Infringement proceeding are 'no indicator of the actual or absolute level' of non-implementation in the EU (Börzel, 2001: 808). Since they only cover a fraction of the violations of Community law in the member states, infringement proceedings can only serve as indicators of *relative* non-implementation (Bursens, 2002). Mbaye (2001: 268) argues that a selection bias could even lead us to question the representativeness of the infringement data. The Commission may strategically select cases to be brought before the ECJ (Börzel, 2003).

All in all, the shortcomings of the existing data show that the Commission's records would be helpful only if the non-implementation cases prosecuted by the ECJ and the Commission were a random sample of all non-transposition cases. Börzel (2001) concludes that there are no existing data that allow us to draw any valid conclusions about whether the EU has an implementation problem.

Second round of statistical data:
More recent larger-n work, which still represents an exception in the case study dominated field of EU implementation studies (Gabel, Hix and Schneider, 2002; Nyikos and Pollack, 2003), has succeeded in improving the quality of existing EU data. In line with the notion that the Commission's data on member states' infringements and its scoreboards on monitoring the application of Community law, in particular, can serve as indicators for non-compliance (as long as scholars carefully control for potential selection bias), Mastenbroek (2003) created a more reliable database on non-transposition. She constructed a database, derived from Celex, containing all EC directives enacted in the Netherlands from 1995 to 1998. In addition, she consulted extra overviews from the Ministry of Foreign Affairs, a list of measures notified to the Commission by the Dutch government, and a database compiled by the TMC Asser Institute (see also Steunenberg and Kaeding, 2007) for all 229 directives. In the end, she and others following her example (Steunenberg and Rhinard, 2005; Berglund, Gange and van Waarden, 2006; Haverland and Romeijn, 2007; Kaeding, 2006), have demonstrated that around 60 per cent of the *acquis* is not notified on time. Although cross-checking with national data is cumbersome and time-consuming, it is, for the sake of data quality, necessary. Furthermore, it shows the direction by which further quantitative studies in the field can enrich and further improve the mainly small-n scholarly work in the field.

2.3.5 *Bias in selection of member states and policy areas:*

A final characteristic that resonates throughout the remainder of the book is that existing implementation literature covers only a marginal number of policy areas and member states alike. As is the case for EU studies, in general

(Franchino, 2005), environmental policy and social policy clearly rank highest as the most-researched policy areas in the implementation literature (Ostner and Lewis, 1995; Eichner, 1995; Knill and Lenschow, 1998; Haverland, 2000; Falkner et al., 2005; Haverland and Romeijn, 2007; Linos, 2007; Falkner, Hartlapp and Treib, 2007; Toshkov, 2007).

Although they clearly represent a considerable percentage of all EU directives (environment 9,3%, social policy 8%) there are 'some worrying signs that we are spending too much time and resources on some clearly secondary policies and ignoring core ones.'(Franchino, 2005: 246). Some important areas, such as free movement, agriculture, transport and competition deserve at least as much attention as do social policy and environment. For a better understanding of the EU policy outcomes, scholars may invest more in older policies that are at the core of the Union. While agriculture represents on average 23.4 % of all EU directives, transport directives represent 6% of the total amount of EU directives (Alesina, Angeloni and Schuknecht, 2005). Acknowledging the requirement of a theory-driven case selection of policy areas, transport follows the regulatory style underlying the well-researched policy areas such as environment and social policy.

Next to the dominance of environmental and social policy areas in the implementation literature which are exemplary for the regulatory style of EU policies, a group of member states is almost always part of comparative research designs, namely: the UK, Italy, and Germany. The smaller member states, such as Austria, Finland, Luxembourg, Portugal and Sweden, have attracted almost no scholarly attention (Mastenbroek, 2005). France, despite its importance for European integration and its theoretical relevance in terms of its centralist polico-administrative structure in Europe, is, relatively, not often covered in comparative implementation projects. However, Mbaye's study (2001), for example, would have been more powerful had Greece not been dropped out of the analysis because the unavailable data on veto players for Greece. To account for the number of veto player shaping both the speed and the quality of implementation of EU law (Haverland, 2000) Greece would have been a theoretically interesting case scoring, between 1974 and 2000, unspectacularly '1' such as the UK and Spain.[12] The UK and Spain have performed well in terms of EU implementation, whereas Greece has been one of the main laggards since its membership to the EU.

Outstanding in the field, however, is the work by Falkner et al. (2005; 2007), who held numerous in-depth interviews for six social policy directives in all 15 'old' Member States. Their study, therefore, represents the first research that provides first-hand evidence to suggest that the EU suffers a pan-European implementation problem.[13]

12 The figures differ only in 1989 (1,50) and 1990 (1,24).

13 For a critical assessment see Toshkov (2007).

2.4 Conclusion

This literature overview has given a critical assessment of the mainstream Europeanization literature that discusses the implementation of EU policies across member states in particular. Screened to assess its potential to answer the research question *Why do member states miss deadlines when transposing EU internal market directives?*, this chapter distilled five theoretically major problematic characteristics that will be subsequently addressed in the remainder of this study.

In order to advance the scholarly understanding of why member states miss deadlines while transposing EU directives, a well-founded conjecture needs to be put forward for scrutiny. Since ontological debates about perspectives that are not meant to be refuted seem good at inspiring scholars to think in new ways, such debates, however, must not be taken for advances in knowledge (Goldman, 2005). Methodologically speaking, whatever the connection may be between factors, on the one hand, and outcomes, on the other hand, the relationship between a factor and an outcome are logically independent of each other (synthetical). Thus, the relationship is not only an analytical one, but an empirical regularity. Second, the nature of that regularity can only be discovered by means of empirical research, for example, by testing hypotheses against a body of data. Thus, there is no *a priori* valid knowledge about the relationships between factor and outcomes, as any hypothesis about such a link can be refuted by empirical evidence.

The assessment of the implementation literature shows that there is still area for improvement. The *third wave* of the implementation literature points to a promising direction for improvement. Scholarly work may further elaborate particular frameworks within the *third wave* of the implementation literature by researching the role of domestic politics on processes of implementation, in order to generate clear predictions that can be tested empirically to answer the research question. Therefore, more attention may have to be given to data quality improving designs, following the study by Mastenbroek (2003). Research should include often untended but theoretically relevant member states and address under-researched and theoretically relevant policy areas, however well fitting the regulatory character of EU policies under which environment and social policy can be subsumed. Last but not least, this review realises that the implementation literature has not yet profited from a so-called mixed-method research design which, however, has brought some helpful insights to other fields of research (Brady and Collier, 2004) and therefore seem well worth the effort of following here.

Before sketching a theoretical framework to explain why member states miss the deadlines while transposing EU Internal Market directives, I, however, assess the characteristics of the development of another regulatory policy area (Lowi, 1964; Hood, 1983), namely: EU transport policy. Whereas the selection of the sector will become fully clear when discussing the data set in chapter five, these policy-related characteristics will guide the set-up of the theoretical framework in chapter four, in particular, and the overall analysis, more generally.

Chapter 3: Economic integration in transport services

'Time and again the common transport policy has been the saddest chapter in the history of European integration.' (Jürgen Erdmenger, Senior member of the Commission's transport directorate in 1983)

3.1 Introduction

The EU is the most advanced model of economic integration [14] in the world. Beginning as a preferential trading area in 1958, it has evolved into a single market in which goods, services, capital, and labour can move between its 25 Member States with virtually no restriction – theoretically. Practically, the EU has been very successful in creating a single market for goods. However, recent discussions about the European stock markets, the so-called national champions in the energy market and the transitional arrangements for workers from the 'new member states' illustrate that the EU does not have a strong single market with regard to services, capital, or labour.

In the service sectors, a striking contrast to a single market is exemplified by the 30-year-old policy of anthemion, which bestows national exclusive rights for network industries independent as if they were independent of the internal market. The implementation of Article 86 was a 'taboo' in the EU for decades (Pelkmans, 2001: 140). 'The Member States have continued to go their own ways on economic strategy, protecting national markets and corporations, and wrestling independently to deal with high unemployment, low investment, and slow growth.' (McCormick, 2005: 159).

Transport is an important policy area affected by the Lisbon strategy (2000) and linked to the worldwide growth of trade flows. It is an example of network industries in general, and another regulatory EU policy area in particular whose 50-years history this chapter will trace back through the major developments. Generally speaking, it could be characterized as one of the saddest pieces in the history of European integration. More clearly, the economic integration of transport in the EU can be characterized as *recent, gradual, uneven, complex and crisis-driven*.

This study will show that three main driving and/or constraining factors account for its development, namely: member states' attitudes preconditioned by their geographical characteristics, EU institutions with the European Commission (Commission) as the agenda-setter, the Council of Ministers

---

14 Economic integration describes a process in which the economies of independent countries are progressively unified as a result of the removal of barriers to trade (Pelkmans, 2001).

and the European Parliament (EP) as co-legislators, the European Court of Justice's (ECJ) as the judicial power, and the occurrence of transport-related crises. Subsequent rounds of enlargement in economic policies extended the group of member states and with it the transport sub-sector specific attitudes. In addition, the policy approach towards EU transport policy by the Commission has shifted over the years. Whereas the first decades of EU transport policy were characterized by so-called negative integration (Tinbergen, 1965; Rehbinder and Stewart, 1984), i.e. the removal of impediments to the establishment of single market), from the late 1990s the Commission implemented positive integration measures, setting up transport policies to shape the conditions under which markets operate (Scharpf, 1996). A final characteristic of the development of the transport sector is its vulnerability to influences from the external environment. Recent ecological disasters in the seas and rivers have affected water travel, whereas strained economic conditions have affected air travel; both kinds of travel occur in our more complex and globalised world. With regard to train and automobile travel, the decreasing market share of the rail sector along with devastating railway accidents across Europe and the rising number of casualties in car accidents resulted in further EU legislation. To conclude the different environmental factors in the different transport sub-sectors have led to the gradual adoption of EU legislation in the form of packages unevenly distributed across the different transport sub-sectors since 1992.

The chapter is structured as follows. First, it reviews the very scarce political science literature on EU transport policy, and argues that the EU transport policy debate is conducted mainly in policy specific, technical and economic journals, leaving EU scholars only a few studies to reference. Second, this chapter presents the European institutional setting for transport policy, which illuminates the historical development of EU transport policy. Third, four phases of integration are identified; it is put forth that, in general, the integration process can be characterized as recent, gradual, uneven, complex and crisis- driven. This is especially clear from the closer transport sub-sector point-of-view. Fourth, it is argued that the EU's transport policies were formed by the subsequent rounds of enlargement in economic policies, as well as the shifting of the Commission's approach towards transport. Finally, it is reasoned that, over the last decades, EU transport policy has further been shaped by transport sub-sector specific crises.

3.2 Literature on EU transport

Scholars' attention to Common transport policy has been, for years, condemned to insignificance in all first-class edited volumes, which cover standard policy areas such as common foreign and security policy, environment, monetary union, social policy, and agriculture (Wallace and Wallace, 2000; Wallace, Wallace and Pollack, 2005; George and Bache, 2001; Bomberg and

Stubb, 2003; Cini, 2003; Dinan, 1999; Nugent, 1999; Hix, 2005; Graziano and Vink, 2006). Although Common transport issues have always been considered important for the economic integration of the EU, their practical significance is not mirrored in scholarly output (Franchino, 2005).[15] Transport policy has intrested those scholars as the fringe of economics and infrastructure issues (Lewis, Semeijn and Vellenga, 2001; Bolden and Harman, 2002; Nash and Sansom, 2001). Subsequently, research on transport policy is often very technical in nature, and covers expectations of traffic growth, infrastructure and vehicles design, traffic restraint, economic and commercial pricing policy, and the methodological tools available to predict and assess the effects of alternative policy options.

However scarce, the scholarly work in the field of EU transport policy in political science can be divided into two groups: studies covering all different modes of transport, and those focusing on only a single mode. In discussions primarily focused on the slight advancement in the Common transport policy as a whole, Erdmenger (1983) and Abbati (1987) investigate why European transport policies failed to make the expected progress in all five modes: road, inland waterways, rail, air and maritime. With more theoretical motivations, Aspinwall (1999) identifies the parameters of two distinct governance subsystems in EU transport: domestic security, and supranational regulatory network. He traces the changes that have occurred in the EU transport policy, accounts for them, and describes the emerging system of governance in EU transport in general (see also Schmidt and Giorgi; 2001; 2003). Stevens (2004), in another blend of practioner insight, focuses on the very different considerations that affect transport by land, sea, and air. Inspired by a rather eclectic approach, namely, neofunctionalism, liberal intergovernmentalism, and institutions and networks, he advances a new model of how three policy-making environments – practical, political, and organizational – interact with each other over time to open windows of policy-making opportunity.

Next to these comprehensive contributions covering transport in general terms, studies of specific modes of transport have emerged, namely: road, inland waterways, rail, air and maritime. Most of these studies came to fruition in the late 1990s. It is worth noting that not all transport sub-sectors have attracted the same attention. Table 3.2 refers to the different accounts.

Whereas inland waterways transport has not yet been investigated, and maritime transport has garnered scholarly attention only recently (Aspinwall, 1995; Paixoa and Marlow, 2001; Pallis, 2002), the aviation sector has enjoyed the most research of any transport sector. Demands from society for the opening of competition in the air transport industry brought forth a supportive

15 Note, however, recent descriptive studies on transport issues by Zeff and Pirro (2006; 2007)

Table 3.2: Overview of scholarly work in the field of EU transport policy.

General scholary contributions	Erdmenger (1983); Abbati (1987); Whitelegg (1988); Ross (1998); Aspinwall (1999); Banister, Dreborg, Hedberg, Hunhammer, Stehen and Akerman (2000); Greaves (2000); Schmidt and Giorgi (2001; 2003); Kerwer and Teutsch (2001a); Baur (2004); Stevens (2004)				
Mode-specific contributions	**Road (6)**	**Rail (5)**	**Maritime (3)**	**Air (8)**	**Inland waterways (0)**
	Button (1984); Young and Wallace (2000); Héritier (1997); Héritier et al. (2001); Kerwer and Teutsch (2001b)	Dobbin (1993); Knill and Lehmkuhl (2000); Héritier et al. (2001); Dobbin (2001); Kerwer and Teutsch (2001); Héritier (2002)	Aspinwall (1995); Paixoa and Marlow (2001); Pallis (2002)	Wheatcroft and Lipman (1986); Stevens (1997); Amstrong and Bulmer (1998); Button, Hayes and Stough (1998); Dienel and Lyth (1998); O'Reilly and Stone Sweet (1998); Lawton (1999)	n.r.

n.r. = no reference; numbers in brackets refer to the number of contributions

response from the Commission, which was initially rejected by the national governments (O'Reilly and Stone Sweet, 1998). Continuing internal and external pressures, as well as the supportive rulings of the ECJ, which invited the application of the EC's competition rules to air transport, together brought forth a succession of EC agreements. By 1997, these agreements had removed internal barriers to competition in air transport and moved Regulation to the EC level. Armstrong and Bulmer's (1998) rendition of air transport liberalisation closely follows O'Reilly and Stone Sweet's analysis. Armstrong and Bulmer emphasize the pressures of transnational business, the mobilizing activities of Etienne Davignon, the leadership of Jacques Delors, and the inspiration of Arthur Cockfield as four major catalysts to air transport liberalisation. Assessing CTP up to the mid-1990s, they show that conflicting member states' preferences and autonomous supranational organizations are constant factors in EU policy-making. Moreover, Armstrong and Bulmer suggest that varying outputs may, therefore, be explained more efffectivly by the opportunities offered through institutional structures in which these decision-making processes are embedded, and also by the availability of credible solutions for the policy problems under discussion (see also Lawton, 1999; Button, 1996; Buttton et al., 1998; Kerwer and Teutsch, 2001; Wheatcroft and Lipman, 1986; Stevens, 1997; Dienel and Lyth, 1998).

Dobbin (1993) illustrates the diverse conceptions of the railway market and the very different conceptions of the relationships between state, market, and individual economic actors. Dobbin argues that these conceptions must be reconciled if Europeanization is to be successful in exploring the different varieties of markets found in French and British high speed train policy. Focusing on the liberalization of the rail sector, Héritier (2002) concludes that technological innovation accounts for the different performances in the United Kingdom, Germany and France.

Focusing on road haulage in the UK, the Netherlands, Germany, and Italy, Héritier (1997) finds four different profiles of responses to the European invitation to reform domestic policies; responses varied by nation. In the same vein, Kerwer and Teutsch (2001) conclude that domestic factors were more important than European factors in bringing about this change. European influence did not severely curtail national policy-making autonomy. Apparently, in transport policy, Europeanization was elusive because national institutional intermediation largely muffled the impact of European policy-making.

Covering the last two modes of transport comparatively, Kerwer and Teutsch (2001: 26) show that both road and rail transport reflect the high demand of consensus as a basis for European decisions. Although the researchers' assessments of common transport policy development focus on two of the five modes, they make strong claims about the overall developments of common transport policy. Yet, without research about maritime shipping, air, and inland waterways transport, such claims may not be warranted. This tendency of generalisation can also be found in the other modal contributions. Whereas case studies from within the different modes of transport are helpful to account for causal mechanisms at a specific time in EU transport history, they 'block the view on the whole.' Comparing different modes of transport with such case studies focus is methodologically problematic. Researchers can rightly assume that member states' preferences have not considerably changed over the years (Scheerlinck and S'Jegers, 1998). Holding this variable constant, they could investigate the influence exerted by the EU and national institutional settings upon member states' preferences. This is, however, methodologically debatable if one wants to deal with more than one mode of transport, because enlarged member states' preferences, and institutional settings' preferences, too, differ also for every single mode of transport. This variability will be accounted for in the remainder of this study.

3.3 Driving and constraining forces of EU transport policy-making

3.3.1 *Basic attitudes among member states:*

Two 'ideal types' of transport policy describe the main 'rupture points' or cleavages across member states, namely: the state-led approach, and the liberal market approach (Schmidt and Giorgi, 2001). The traditional *state-led approach* assumes that transport primarily serves structural inequalities, especially in regard to the regional level. Under this policy framework, transport planning is guided by the goals of regional cohesion and development, and emphasis is placed on infrastructure investment by the state as the main instrument for achieving these goals. Environmental sustainability, in this respect, is important, but must be balanced against social sustainability and regional cohesion. The *liberal market approach* to transport development considers regulation of the transport sector important, and this is achieved primarily through economic instruments. Particularly relevant under this scheme are pricing instruments and taxation, and so are liberalization and privatization when associated with greater accountability and transparency in operations. Ultimately, however, the role of transport is said to support economic development through faster and more efficient mobility of goods. Environmental impacts are recognized as negative externalities and, as such, also pose questions of fair pricing in conjunction with technological upgrading. Although reallife transport policy cannot be confronted clearly with the two-fold typology, I try to group the member states accordingly.

State-led approach towards transport
Large member states tend to favour the traditional state-led approach. France is a large country that is relatively less dependent on international trade, with a widely dispersed population, and a large domestic transport market. France's deep roots in the tradition of government support for domestic objectives of economic policy, have made French transport policy-makers notably reluctant to open France's markets to foreign competition. Germany is also a large country that favours the state-led approach. Its surface transport industries are potentially exposed to competition, particularly from operators based in the the Netherlands and in the new Eastern member states. In Germany, there is a corporatist tradition supported by government policy and reinforced by a strong partnership between unions and management, which has tended to make transport policy officials cautious about competition, particularly foreign competition. The traditional state-led approach has also been supported by some smaller EU member states. For example, the social importance of its dense network of island services led Greece, until very recently, to defend a protective regime for coastal shipping whilst supporting a more liberal regime in international relations, and particularly in the bulk shipping trades, where Greek owners are strongly represented.

Liberal market approach towards transport
Other member states tend to follow the liberal market approach. The UK and the Netherlands, in particular, advocate this approach. Their motivation in this respect is obviated by their positions as key players, with high stakes in the evolution of international air transport policies. The world-wide network of air routes link Britain and the Netherlands with their colonies and dominions. London is a natural hub for air traffic between North America and much of Europe, and Amsterdam is a connecting airport. The Netherlands, furthermore, is a small country with a great river whose ports link the North sea to the industrial heartlands of Northern Europe. Its transport industries could not prosper on the business generated by the Dutch economy alone. They need competitive open markets.

3.3.2 European institutional setting:

Member states' attitudes towards transport policy hinge on their respective European institutional settings. The Commission as the agenda setter, the Council and the European Parliament (EP) as the legislative powers in EU decision-making have gained and lost institutional power, i.e. the rules constraining and enabling actors in EU policy-making have been amended with every proposed revision of the existing treaties.

With the Single European Act (SEA) since 1987, transport including air and sea has been subject to qualified majority voting (QMV). Taking measures further, the Maastricht Treaty in 1992 gave the European Community (EC) infrastructure. In the Council, there are two basic voting rules, namely: unanimity (UV), and QMV. Changes of voting strengths and the QMV threshold have affected the relative power of member states. During the second European Free Trade Agreement (EFTA) enlargement, the UK, Spain, and Italy argued that the addition of Austria, Finland and Sweden would alter the type of coalition needed to achieve a QMV. Their arguments resulted in the 1994 Ioninna Declaration, which foresaw 26 votes (30%) as the blocking minority (Hix, 2005: 85). A similar argument arose in the negotiations on voting weights in the Nice Treaty, where a blocking minority was reduced from 30% to 26%.

The Commission's approach towards transport policy has evolved over the years as well. Its approach towards EU transport policy, as the agenda setter in EU policy-making, can be characterized by either a sub-sectoral or an integrated approach. Whereas the sub-sectoral approach calls for equal competitive conditions to be achieved within each transport sub-sector, the integrated approach to transport demands a greater equality of competitive conditions between the different transport modes.

In addition, over four decades the EP has changed from a largely consultative assembly to a genuine co-legislator that has itself evolved considerably beyond the original EC, both in scope and in powers (Corbett, Jacobs and Shackelton, 2005: 5). The EP's transport committee actively influences policy-making in the field (Häge and Kaeding, 2007) and actually happens to be one of the most active committees in EP (EP conciliation committee report, 2004).

The ECJ represents the last important player in the policy-making process. It hears actions brought against member states for failures to comply with obligations, and the ECJ has the power of judicial review, as well as the power to issue preliminary rulings on references by national courts. Importantly, the ECJ's rulings in the 1970s obliged member states to construct an internal market in transport services.

3.3.3 *Transport specific crises:*

Last but not least, it is transport specific crises that instigate European integration in the transport sector. Next to the divide between member states along the state-led and the liberal market line, and the European institutional setting – which allowedly holds true for a lot of policy areas – it is this third factor that plays an important role for the overall development of EU transport policy and its sub-sectors, in particular. Be these crises the actual numbers of fatalities in car accidents, the ecological disasters in the maritime or inland waterways sector, the shrinking market shares of railways, or the economical challenges faced by the aviation sector in a globalized and terror- plagued world, crises in any transport sub-sector have considerable impact on the policies of the transport sector.

3.3.4 *Summary*

This study argues that the EU's transport policy developed as it has because of three important factors: First, member states' approaches toward transport shaped by economic geography and national needs in the different transport sub-sectors. Second, the underlying institutional settings with the Commission as agenda-setter, the EP as co-legislatior and the ECJ as the guardian of the treaties; second, the member states' approaches towards transport (both in general and towards specific modes of transport), and the conflicts surrounding these –conceptually, as well as on in practice with reference to actors' strategies and alliances. These conflicts can be seen, on the one hand, in the significant disagreement as to the role of the market and the role of the state, and on the other hand, in the executive, judicial and legislative powers of the Commission, ECJ and the EP respectively, which have evolved over the last 50 years, shaping the development of the policy area. The agenda -setter's approach towards the policy is decisive, initiating transport legislation in terms of sub-sectors or integrated. The third important factor in the EU's transport policy development is the transport related crises. They clearly affect the shape of EU transport policy. Adopted in so-called packages, a number of regulations and directives spawned from crises indicate the need of response to situational changes of the external environment.

After having outlined the driving and constraining factors accounting for the development of the EU transport field, I approach the analysis as follows. Taking the Treaty of Rome (1957) as the starting point, the following chapter assesses the developments in the field up to 2006. Newspaper articles and official documents of the European communities will help me trace back the major steps in EU transport policy in general and the different sub-sector specific developments in particular. Interviews with Commission and member states' civil servants serve to complement the overall assessment which follows.

3.4 The paths of EU transport policy: Recent, gradual, uneven and complex

The overall development in EU transport policy can be divided into four phases of distinct time periods: 1957-1984, 1985-1991, 1992-2000, and 2001-2006. This analysis focuses on these phases, in addition to its particular attention to all five sub-sectors of transport, namely: road, rail, inland waterways, maritime, and air. In the following discussion, each phase is addressed separately, starting from a general assessment of Common transport policy (CTP) and moving to a sub-sector specific analysis. Tables 3.3.1-3.3.4 summarize the key developments for the different periods in the policy sub-fields, identifying the member states' general purposes of CTP, the Commission's key goals and specific proposals, and the crises that occurred over the last six decades.

3.4.1 30 years of deadlock (Phase I: 1957-1984)

Between 1957 and 1985 the CTP did not amount to much more than the stated intention to facilitate pan-European transport between the member states. During the first thirty years of the EC, transport policy was to a large extent under the control of individual governments, and was 'dominated by deadlock' (Knill and Lehmkuhl, 2000: 7) and 'false starts, of politically inept Commission proposals, or persistent Council inaction, of divided government views' (Héritier, 1997: 31). The 1961 Schaus Memorandum, for example, presented the first guidelines for a community-wide action programme in transport, but member states showed little real interest in following up with these guidelines Commission proposals were debated, but few of any significance were adopted. Most European governments, especially until the first round of enlargement in 1973, regarded transport as a public service which could not be left solely or even primarily to the private sector. Consequently, member states often intervened extensively in transport policy at the national level, not just to ensure that services were provided, but also to guarantee that peripheral regions were not disadvantaged, so that interventions were used as instruments of regional development policy.

Road and railway
In the *road* sector, the European rules did not oblige member states to deregulate inland transport until the first enlargement in the mid-1970s. In the *railway* sector, also, there was practically no competition. The national railway companies had traditionally 'cooperated' for cross-border services, but the efficiencies in pricing, work practices, allocation of slots on the networks, terminals procedures, technical incompatibilities, service quality, and frontier problems 'confirmed people's worst beliefs about monopoly practices' until the early 1990s (Pelkmans, 2001: 146).

Inland waterways
In *inland waterways,* too, there were hardly any provisions of secondary Community law. The important reason is the existence of the Revised Convention for the Navigation of the Rhine, signed in Mannheim on 17 October 1868. This and later additions have given the Rhine an international river regime, providing the principle of the freedom of navigation. This regime applying to the Rhine seriously hindered the achievement of economic integration in the inland waterways sector. Certain national delegation repeatedly rejected the Commission's proposal by invoking the Mannheim Convention (Stevens, 2004).

Maritime
For a long time, *maritime* navigation was not even considered to fall under the EC responsibility. Twenty years after the Treaty of Rome, in 1974, finally, the ECJ in Luxembourg dispelled the controversy about Article 84 (2). Its judgment overturned the arguments against including sea transport in the integration process. The Court ruled that sea transport was not covered by the provisions on transport (Articles 74 and 83) but that the general rules of the EEC Treaty nevertheless applied unless express exemption was made in the Treaty or by the Council. This particular judgment, shortly after the enlargement of the Community, helped 'to start the ball rolling' (Stevens, 2004). This was especially seen after the accession of the UK and Denmark, which brought two major shipping nations into the Community, and with them, their special interest in world shipping. However, the Community did not enter shipping safety until Spring 1978, following the Amoco Cadiz accident off Brittany. Pressured by their constituencies, the Council adopted decisions including checks on tankers entering Community ports, employment of deep-sea pilots in the North Sea, and ratification of the various IMO (International Maritime Organisation) Conventions on the safety of life at sea and on the prevention of pollution from ships.

Table 3.3.1: Mode-specific developments in Common transport policy (CTP) 1957-1984.

	Rail	Road	Air	Maritime	Inland waterways
I. 30 years of deadlock (1957-1984)	Despite several Commission attempts to introduce transport legislation, member states adopt actions only in the road sector, due to already existing international agreements in other transport sectors.				
	Safeguarding the status quo: Regulation 1191/69 allows compensation for public service obligations. Regulation 1107/70 pro-ides extensive justification for State aids.	**Application of competition rules:** Regulation 141/62 exempts all inland transport from competition rules. **Regulation of market access:** **Licensing:** Directive 74/561 sets minimum standards for road haulage companies **Social harmonization:** Regulation 543/69 (amended by Regulations 3820/85 and 3821/85) sets minimum ages, working time limits for transport crews **Harmonization of operating conditions in road passenger transport:** Directive 74/562 sets minimum standards for road passenger transport service operators.	**Economic liberalisation:** Memorandum No.1 1979 leads to liberali-zation of most interregional services for planes with less than 70 seats. Memorandum No. 2 COM(84)72 , launches EU liberalization in accordance with the Chicago Convention	ECJ dispels the controversy about Article 84(2) in 1974 by overturning the arguments against including sea transport in the integration process. Council rejected all Commission's proposals and preferred to rely on the existing institutional framework guaranteed by International Maritime Organisation (IMO).	No action – relying on Mannheim Convention from 1868

Source: ECE documents and publications; newspaper articles, interviews with policy experts in the EU institutions and Stevens (2004: 94-95; 104-105; 118-119; 130; 148-149)

Aviation
The 1974 ECJ ruling dispelling the controversy about Art. 84 (2) applied not only to maritime, but also to *air* transport. In 1978, the Council of Ministers, lead by the UK, decided on the basis of preliminary work by the Commission to adopt a first priority program of measures in the field of air transport. This program was based on the Chicago Convention, whose article 82 expressly states that member states must annul all obligations that are inconsistent with the terms of the Chicago Convention.

3.4.2 *Watershed (Phase II: 1985-1991)*

The year 1985 is often regarded as a 'watershed for supranational transport policy' (Krewer and Teutsch, 2001: 29). The volume of passenger numbers and goods kilometres by car, train, shipping, air, and inland waterways transport in the EU had increased by 246% between 1965 and 1989 (European Commission statistical yearbook, 2000; 2001; 2002). In addition, Europe was experiencing a general shift towards regulatory policies favouring market mechanisms (Majone, 1994). Responding to increasing demands for mobility and the ideological shift in politics, the SEA changed the institutional settings for the Council of Ministers by replacing unanimity with qualified majority voting for measures in the fields of sea and air transport (Article 80.2). Furthermore, accession to Spain, Portugal and Greece shifted the balance of sub-sectoral interests in favour of maritime and road transport. By the end of the 1980s, transport policy as a European policy area finally got off the ground, leading to liberalization.

Some ECJ rulings and the Commission in particular helped stimulate the development of EU transport policies. On 22 May 1985, the Court of Justice ruled on case 13/83. These proceedings, which were instituted by the Parliament, ruled against the Council for failing to bring about the freedom to provide international transport services, and failing also to create the conditions required for non-resident carriers to have access to national transport services in a member state. This ruling was given immediately after the Commission's White Paper, '*Completing the Internal Market.*' The White Paper identified restrictions on the provision of transport services as a serious barrier to open trade. In order to achieve the SEA's 1993 objectives, the Commission decided that developing the CTP according to a sub-sectoral approach, i.e. achieving equal competitive conditions within each sub-sector, was an absolutely necessary measure.

Road
In the sub-sector of *road* haulage, the EU introduced the right of non-resident transport haulers to operate in foreign markets. The Cassis de Dijon case confirmed that the Council should induce the member states to liberalize the inland transport sector according to the principles of the European Treaty.

In the 1980s, the member states started to abolish all quantitative restrictions on entries in road, and to limit their interventions to regulate the qualitative conditions that operators were obliged to meet in order to obtain access to the profession (Ponti and Cappiello, 2000).

Inland waterways
Whereas Regulation 3921/91 granted cabotage on *inland waterways* from 1 January 1993, with derogations for FR and DE until 1 January 1995, the late 1980s marked a difficult period for the Community fleet, and demanded a European approach. The size of the EC-registered fleet in worldwide *shipping* had decreased from 32% of world tonnage in 1970 to 14% in 1995. Over-capacity in the world market had worsened the conditions of competition for EC shipping lines as compared to those from countries with lower costs. In 1986, the Council was enlarged by Spain, Portugal and Greece, which had been traditionally powerful maritime actors. Subsequently, the Council adopted four measures which were important landmarks in the development of the Common maritime transport policy (see table 3.3.2). Just two and a half years later, in August 1989, the Commission sent the Council a second package of key measures to improve the operating conditions and competitiveness of Community shipping.

Aviation
The ECJ's *Nouvelles Frontières* case in 1986 represents the turning point for EU aviation (EU Court reports, 1986: 1425-1473). Since 1987, the policy has been set to phase out the bilateral system between states and inter-airline agreements in Europe so as to establish a genuine Single Market in civil aviation. The first package of measures was adopted in December 1987. It limited, among other rights, the right of governments to object to the introduction of new fares. In June 1990, a second package of measures opened up the market even further, allowing greater flexibility over the fare setting, and capacity sharing.

3.4.3 *Enlarged set of objectives (Phase III: 1992-2000):*

Whereas the Treaty of Rome described the tasks of the EEC in purely economic terms, the Single European Act (SEA) and the Treaty of the European Union (TEU) granted the Commission new powers for transport safety and for transport infrastructure. The Commission's influence as the principal spokesman and negotiator for the Community in international bodies dealing with transport policies, especially within Europe, was continuing to grow (Rhinard and Kaeding, 2006). This development was bolstered by the third round of EU enlargement with Sweden, Finland and Austria, which were all known for their high environmental standards. These developments coincided with the Commission's new approach of 'sustainable mobility for the Community as a *whole*.' The approach was signalled in the 1992 White Paper,

Table 3.3.2: Mode-specific developments in Common transport policy (CTP) 1985-1992.

	Rail	Road	Air	Maritime	Inland waterways
II. Watershed (1985-1992)	ECJ ruling of 22 May 1985 against Council for its failure to adopt measures put forth in the treaty as well as the Commission White Paper *Completing the Internal market*. Both documents identify restrictions on the provision of transport services sub-sectors as serious barriers to open trade.				
	Economic Regulation of the internal market: Directive 91/440 requires sepa–ration of infra-structure and operations.	**Regulation of capacity:** Regulation 4059/89 grants cabotage quotas. Regulation 3118/93 phases out all quota restrictions by 1 July 1998. **Technical harmonization:** Directive 85/3 (amended by Directive 96/53) sets maximum weights and dimensions for road vehi-cles. Directive 89/460 allows derogation for UK and Ireland to 1 January 1999. Directive 94/55 (amended by Directive 2000/61) concerns harmonization of national legislation for transport of dangerous goods by road.	**Economic liberalization:** Market access, capacity and tariffs progres-sively liberalized under three package deals (1987, 1990, 1992). Regulation 240/92 lays down common rules for airline licensing policies. Regulation 2408/92 provides for cabotage to be phased in by 1997. **Social and economic harmonization:** Judgement in the Nouvelles Frontières case (ECJ case 209-213/84) undermines national Regulation of competitive conditions.	**First package of EU measures COM (85)90:** Regulation 4055/86 establish-es freedom to provide serv-ices between member states. Regulation 4056/86 applies competition rules to maritime transport, and revises 1988, 1992, 1995. Regulations 4057/86 and 4058/86 make provision for EC action to deal with pro-tectionist practices of third countries. **Second package of EU measures, COM (89)266:** Reg 3577/92 grants cabotage, with derogations to 1999 for Mediterranean services and Atlantic coasts of FR, ES and Portugal, and to 2004 for the Greek islands.	**Geographical extension of market access:** Regulation 2919/85 implements licensing provision of Mannheim Convention, extending equal access to all EU member states **Liberalization:** Regulation 3921/91 grants cabotage on inland waterwayss from 1 January 1993 with deroga-tion for FR and DE until 1 January 1995. **Harmonization:** Directive 87/540 requires mutual recognition of car-riers' qualifications and certificates in relation to goods transport, extended to passenger transport under Directive 91/672.

Rail	Road	Air	Maritime	Inland waterways
	Directive 95/50 (amended by Directive 2001/26) sets uniform control procedures. **Fiscal harmonization:** Directives 92/81 and 92/82 set minimum rates of fuel duty. Directive 93/89 (replaced by Dir 99/62) sets minimum rates for vehicle tax, maximum rates for road user charges, and a regulatory framework for setting tolls. **Harmonization of operating conditions in road passenger transport:** Directive 91/439 (amended by Directive 2000/56) lays down common requirements for driving licences. Directive 96/47 provides optional alternative in credit-card format.	Regulations 3975 and 3976/87 (which are part of the first package) establish framework for Community Regulation of competitive conditions, and state aid. Regulation 295/91 lays down rules for denied boarding compensation. Directive 91/670 requires mutual acceptance of personnel licences. **Technical and safety harmonization:** Reg 3922/91 provides for implementation of safety certification rules agreed by Joint Aviation authorities		

Source: ECE documents and publications; newspaper articles, interviews with policy experts in the EU institutions and Stevens (2004: 94-95; 104-105; 118-119; 130; 148-149).

'The Future Development of the Common Transport Policy' and was followed by, and specified through, the common transport policy Action Programs from 1995 to 2000 (European Commission, 1995), and 1998 to 2004 (European Commission, 1998). The sub-sectoral approach was exchanged by an integrated approach, i.e. increasing attention was given to achieving greater equality of competitive conditions *between* the different transport sub-sectors. Furthermore, the approach enlarged the set of objectives to be achieved by the CTP to include sustainability and social cohesion, both of which led to a shift toward more environmental friendly sub-sectors through the support of better transport system management that included combined transport and an emphasis on inter-modality. However, like the first and the second phases, the third phase was still a (narrow) triumph on points for the market-led tendency (see listing of EU transport legislation in the Appendix). Especially in the railway and inland waterways sub-sectors deregulatory legislation dominated, whereas in the road and maritime sub-sectors, harmonization hold sway over the agenda.

Inland waterways and railways

Regulation 1356/96 extended equal access to all *inland waterways*, but the first attempt to liberalize the European *railways* was made in 1991 by a Directive on the development of the Community's railways. In 1995, two pieces of legislation were adopted on the licensing of railway companies and the allocation of and charging for infrastructure. A year later, in 1996, a Commission White Paper was published on the revitalization of the European railway companies, which stated, notably, that the recovery could be achieved by rationalizing their financial situation, ensuring freedom of access to all traffic, and public services and promoting the integration of national systems and social aspects. At the end of year 2000, a first rail liberalization package was agreed upon.

Aviation

Like the 1980s for the maritime sector, the early 1990s were problematic for the *air* industry. Europe's leading airlines suffered heavy losses between 1990 and 1993 due partly to the Gulf wars. Additionally, in a climate of increasingly fierce international competition, airlines continued restructuring their progress in hopes of improving productivity. The three Regulations (2407/92, 2408/92, and 2409/92) that constitute the third package of internal liberalization make up the core of what is called the *acquis communautaire* in air transport. They provide for free access of European airlines to any European airport on merely commercial considerations (air cabotage).

Maritime

The Community continued to build its *maritime* safety policies on the basis of the IMO Conventions and rules. Nevertheless, a number of stricter EC measures were deemed necessary in the aftermath of dramatic shipping accidents, such as those involving the Herald of Free Enterprise (1987) and the

Exxon Valdez (1989). In particular, concerned member states, such as the UK, France, Spain, Sweden and Geramny, pushed for stricter regulations. In 1994, the Council adopted a Directive on the minimum level of training of seafarers, a Directive on ship inspection and surveys, and a Regulation on tonnage measurement of ballast spaces in segregated ballast oil tankers. A Directive on Port State Control was adopted in June 1995, and in December 1995, the Council adopted a Regulation on the safety management of ro-ro passenger ferries. The grounding of Aegean Sea (1992) and the Braer (1993) led to a common policy on safe seas–another safety package with a total of 8 Directives.

Road
In *road* transport, traffic related accidents attracted major EU attention, with more than 40,000 lives and more than 1.7 million people injured. On 30 November 1993, the Council created a Community database (CARE) on road accidents, which would lay the basis for further harmonization of operating conditions in road passenger transport, and recommend maximum permitted blood alcohol levels.

3.4.4 *Consolidation (Phase IV: 2001-2006)*

Whereas the 1999 Treaty of Amsterdam led to further reinforcement of environmental provisions in the transport sector and strengthened the EP's role in the co-decision process, the Treaty of Nice did not change any articles concerning transport policy. In September 2001, the Commission released its '*White Paper on transport policy: European Transport Policy for 2010: Time to Decide*' (European Commission, 2001) which emphasised the integrated approach towards transport policy, with inter-modality playing an important role. The idea behind the integrated approach was to bolster the railway's share in the transport sector, which had dropped considerably, while road transport then accounted for more than 63 percent. Consequently, the emphasis was placed on road pricing for freight and especially heavy goods vehicles, which was considered the way forward for redressing the balance between modes (especially road and rail). This redressed balance, in turn, is expected to contribute to resolving both the congestion and the environmental problems facing transport. The 2001 White Paper has carried the ball deep into the state-led approach of transport policy which , however, has been relaxed recently by the mid-term review of the Commission's 2001 White Paper (2006; Kernohan, 2005).

Road
For *road* transport, a decision was made concerning a genuine European electronic road toll service. The toll is predicted to guarantee interoperability of road toll systems in the internal market, and also contribute to the develop ment of infrastructure charging policies on a European scale. By 2009, at the latest, road cabotage will be opened with respect to all new member states.

Table 3.3.3: Mode-specific developments in Common transport policy (CTP) 1993-2001.

	Rail	Road	Air	Maritime	Inland waterways
III. Enlarged set of objectives (1993-2001)	With the establishment of the Single Market in 1993, *the Commission launches an integrated approach of 'sustainable mobility for the Community as a whole' by the 1992 White Paper*, The Future Development of the Common Transport Policy.				
	Directive 95/18 on the licensing of railway undertakings Directive 95/19 on the allocation of infrastructure and charging for its use **Technical harmonization:** Directive 96/49 applies United National Economic Committee for Europe (UNECE) rules on transport of dangerous goods by rail, amended by Directive 2000/62. Directive 96/48 provides for interoperability of high-speed railways.	**egulation of market access** Directive 96/26 (amended by Directive 98/26) grants unrestricted access under harmonized conditions, including professional competence and financial standing. **Harmonization of operating conditions in road passenger transport:** Directive 99/37 harmonizes form and content of vehicle registration certificates.	**Economic liberalization:** Regulation 95/93 regulates airport slot allocation to encourage market entry. Directive 96/67 opens ground handling services to competition. **Social and economic harmonization:** Regulation 2027/97 implements provisions of revised Warsaw Convention, leading to Community membership alongside member states.	**Grounding of Braer and Aegean Sea leads to:** A common policy on safe seas, COM(93)66. Directive 94/57 sets standards for ships inspection and survey organizations. Directive 94/58 based on International Convention on Standard of Training, Certification and Watchkeeping (STCW), sets standards for approval of training certificates, amended by Directive 98/35. Directive 2001/25 consolidates texts applying to minimum levels of seafarer training. Directive 95/21 on higher standards of port state control **Sinking of Estonia leads to:** Directive 98/18 on international safety standards for passenger vessels	**Geographical extension of market access:** Regulation 1356/96 extends equal access to all Community waterways. **Liberalization:** Directive 96/75 phases out rotation chartering by 1 January 2000. **Harmonization:** Directive 96/50 harmonises national conditions for a single boatmaster's certificate.

	Rail	Road	Air	Maritime	Inland waterways
	Directive 2001/16 provides for interoperability of conventional railways. **Social dimension:** Directive 2005/47 giving a legal status to the concluded Agreement between the Community of European Railways (CER) and the European Transport Workers' Federation (ETF) on certain aspects of the working conditions of mobile workers engaged in interoperable cross-border services in the railway sector	Regulation 2000/115 on maximum permitted blood alcohol levels, endorsed by Council on 4/5 April 2001	**Technical and safety harmonization:** Directive 93/65 establishes rules for procurement of some air traffic management equipment. **Social dimension:** Directive 2000/79 concerning the European Agreement on the Organisation of Working Time of Mobile Workers in Civil Aviation concluded by AEA, ETF, ECA, ERA and IACA	Directive 98/25 raises standards of port state control. Directive 98/41 on registration of passengers Directive 99/35 on mandatory surveys for ro-ro ferries **Pollution control:** Regulation 2978/94 requires port fees to be discounted for modern segregated ballast tankers. Directive 2000/59 on provision of and charging for port reception facilities for ship-generated waste **Social dimension:** Council Directive 1999/63 concerning the Agreement on the organisation of working time of seafarers concluded by the ECSA and the FST	

Source: ECE documents and publications; newspaper articles, interviews with policy experts in the EU institutions and Stevens (2004: 94-95; 104-105; 118-119; 130; 148-149).

Aviation
To deal with the disaster of 9/11, the Council adopted Regulation 2320/2002, which establishes common *aviation* security arrangements based on ICAO and ECAC recommendations. In the air transport sector, a Regulation was adopted to safeguard European airline industries against unfair third country airline practices. The European Parliament and the Council also agreed on a package of Regulations establishing common rules of air traffic management throughout the Community,hereby, creating a single European sky.

Maritime
Europe's enlarged coastline and numbers of ports means that the maritime sector is a valuable alternative to land transport as illustrated by the Commission's concept of the 'motorways of the sea' (2004). The expected growth of sea transport has already started to be absorbed through an improved EU's ports infrastructure. Where *maritime* transport is concerned, the Commission adopted a proposal for a Directive on access to the port service market. The prosposal´s scope was to improve the competitiveness of Community ports, to establish a legislative and regulatory framework for the provision of port services, and help reduce port congestion and environmental pollution. On the question of maritime safety, the sinking of the *Erika* in December, 1999, the Estonia in 2002, and the *Prestige* in November, 2002, prompted new measures in establishing European policy on maritime safety, aimed in particular at the environmental risks caused by oil tankers. The measures proposed cover, among others effects, the ban on single hull tankers, the establishment of a Community monitoring, inspection and information system for maritime traffic, and the establishment of a compensation fund for oil pollution damage.

Inland waterways
In regard to *inland waterways*, the Commission approved a proposal for a Directive on harmonized river traffic information systems (RIS), which is aimed at modernizing inland waterways infrastructure (European Commission, 2004: 1-3). Whereas river transport accounted for only 3% of overall freight transport before enlargement, in an EU-25 on certain corridors (Danube for example) their share exceeds 40%. The Commission's *Naiades* program sets out an action plan for further promoting river transport (2006).

Railway
Whereas the aforementioned legislation for the four sub-sectors of transport has harmonized the sectors, the *railway* sector was to see a couple of liberalizing Directives in 2001 (first railway package on freight liberalization). Another big step towards the integration of the rail transport market was taken in April, 2004 with the adoption of the second railway package. This package intended to ensure a high standard of operational safety on the railways, and to remove obstacles to cross-border services, with a complete liberalization of the European market for rail freight set for January 2007 (Euro-

pean Commission, 2003). The legal framework for rail freight transport will be completed by 2007. At the end of 2004, then, the Commission proposed further instruments with its third railway package. The third railway package will also open international passenger transport. The proposal attempts to influence three issues: first, opening up international passenger transport services to greater competition, second, ensuring that passengers' rights are respected more effectively, and third, ensuring better recognition of the professional qualifications of train drivers and crews performing safety-related tasks. The safety issue, in particular, attracted attention after the fatal Southhall accident (1997), the Hatfield crash (2000), and the Potters Bar crash(2002) in the UK, the Enschede ICE crash (1998) in Germany, and the Paris-Vienna train inferno (2002), which claimed the lives of numerous people.

3.5 Results

In the 1957 Treaty of Rome, which established the European Economic Community, the creation of a single market for intra-Community transport was judged as one of the necessary conditions for achieving the 'four freedoms.' Articles 74-84 of the Treaty of Rome (Appendix) form the legal basis of the Common transport policy.

The study identifies four general phases in the development of transport policy from 1957 to 2006: (a) deadlock (1957-84), (b) watershed (1985-1991), (c) new integrated approach (1992-2000), and (d) consolidation (2001-2006). Although 1992 was the completion date of the internal market for transport it was very much the *starting date*. Until the early-1990s, the EU did not have a comprehensive approach towards transport policy. Despite the Treaty of Rome's attention to its importance, the transport sector was one of the great failures of the single market. For example, little had been done to deal with problems such as an airline industry split along national lines, time-consuming cross-border checks on trucks, national systems of unconnected motorways, air traffic control systems using 20 different operating systems, or 70 computer programming languages. Transport policy is relatively recent EU policy area despite its mentioning in the Treaty of Rome.

From a transport sub-sector specific perspective, the integration process has been very *complex* too. This analysis demonstrates that even a discussion about a comprehensive EU transport policy is difficult because of its complexity. Five different modes of transport have undergone varying developments. The process is *gradual* and *uneven* with respect to advancements. In the road sector, the first liberalizing measures were put forward in the early 1970s. The maritime and air sectors were liberalized in the late 1980s. The first railway packages came in the 1990s. Every mode of transport is de regulated and regulated by different packages, and these packages were adopted unevenly. The first railway directives were not adopted before mid-1990s, road legislation started in the 1970s.

Table 3.3.4: Mode-specific developments in Common transport policy (CTP) 2001-2006.

	Rail	Road	Air	Maritime	Inland waterways
IV. Consolidation (2001-2006)	White Paper, *European Transport Policy for 2010: Time to decide*, which resonates deeply inside the state-led ideology, and mid-term review of the Commission's 2001 White Paper (2006).				
	First rail freight liberalization package (2001): Directive 2001/12 grants freight operators access to Trans European Rail Freight Network by 2003, whole network from 2008. Directive 2001/13 (amending 95/18) establishes common rules for railway licensing Dir 2001/14 (replacing 95/19) establishes principles to govern non-discriminatory allocation of capacity, charging for infrastructure use, and safety certification **Second rail freight liberalization package:** COM (2002) 21-25, proposes: access to cabotage, detailed provisions for safety certification, accident investigation, a European Railway Safety	A decision was taken concerning a genuine European electronic road toll service which could be established as from 2006 in order to guarantee interoperability of road toll systems in the internal market, and also to contribute to the development of infrastructure charging policies on a European scale.	**Technical and safety harmonization:** Regulation 1592/2002 establishes European Aviation Safety Agency. Council agrees to provisions for Single European Sky establishing common rules concerning air traffic management based on six lines of action: joint management of airspace, establishment of a strong Community regulator, gradual integration of civil and military management, institutional synergy between the EU and Eurocontrol, introduction of appropriate modern technology, and better coordination of human resources policy in the air traffic control sector.	Proposal for port services Directive, COM (2001)35 **Breaking up of Erika leads to:** Directive 2001/106 raises standards of port state control. Directive 2001/105 raises standards for shipping inspection and survey organizations. Regulation 417/2002 phases out use of single-hull tankers. Regulation 1406/2002 establishes European Maritime Safety Agency.	The Commission approves a proposal for a Directive on harmonized river traffic information systems (RIS) aimed at modernizing inland waterways infrastructure. Com(2006) 6 final of 17.1.2006 on the promotion of inland waterways transport 'Naiades'.

	Rail	Road	Air	Maritime	Inland waterways
	Agency, and Community membership of Berne Convention.		Regulation 2320/2002 establishes common aviation security arrangements, based on work done in International Civil Aviation Organisation (ICAO) and Eurocontrol Navigation Domain (ECAC).	Com (2004) 453final of 2.7.04 on short sea shipping	
	Third railway package (end of 2004 proposed): Ensuring that passengers' rights are respected more effectively; improving the quality of rail freight services; opening up international passenger transport services to greater competition; and ensuring better recognition of the professional qualifications of train drivers and crews performing safety-related tasks			Green Paper: Towards a future maritime policy for the Union: A European Vision for the oceans and seas (Com(2006)275 final of 7.6.06	

Source: ECE documents and publications; newspaper articles, interviews with policy experts in the EU institutions and Stevens (2004: 94-95; 104-105; 118-119; 130; 148-149).

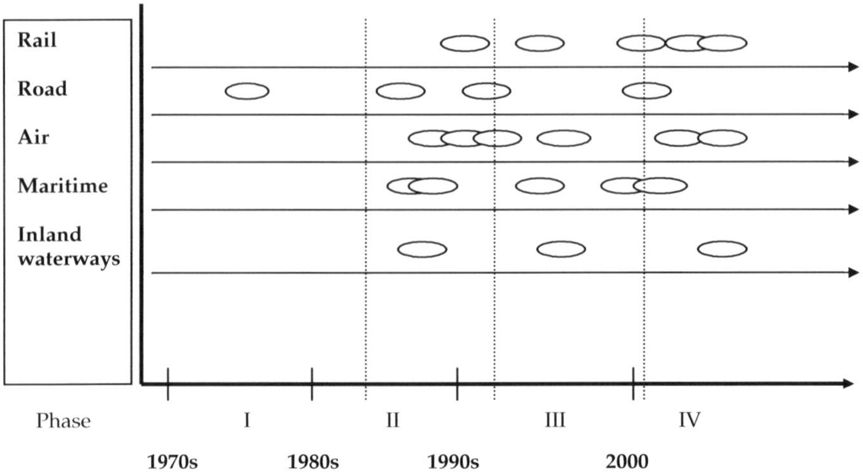

Note: Each ellipse indicates a EU package including regulations and directives applying to the transport sub-sector in question. For further detail on the content of ellipses see Table 3.3.1-3.3.4.

Figure 3.4: Development of EU transport policy- recent, gradual, uneven, and complex.

This chapter shows that the economic integration of EU transport policy has been *recent, gradual, uneven,* and *complex* as a result from the interaction between member states. Important interactions include member states' approaches to transport policy, respectively, in a regularly modified institutional setting with supranational constitutionally guaranteed bodies and, also, responses to crises. Assessing the historical development of EU transport policy in general, this study shows that member states, in the mid-1980s, initially endeavoured to remove impediments to the free movement of goods and services (negative integration). But since the mid-1990s, member states are becoming more and more involved in harmonizing the relevant national policies (positive integration). More specifically, it was the member states' attitudes towards different sub-sectors of transport that shaped EU transport policy actively from the early 1990s. Each round of enlargement and each revision of the existing treaties represented a potential challenge to the institutional balance. Maastricht extended the scope of the existing treaties to include safety and infrastructure issues. The Northern enlargement did not interfere with inland waterways protagonists such as Germany, the Netherlands, Belgium and Luxembourg.

In addition, the Commission's approach towards transport policy has shifted from a more policy sub-sector approach (modal approach) in the 1980s – working to achieve equal competitive conditions within each mode – towards an integrated approach demanding a greater equality of competitive conditions between the different transport modes.

Table 3.4: EU transport policy: Four phases between 1957-2004.

		Member states' approaches towards transport policy	
		Liberal market approach (negative integration)	State-led approach (positive integration)
Commission approach towards EU transport policy	Modal approach	**1957 – 1984** **1985 – 1992** **1993 –**	**2000**
	Integrated approach		**2001 – 2004**

Table 3.4 maps the 50-year history of EU transport policy, focusing on the changing key objectives and paying particular attention to the Commission's modal or integrated approach towards transport policy. In particular, the Commission's White Paper on *transport policy: European Transport Policy for 2010: Time to Decide'* (European Commission, 2001) represented a clear pursuit of the integrated approach towards transport policy, with inter-modality playing an important role. Bolstering the railway's share in the transport sector, which had dropped considerably, while road transport then accounted for more than 63 percent, the ideology-driven emphasis was, then, placed on road pricing for freight and especially heavy goods vehicles, which was considered the way forward for redressing the balance between modes (especially road and rail) and carried the ball deep into the state-led approach of transport policy, which, however, has been relaxed by the recently released mid-term review of the Commission's 2001 White Paper (European Commission, 2006).

Last but not least, the study has shown that EU transport policy has been driven by crises, so to say by political answers to crises – coinciding with the Commission's commencing shift in approach towards EU transport in the mid-1990s. Transport related accidents have affected the development of the EU transport *acquis* considerably since. Situational changes in the external environment evoked actions by the Commission (the agenda setter) in concert with the member states and the EP, the ECJ and following crises within transport-subsectors.

Table 3.5 highlights the major accidents on land, water and air for the last 15 years. While the annual statistics on alcohol induced road fatalities (Euro pean Commission, 2002) have resulted in a serious of EU legislation, in the maritime sector, it was major tanker calamities that initiated new legislation.

Table 3.5: Transport related accidents in Europe.

Accidents	Road	Rail	Inland waterways	Maritime	Air
Phase III: Integrated approach (1992 -2000)	Yearly figures about fatalities in car accidents	Southhall crash (1997); ICE Enschede crash (1998); Landbroke Grove collision (1999); Hatfield crash (2000)	Numerous collisions on the Rhine (Pallas & Co)	St. Ann´s Head (1996); Pallas (1998); Erika (1999); Cherbourg (2000); Ievoli Sun (2000)	Brigenair (1996); Essex (1999); Concorde (2000)
Phase IV: Consolidation (2001-2005)		Puddington rail crash and Potters Bar crash (2002); Paris-Vienna train		Baltic Sea (2001); Prestige (2002)	Milan (2001); Bodensee (2002)

The sinking of the car ferry MS Estonia, for example, which, in September 1994, capsized in a heavy storm in the Baltic Sea and sunk with over 900 passengers, while less than 200 survived, lead to the adoption of four consecutive EU directives dealing with safety standards for passenger vessels, of port state control, the registration of passengers on ferries and the mandatory surveys for ro-ro ferries in particular.[16] Other major fatal incidents in the maritime sector followed with Erika in 1999 and Prestige in 2002.

Furthermore, the Paris-Vienna train inferno in 2002, where a fire swept through on of the sleeping cars of Paris to Vienna killing twelve passengers, and a numerous other fatal train accidents since the mid-1990s on British and German soil lead to the adoption of the second railway package including, among others, detailed provisions for safety certification, and accident investigation.

In the aviation sector, a plane crash over the lake *Bodensee* in Summer 2002 underscored the necessity for additions to a common aviation security arrangements and better coordination of human resources policy in the air traffic control sector. In the night from 1 July to 2 July 2002, an aircraft of Bashkir Airlines and a freight Boeing-757 collided at a height of 11,000 m. The Russian airliner was carrying mainly children who were going on holiday in Spain, but then perished over the lake *Bodensee*. After investigations, the reason was verbal and computer instructions from Swiss air traffic controllers to the Russian crew which put the planes on a deadly new collision course. Also, the reasons for the 2001 Milan Linate plane collision between a SAS aircraft and a business jet on the runway killing 118 people had been traced back to the defective behavior by air traffic controllers who were, later on, charged with

16 Directives 98/18/EC, 98/25/EC, 98/41/EC, 99/35/EC.

manslaughter. The SAS aircraft had crashed into a baggage-handling building when it veered off the runway after hitting the Cessna aircraft, which had crossed its path. Investigators named poor visibility and human error the causes of the accident. But others claimed that the out of service ground radar was liable. The EU adopted regulation 552/2004 on the interoperability of European air traffic management network in 2004 and discuss a Community air traffic controller license (ATCO license) based on the Commission's proposal from 12 July 2004.

In the following, these findings will further guide the analysis of the study more general and the theoretical argument in particular which will be the focus of the next chapter.

Part II

The timing of transposition

Chapter 4: A theoretical framework for apt transposition

'Good things come to those who wait' – *Proverb*

4.1 Introduction

As has been argued in the literature review chapter of this book, comparative politics literature on implementation is rich in sociological (Dimitrova and Rhinard, 2005) and, to a lesser extent, historical institutionalist (Haverland, 2000) explanations. The few rational choice contributions that do exist represent the beginning of what in all likelihood will become a burgeoning field (Treib, 2003; Franchino, 2005; Steunenberg, 2006; 2007). Here, in the second main part of the study, I engage in the theoretical debate on transposition, in particular, by drawing from a simple bargaining model, in particular, that has a number of appealing features: *war of attrition games*. In this light, it refers to the transposition outcome as a bargaining between groups of actors of administrative and political nature who must agree on a new national policy. That is, actors are able to weigh every choice against its alternatives, and they invariably choose the most preferred option. Since their demands are incompatible, the actors can either reiterate the previous demand and waiting for the opponent to lower his demand or lower her own demand. Two parties choose the lengths of time to hold out for the prize in question. Waiting, i.e. delaying national transposition processes, is one of the actors' strategies, but can be costly.

Formal war of attrition models have subsequently been applied by economists to a variety of economic conflicts, such as price wars and economic reforms (Alesina and Drazen, 1991; Drazen and Grilli, 1993; Rodik, 1994; Haggard, 1990; Casella and Eichengreen, 1994; Sachs, 1994). Recently, a small group of political scientists has also begun using the war of attrition games, in a more informal way, to describe proliferation and warfare (Fearon, 1998; Smith and Stam, 2004; Adamsky, 2005). In comparative studies, however, no study has yet applied the underlying logic of those war of attrition models to societal problems. In the following I will present the basic concepts of war of attrition reasoning.

This book will identify three main groups of dynamics that influence timely transposition, such as European specific variables. Having an effect on the cost structures, also examined are member states' individual transposition forms, including the number of actors, and member states' individual methods, including the national transposition package approach[17], general elections, the allotted transposition time and the so-called 'deadline effect'. As a third set of factors this study leans on Hirshman's research (1985) which suggests that crises play an important role in determining when to cooperation in bargaining. Following his argument, here, I assess the effect of timeliness of transport-related accidents across member states.

This chapter is structured as follows. First, it presents the foundations of formal war of attrition games. To determine the outcome of the game (when and who ends the game?) it is necessary to determine the players' expected payoffs, i.e. the difference between benefits and costs. Then, I briefly discuss the individual components of the cost and benefit functions affecting the overall payoffs. Hereupon, the chapter bridges to the transposition setting in member states presenting a theoretical framework. It argues that transposition is a bargaining process over the sprawling rent-seeking costs, the rent proportion and time. Eventually, six hypotheses are generated to explain the timing effects of a) the number of veto players in the national transposition process, b) the amount of discretion granted by the directive's provisions (number of issues), c) the fixed transposition deadline in the directive, d) the so-called national transposition package approach, e) general elections, and f) transport-related accidents.

4.2 War of attrition games – The basic model

Political decision-making is often fundamentally a bargaining problem about *who* gets *when* and *what*. A bargaining problem, hence, is the essence of strategic decision-making between states, parties, bureaucrats, leaders, players – groups of actors. It refers to a situation where actors are confronted with a dilemma. There are multiple agreements or outcomes that would be preferred by all actors to no agreement, but the actors disagree in their ranking of the mutually preferable agreements (Fearon, 1998: 274). A second characteristic of bargaining problems is that they are resolved through time, in sequences of offers and counteroffers or with one or both parties 'holding out' in hope that the other will make concessions (Rubinstein, 1982). A final significant aspect of bargaining problems is that they typically involve uncertainty about the minimum that the other side would accept or private information about what the other side's true preferences and payoffs are. In this section, I describe the foundations of the bargaining model which account in particular for 'waiting' as one of the actors' strategies often referred to as war of attrition.

17 Understood as using one national implementing measure to transpose numerous EU directives.

To start there are two players who try to maximize their expected payoff.[18] In the beginning, both players announce simultaneously what they want from themselves. Player 1 demands her share to be x offering $1\text{-}p1$ to player 2. If $p1+p2=1$, the demands are called compatible and the players will split the money at the middle of their proposals (divide-the-dollar). When the demands are incompatible, the players proceed to the war of attrition stage. The actors are assumed to have conflicting preferences over two issues. Both would prefer coordinating on either one of the two outcomes to noncooperation, but they differ over the ranking of their preferred outcome. So the players' strategies are concerned with the moment *when* they decide to stop the game. Bargaining over which of two possible deals they will implement the players decide simultaneously what to do out of two options: *Reiterating her previous demand and waiting for her opponent to lower his demand, or lowering her own demand.* Eventually, the aim of the game is to find a player who ends the game at a specific date a (agreement).

Who and *when* the game ends, depends on the players' expected payoffs, i.e. the payoff to the actors for choosing a particular waiting time. The expected flow of payoffs to an actor i equals to the difference between benefits and costs: the benefits (Bi) based on the interval from the point of agreement (a) to infinity and the costs (Ci) based on the interval from the start of the negotiations (0) to the moment of agreement (a).

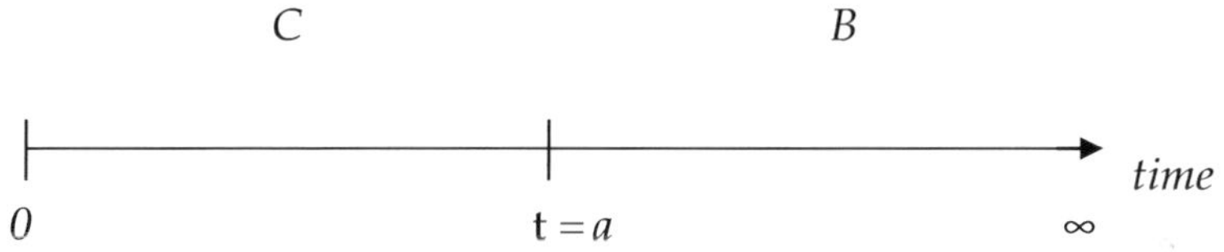

Benefits: The aim of negotiations is rent sharing. Before the deal, actors earn a proportion of the full rent and they want their share (benefit) to rise. If player 1 gets his way through, then, he wins a reward--which is private information to player 1 at the beginning of the game. The rationale behind this is that each individual picks a time that they are willing to display for and that when the lesser of these has elapsed the corresponding individual leaves and the other collects the reward (Hendricks, Weiss and Wilson, 1988). Here, the motto is: the earlier the better. The flow of benefits to actor i for choosing a particular

18 Originally, the war of attrition games was introduced by Smith (1974) in his study of the evolutionary stability of certain patterns of behaviour in animal conflicts. In particular, he notes that they often engage in a fight over prey. If one animal were to back down, its opponent would obtain the prey. If both animals were to back down simultaneously, then each would have an equal chance of obtaining the prey. Smith also notes that, in the animal kingdom, delaying cooperation entails fighting which is costly in terms of energy output and personal injury. Because fighting results in the diminution of strength, each animal prefers as short a fight as possible.

waiting time is positively related to the rent proportion, *pa*, and negatively related to time, *t*: *Bi (pa , t).*

Costs: Next to benefits, costs represent the second element of actors' payoff functions. Actors pay so-called rent-seeking costs. As Tullock (1967) has pointed out for market-distorting effects of monopolies, the real costs of acquiring rents can be much bigger than the 'second-order triangle losses from allocative distortions'; the big losses from an existing policy might not be the reduced trade in monopoly settings, but the *cost of the battle* to gain the monopoly. So-called rent-seeking costs emerge when players use advertising to increase their influence. Informative advertising has some social benefits, but to the extent that advertising is just 'gloss and glitter', it represents wasted resources. Studies, meetings, legislative hearings, and floor debates are all part of the political process needed to make expropriation threats credible whenever milder bills are proposed or the other way around. Hiding resources to avoid their expropriation likewise imposes deadweight losses (Shughart II and Razzolini, 2004: 387). Competition for benefits will cause scarce resources to be diverted from other, more socially valuable purposes and the cost to society of this *competition* might be as large as the value of the benefits themselves. Furthermore, these costs represent the costs of the status quo. The players' costs depend on the rent-seeking cost determinant, but also have to be paid per unit of time as long as the actor competes and until the second actor has quit. So, the flow of costs is determined by the player's cost determinant, *Xi*, and time, *t*: $C_i\,(X_i\,, t)$.

Expected payoff:
The actors' payoff structures consist of both, benefits and costs while both elements are affected by particular factors. Whereas both include the time component determining the flow of benefits and costs respectively, they vary in terms of additional elements which determine the actors' payoff flow. Generally speaking, the expected payoff of both players depends on the benefit indulged by the new policy and the total amount of time the player can expect to wait during the encounter. In addition, it is the rent-seeking costs, i.e. the cost of the battle in the pursuit of these benefits. The players' payoffs are similarly affected by the amount of time they wait. Waiting is assumed to be costly to both players for a number of reasons. Payoffs decrease over time. For the time being and simplicity, I assume that the loss in payoffs of both players while waiting is a linear function of the total amount of time they wait during the encounter. However, last but not least, however, players discount future payoffs. If the discount factor is low, the future cost/benefits are currently perceived as almost negligible; if the discount factor is high, future cost/benefits are perceived as being similar in value to the current ones.

$\mu_i = [\, B_i\ (p_a, t, d) - C_i\,(X_i, t, d)]$ with

t = time;
p_i = is player i rent proportion; $p_t^{\ i}$ is the player i rent proportion before agreement; p_a is player's i rent proportion claiming after agreement; with a = moment of agreement (when a player takes decision to accept his opponent claim);
X_i = rent-seeking cost determinant;
d = the percentage rate required to calculate the present value of a future payoff;
$B_i\,(p_a;\,t)$ is the benefit function positively related to *pa*; and negatively related to *t*;
$C_i\,(X_i,\,t)$ is the player i rent seeking cost function positively related to *Xi*; and negatively related to *t*.

In order to maximise the payoff, each player must choose a moment of agreement *a* at which he plans to concede in the event that the other player has not already conceded. An actor quits on time (*a*) which determines how long he will incur the rent-seeking costs in the hope of getting a better deal, because at any time player *i* earns a higher return if the other concedes first. The actor conceding first is normally referred to the leader (*L*), whereas the actor who does not end the game is the follower (*F*). The follower's payoff function is:

$F = B\,(p_0,\,t) - C\,(X_i,\,t,\,d);$
if $p_0 + p_a = 1$ then $p_0 = 1 - p_a$, and $F = B(1-p_a,\,t,\,d) - C\,(X_i,t,\,d)$

As a leader the player receives an expected payoff of:

$L = B(p_a,\,t,\,d) - C\,(X_i,\,t,\,d)$

All four payoff parameters, *p, X, t, d,* affect the benefits and costs of player *i* differently. Both actors choose lengths of time to hold out for the reward in question (here, the better cooperative deal) i.e. waiting in the hope that the other will make some significant concession first (back down). The first player to quit the contest cedes the reward to the other side. Increasing the rent proportion *p* increases the benefits and increases the risk of waiting. The point of waiting is to let someone else volunteer first, but waiting can be costly. Increasing the cost determinant increase the cost-side of the difference and decreases the likelihood of a complicated and time-consuming negotiation process. Increasing the waiting time *a* of the player increases the waiting costs with every additional unit per time while reducing the benefit. In this respect, discounting the future plays an additional important role. Players discount the future flow of payoffs affecting the perception of them. With a discount rate close to 1, the less player discount future payoffs and the more future cost/benefit payoffs are perceived as similar in value to the current ones. On the other hand, a discount rate close to 0 entails cost/benefits to be almost negligible.

In the following, I apply this waiting game logic to the EU's transposition problem without any claim for formalisation since there are a few difficulties in the basic war of attrition model which would make a formalisation very cumbersome. On the one hand, the assumed two actors' logic does not apply to most real applications in political science; in particular, it bears almost no relation to national transpositions of EU directives. The transposition process at the national level, for example, normally involves more than two actors. The need to forge a parliamentary majority in both chambers in case of legislative acts or a domestic consensus among relevant bureaucracies and other transposition actors may make it very costly for a state in general and ministers in particular to generate a new policy that they had signed at the Council of Ministers meeting. In addition, actors often bargain about more than two issues with EU directives' number of articles varying between a few to dozens (Kaeding, 2006). Furthermore, national transposition processes are constrained by so-called transposition deadlines set in the EU directive. So, we must add an additional factor that reflects the ability of the EU to legally open cases, and impose sanctions on the players, after the passing of the deadline in the directive.

Examining the timeliness of national transposition processes across member states, the following theoretical framework will adapt some of the basic components of the basic game described here, follows its reasoning in broader terms.In summary, this study will account for a transposition deadline that alters the payoff structure of *n* transposition actors. Furthermore, these actors, who are administrative and political in nature, are said to deal with several policy issues at once. Finally, I determine additional factors that may affect the players' expected payoffs, namely: effects of national transposition packages, general elections and external shocks. The next section reviews the study's theoretical framework.

4.3 The timing of transposition – what makes national transposition processes timley? – The theoretical framework

As an empirical matter of fact, Fearon (1998) argues that international bargaining often take the appearance of a war of attrition – two sides holding out, waiting in the hope that the other will make some significant concessions first. I argue that this holds also true for the transposition of EU legislation across the Member States. Member states must comply with new legislative measures passed by the Council of Ministers. Compliance is achieved through both the legal transposition process and the practical implementation of new, national legislation. In the following, this study focuses exclusively on the first stage, the legal transposition process which 'denotes the process of transforming directives into provisions of national law by the competent national legislative body or bodies' (Prechal, 1995: 5) within the margins of discretion guaranteed and the transposition deadline in the EU directive. In the following, I address every single component of the transposition bargaining process, namely: number of actors, set of possible deals, the transposition deadline and other effects on the expected payoffs determining the timeliness of national transposition processes.

Number of actors:
To start, this study argues that a transposition process normally induces policy change at the national, member state level. This policy change must be implemented by national transposition actors, who must come to an agreement of how to implement policy in a manner complying with EU legislation. Transposition actors are administrators and politicians, responsible for the adoption of national legislation. Whereas ministers and political appointees sign the ministerial orders and control the interpretation of the content of the directive, respectively, it is the ministry's administration that provides the technical and juridical know-how in the legal transposition stage.

The number actors on the state is contingent on the chosen type of national transposing instrument. Whereas member states transpose EU directives by using national implementing measures, the types of the legal instruments differ. Questions about how many ministries to be involved, and how many national legal instruments needed may depend on strategic calculations or may be preconditioned by national trajectories. Predicated mostly on administrative and ministerial traditions, one legal instrument is preferred over another. For example, in France the choice of an instrument to transpose an EU directive is affected by the question of whether its contents requires 'legislative' or 'executive' actions, that is, the introduction of law, or the introduction of government regulations. It is the State Council of France that determines to which branch the content of a directive belongs (Steunenberg and Voermans, 2005). Based on this advice, preparations to transpose a directive can begin. In Denmark, the bulk of transposition, about 85% of all directives, takes place by means of Ministerial orders. Over time, the trend has been to 'use more and more delegation to a Minister to pass certain provisions' (Steunenberg and Voermans, 2005: 83). In Italy, laws and legislative decrees represent 40% of all implementing measures, whereas ministerial orders are applied in about 60% of the cases. In 2004, for example, 52 of 87 notified Italian transposition measures were ministerial orders, 31 were ordinances, and only 1 was a law (Steunenberg and Voermans, 2005: 190). Obviously, the number of transposition actors varies considerably and not seldom go beyond two.

In general terms, the classical war of attrition literature, however, has focused on games with only two players, competing for rewards which is private information by actor *i* from the beginning of the game. While many of the examples do involve only two players, multiple player games are important. In line with Bulow and Klemperer (1997), I consider a generlised war of attrition in which n-persons are competing for n-rewards, so that *n-1* players must concede for the game to end. More players, however, create coordination problems (Shepsle and Boncheck, 1997). So to say, n-games are more complicated to resolve due to problems common to group interaction (Raiffa, Richardson and Metcalfe, 2002: 390):

- 'People talk at the same time. No one can make himself heard or, worse, hear anybody else;
- People don't listen carefully. They think about their next input;
- Too much time is spent on trivia and not enough on substance;
- Often the discussion breaks down into several parallel meetings, reaching inconsistent understandings'.

Imagine a handful of groups of transposition actors that want to pick an interpretation of an EU directive. Player A wants to opt for *a* and player B want to defend *b*. It might be possible to link those two. But now add some more parties, who will impose additional restrictions on the decision. Player C wants to push c; player D wants d. Now it does not seem very easy to make everyone happy. The difference is that in a game with two players we get down to one actor immediately, and so only have to incur costs running through the highest value of actor A and highest value of actor B. In a n-actors setting, *all* possibilities must be run through in real time, and the amount of time required for the transposition actor to shake down from n-actors to the remaining winner (follower) may far exceed the time needed to get from 2 to 1. To put it differently, complexity increases with the number of players. A deal between two players is less complex than a deal with four because the number of possible combinations is much greater. Complexity can delay the process considerably. The more actors involved the more time needed for policy change.

Set of issues:
A directive has to be transposed into national legislation, which requires 'the adoption of general measures of a legislative nature' (Prechal, 1995: 5). A directive's text determines the baseline policy and the latitude enjoyed by the member state in the transposition of the policy (Steunenberg, 2006). In accordance with Article 249, third paragraph, EC, a directive is binding in terms of the result to be achieved in each member state to which it is addressed. But, directives leave the choice of form and methods to the national authorities. The leeway afforded to member states in this regard, however, invariably depends on the result that the Council or the Commission wish to see achieved, i.e. the set of issues granting some degree of discretion.

National transposition actors, regardless their number, cannot modify the policy in ways that are substantially different from the draft adopted by the Council of Ministers. Otherwise, their action can be subject to infringement procedures (Art. 223) and, eventually, a Court's judgment of failure to comply with Treaty obligations. Since Maastricht (1992), member states can also expect to be charged with penalty payments. However, the Commission only challenges adopted national implementing measures that take extreme liberty with the competence, also known as margins of discretion, assigned to member states by the directive. Hence, if already existing national measures lie within the margins of discretion, then no new national transposing instrument has to be agreed upon. The member states simply notify the Commission directly about the existing legislation before the deadline of transposition. Whereas most transposition processes require new national implementing measures, i.e. the national policy status quo lies outside the directive's margins of discretion, the new European policy determines each member state's ability to interpret a directive's provisions.

But transposition bargaining often deal with more than two issues (points on which actors may disagree). EU Directive 2001/14/EC of the European Parliament and of the Council of 26 February 2001 *on the allocation of railway infrastructure capacity and the levying of charges for the use of railway infrastructure and safety certification*, for example, left the transposition actors with a comparatively high amount of discretion. It was for the transposition actors to decide whether the infrastructure manager were to provide all necessary information on the charges imposed (Article 7), whether member states were to levy mark –ups on the basis of efficient transparent and non-discriminatory principles (Article 8), whether member states were to establish a framework for the allocation of infrastructure capacity (Article 14), whether applications for infrastructure capacity were to be made by railway undertakings and their international groupings and member states were to allow other applicants to apply for infrastructure capacity on their territories (Article 16), and, finally, whether member states were to require railway undertakings to be involved in assuring the enforcement and monitoring of their own compliance of the safety standards and rules (Article 29). Hence, this example illustrates that transposing this specific EU directive raised six issues with considerable leeway for interpretation. If we apply a dichotomous interpretation, alone they already stand for 6! (240) different combinations – policy combinations that have to be addressed one by one which is very time-consuming and rent-seeking cost-intense.

Again, the coordination of different interpretations are cumbersome and complicated. Those at a meeting may fail to agree on the purpose of their gathering. They do not agree on what they should be talking about at any particular moment – what they need to decide, what information to share and so on. Combined with a growing number of actors the negotiations are easily sidetracked, and time wasted on irrelevancies. Each additional person has a new interpretation of an issue to discuss, and the same arguments are rehearsed again and again, 'without persuading anyone' (Raiffa, Richardson and Metcalfe, 2002: 392).

Transposition deadline:
Whereas most war of attrition models allow negotiations ample time as infinity, most real applications of the war of attrition models simply cannot allow infinity. i.e. there is a change in the payoff structure after some moment in

time. This also holds for the transposition of EU directives. After being adopted at the European level, EU directives must be transposed within a specific allotted timeframe set in their texts that can be normally found under the penultimate article of the EU directive. Therefore, this study takes a fixed deadline into the timing game (Ponsati, 1995) into consideration, which yields a discontinuity in the payoffs that actors can enjoy over time by leaving the assumed constant-cost but allowing costs to shoot up with the expiry of the deadline.

As long as the transposition actors have not settled their bargaining game, the status quo can proove very costly for the government. After the deadline has expired lawsuits at the national or European level become a real threat – representing additional costs to the already existing rent seeking costs of player *i*. A well-known example of such a lawsuit is the Francovich case. [19] The costs of being among the non-transposers of a European directive, individual transposition actor's costs of holding out which may differ for actors, i.e. delaying the transposition of the EU directive, include the private costs of enduring pressure from the administration, and the public costs, borne by all actors, of delaying passage of the legislative text. The delay increases public frustration with the political process, delays the legislative text's benefits, increases the probability of the text failing and left the actors less time to work on the rest of their agenda.

To put it differently, whereas in an infinite time horizon rent-seeking costs per unit of time are constant until the date of agreement, with the expiry of the transposition deadline the pattern changes. Additional costs of noncooperation occur reflecting the potential threat of a likely infringement procedure which is cumbersome, time-consuming, image damaging, distracting and with a possible costly outcome.

Both, the constant and variable element form part of the cost-side of the payoff function. Whereas until now players would spend an amount smaller than the benefit in their pursuit of the benefits, costs to society of this competition might be as large as the value of the benefits themselves or could even exceed the benefits. Introducing a deadline allows the rent-seeking costs to rise exponentially.

So, altering the game to one in which individuals must meet a deadline entails two consequences. One consequence: evolving around the fixed transposition deadline itself. The second consequence is the length of the transposition period granted in the EU directive. A fixed transposition deadline adds to the assumed constant rent seeking cost function a second cost component; This

19 Additional examples include, among others, Commission vs. UK, Case C-218/02, Commission vs. Ireland, Case C-494/01; Commission vs. Belgium, Case C-27/03.

component reflects the potential national court and European infringement costs (Conant, 2002). Furthermore, the length of the transposition period defined by the EU directive has an impact on the date of agreement. The longer the transposition timeframe the more costs accumulate per unit. This accumulation leads to an agreement while costs exceed the benefits of delay. The flow of benefits to actor *i* for choosing a particular waiting time is negatively related to time. Whereas a comfortable generous timeframe allows the actor to transpose timely and correct, consequently, the less transposition time guaranteed by the directive, the more prevalent are the players' benefits – leading to more complex and time-consuming bargaining.

Additional effects on players' expected payoffs

Effects of national transposition packages:

European directives rarely require more than one national transposing measure in order to be adequately implemented. But member states often use one national legal instrument to transpose a handful of EU directives at the same time, in what is known as a national transposition package approach. These national transposition packages can include two or more EU directives whose full transposition is, quite often, not due in the same year. They are applied to reduce coordination costs within the ministries since they allow to transpose a couple of directives with only one national legal instrument. Decisions on whether to apply the package approach, and how many EU directives the package would include, are made by the same institutional actors who decide what national legal instrument to use and how many are needed in terms of correct transposition. For example, in France, the decision-makers are the SGCI (*Secrétariat Général du Comité Interministériel pour les questions de coopération économique européenne*), who consult with the State Council and the SGG (*Secrétariat Général du Gouvernment*); in Spain, the *Potestad Reglamentaria* (*Article 23 of ley 50/1997 de 27 noviembre, del Gobierno*) is responsible for indicating what circumstances require a law (Steunenberg and Voermans, 2005: 129).

Due to its endogenous character a national transposition package should only positively affect the transposition speed assuming that member states always try to meet the deadlines. However, to what extent the package approach accounts for the timeliness of the national transposition process is contingent on when it occurs (timing). Since a transposition settlement will be reached as soon as the costs of non-transposition surpass the benefit of the existing policy, the package approach will trigger policy change at different pace by increasing the costs of non-transposition steadily. Depending on the position of the EU directive within the national transposition package, the costs may remain for a longer period below the costs for policy change. However, a break-even point will occur when costs of maintaining the status quo surpass the rent-seeking costs of implementing the new policy. Hence, the usual time margins of transposition are set by the deadlines in the first and last directives in the package. Depending on those and following the earlier mentioned logic of an additional 'infringement threat' cost component, the accumulated costs may increase considerably for the first EU directives after the deadlines and remain relatively low for the last directive whose allotted timeframes are longer.

Effects of general elections:
Elections are the usual mechanism by which modern democracy fills offices in the legislature. They are universally accepted as a tool for selecting representatives in modern democracies. Elections can be set and postponed by Presidents and Head of States, and they vary in frequency and time needed for execution. Because elections attract a lot of attention by voters and office seekers, they have an impact on the internal policy-making procedures in a member state. Whereas elections can cause political crises, as in the case of Ukraine general elections in 2004 or the Italian general elections in 2006, elections are often characterized as destabilizing and disequilibrating factors in a country's policy-making system. Incumbent decision-makers perceive general elections as a threat to the status quo to which a responsive decision is necessary (electoral campaign). It unbalances the regular heartbeat of day-to-day politics and directly affects the size of actors' rent-seeking costs.

National general elections reduce rent seeking efforts of government officials by channelling all their attention away from day-to-day policy-making toward the electoral campaign (keyword: parliamentary recess). With regard to transposition, depending, however, on when a general election occurs in the point in time of the transposition process (timing), a general election can have either a retarding or accelerating affect. For analytical reasons, I distinguish between general election falling at two points during a national transposition process: either *at the beginning*, or *at the end*. Although elections reduce rent-seeking costs in general, elections that fall at the end of a national transposition process increase the cost of waiting dramatically. The underlying reason, here, is with the potential threat of infringement costs, which coincide with the 'legislative deadline'. Future payoffs shadow on the national transposition process with a discount factor close to 1. National implementation procedures that have not been finalized by the end of the parliamentary term often expire and must be re-tabled in the new legislative term. If they are not *adopted* before the end of the legislative term, however, they automatically extend the duration of a national transposition process considerably. Any legislative project that the institutions have not passed by the 'legislative deadline' must be reconsidered from scratch, which is a time-consuming endeavour. Considering the potential infringement costs after the expiry of the transposition deadline, such reconsideration represents a financial and image marring threat. Therefore, on the one hand, it is the national administrations that use the 'political vacuum' to push their efforts of special interests in order to obtain preferential treatment by using the machinery of government – regulations and legislation. A member state's administration increases its standing with other ministries if it takes the lead in more and more dossiers from

Brussels. On the other hand, politicization of public administrations across political systems has become a 'reality of modern government' (Peters and Pierre, 2004: 288). Some positions in the public service will always be political which makes administrations very much dependent on politics and general elections respectively.

To the contrary, general elections that fall at the beginning of a national transposition process do not encounter infringement costs in the short run. Politicians still have all the legislative term ahead and, first, probably prioritise election pledges. Administrators have less incentive to maximize their influence at the beginning of a legislative term compared to the end of a legislative term. Generally speaking, they regard transposition of EU law as a low priority, not in the least because they associate it with a lot of additional workload from Brussels. This work is believed, and rather accurately so, to be in terms of prioritizing and coordinating across different units (of one or more ministries).

Effects of external shocks:
Exogenous shocks that aggravate economic conditions increase the cost of not adopting reforms and thus prompt a solution to the bargaining problem (Drazen and Grilli, 1990; Alesina and Drazen, 1991). Regardless of the kind of crisis[20], considerable influence is enacted on the timeliness of the transposition process by such upsets. According to Brecher's definition (1977:32) a crisis is a

> sudden and unforeseen '*situational change in the external or internal environment which creates in the minds of the incumbent decision-makers of a state a perceived threat from the external environment to the basic values to which a responsive decision is deemed necessary.*' (italic added)

In the context of transposition, crisis add to the constant rent-seeking costs additional costs of external shocks. A crisis that immediately shoots up overall costs, increases the cost of non-transposition more general, and thereby increases the probability of a fast settlement.

Thus, the external shock costs reduce the benefits, settles bargaining issues, and increases the probability of settlement in even the most conflicted bargaining processes. In line with this theoretical framework, the following section proceeds with the presentation of seven testable hypotheses.

---

20 The word crisis comes from the Greek word *krinein* meaning 'to decide.' It is defined as a crucial time, a climax, or a juncture and is often depicted by the Chinese symbol that means danger and opportunity. This paper argues that crisis may raise welfare if it is the only way to induce necessary policy change.

4.4 Hypotheses

Number of veto players:
Depending on the form of the national transposing instrument, the number of actors varies, and this affects the timeliness of transposition in general. A Dutch Ministerial Order, for example, is faster than statutes or orders in Council, because consultation of advisory boards is very rare, and neither the Council of State nor the Parliament needs to be consulted (Bekkers, Bonnes, De Moor van Vugt, Schoneveld and Voermans, 1995: 412). In France, a Legislative Act with the format of an omnibus bill that transposes a number of directives, preferably in one policy area, requires the State Council's advice and a parliamentary approval with a simple majority. A ministerial order, however, represents a provision issued by the minister without explicit authorization through a law, and requiring nothing more than a signature by the minister. National governments that must satisfy many coalition partners, as well as other veto players, have through all possibilities in real time requiring a lot of time for the actors to shake down from *n* to one player. Since waiting i.e. delaying is costly, the model suggests, in line with Haverland (2000); Giuliani (2003); Steunenberg (2006), that policy change is adopted later in countries with more political fragmentation.

> *Veto-player matters – hypothesis*: The fewer actors involved in the making of a legal instrument, ceteris paribus, the less likely a delayed transposition process.

Level of discretion:
The more discretion guaranteed in the EU directives reflected by the amount of issues, the more difficult it will be to find an agreement across the numerous transposition actors. The higher the directive's number of issues, guaranteeing a certain degree of flexibility, the more complex the transposition process, i.e. the more issues to be pondered and negotiated, the more strategic and time-consuming bargaining involved, the longer it will take for an agreement to be reached. Since waiting is costly (and a considerable number of issues given leeway in interpretation entaisl longer rounds of bargaining), there is a positive relation between the number of issues, member states' discretion and the timeliness of national transposition processes.

> *Discretion matters – hypothesis:* The higher the amount of discretion, *ceteris paribus*, the more difficult to settle an agreement on time.

Time set for transposition:
Two effects on timeliness with regard to the transposition time set in the directives are important. First, the length of the transposition time matters. Especially highly detailed and complex directives are transposed slowly (Ciavarini Azzi, 2000: 56) and need to grant more time for transposition than fairly straightforward directives. This is especially true when technical decisions about complex directives are decided in implementation committees

after the directive has been accepted. For example, changes to labelling requirements should allow sufficient time to exhaust existing label stocks. With longer transposition timeframes the flow of benefits to actor *i* for choosing a particular waiting time decreases and with it this overall utility. To the contrary, a short transposition time set in the EU directive limits the rent seeking costs of actor *i* and increases the benefits. Member states are more likely to comply in case of longer deadlines.

> *Transposition time matters- hypothesis*: The more time a member state has to transpose a directive, *ceteris paribus*, the swifter the national transposition process.

Furthermore, a comfortable transposition timeframe increases the probability that the adoption of the national transposing measure will occur around the deadline. In politics, each actor chooses the time at which he or she intends to concede his or her position. In situations where there is a known final period, or even when the number of negotiation rounds is known, a settlement is agreed upon around the time of the deadline. Whereas the average benefits of bargaining without a deadline are close to zero (since conceding means giving up almost all the surplus), a deadline, and especially an early deadline, yields positive average benefits. Whereas the costs of non-transposition remain constant before the deadline, they shoot up after the expiry of the deadline by adding the 'infringement cost'component. The costs of non-transposition increase considerably after the deadline because, after that set date, citizens and businesses can file costly court cases in hopes of eking out their rights. Since delays are so costly, this study predicts that introducing a deadline with the directive results in a so-called *deadline-effect* (Carré, 2000). This study argues that there is a positive, unidirectional, probability of a compromise at the transposition deadline set by the Council of Ministers.

> *Transposition deadline effect – hypothesis*: Actors come to an agreement around the date of expiry.

Coherence of national transposition package:
First directive in the national transposition package: Delaying effect
Normally, a European directive is followed by more directives on the same issue at hand, so the costs for the first directive are relatively high compared to the costs of maintaining the existing status quo. As long as the responsible unit is aware of the fact that forthcoming amendments are common to recently adopted directives, the costs of the status quo are bearable because the possibility of future EU legislation illuminates the actual costs of non-transposition. Ministries may strategically delay engaging in a cumbersome transposition process. As long as the costs of the existing policy remain lower than the costs for policy change – which, however, decreases with every additional directive in the transposition package – the settlement of transposition bargaining for the first instrument in the package will be delayed.

Last directive in the national transposition package: Accelerating effect
In most cases the national transposition process is already underway when the last European directive (of a transposition package) has been adopted by the EU Council of Ministers, so the national package approach will have an accelerating effect on the last directive in the perceived transposition package. While time will have helped to settle allocation quarrels about the costs before the adoption of the last European directive, costs of non-transposition will have surpassed the costs for policy change.

> *National transposition package approach – hypothesis*: A national package approach increases the probability of a delayed settlement of the first European Directive in the package, whereas, in turn, it accelerates a settlement of the last European Directive.

Timing of general elections:
Beginning of transposition process: Retarding effect
Ministers are office seekers. To get (re-)elected, politicians must please and spend time with their constituency. Although they are not always Member of Parliament, due to their popularity Ministers spend much of their campaigning time with their constituency. Consequently, during general elections, ministers who are key players in the legal transposition process have less time for day-to-day policy-making. Electoral concerns that occur in the beginning stages of the transposition process may persuade policy makers to stick with the status quo. At the beginning of a transposition process the costs are lower than the benefits from possible re-election. When the discount factor for future payoffs is comparatively low the overall utility to settle an agreement low. If the timing of general elections falls within the starting phase of a national transposition process the drafting process of new legislative instruments, hence, will be retarded. In addition, a change in domestic political circumstances may lead government leaders to see new potential gains from alternative policy options, as when a political party with stronger commitments to liberalizing trade come to power or the implementation of a European directive generates new domestic political pressures (Börzel and Risse, 2003). For administrators a new legislative term means increased workload. This workload includes all non-adopted legislation from the former legislative term that must be re-considered from scratch as well as delving into new legislative texts that have not yet seen the light of day.

End of transposition process: Accelerating effect
The end of a legislative term coinciding with a national transposition process has the opposite effect. At the end of a legislative term the so-called 'legislative deadline' triggers the need to act fast. Directives that have not been transposed by the end of the parliamentary term expire or have to be tabled new. Since, here, the threat of additional infringement costs with the date of expiry is potentially high, the discount rate is almost equal to 1, national transposition processes are very likely to be adopted on time. If transposition is not concluded before the next legislative term, a general election will shelf it,

along with all legislative projects that have not been adopted before the next legislative term. Hence, all non-adopted legislation in the concluding legislative term would have to be re-introduced in the forthcoming term, which would increase the costs unbearably for politicians and administrators alike. Administrators profit from a political vacuum; it increases their influence in day-to-day policy-making. The certainty of a legislative deadline makes transposition before the end of the legislative period possible.

> *Election matters – hypothesis:* Whereas a general elections falling at the beginning of the transposition procedure decreases the probability of a problem-free settlement, a general election at the end of a transposition process accelerates the adoption of new national legislation.

Transport related accidents: Accelerating effect

Considering the findings of the transport chapter, accidents apply to transport sub-sectors in particular. [21] This study has identified a crisis-driven approach behind the overall European development of transport. EU policies for all modes of transport, (maritime, air, inland waterways, road, and rail) have been often initiated by accidents and crises, leading to the adoption of numerous packages in the transport sub-sectors by the Ministers of Transport. So, accidents in all modes of transport have not only shaped the development of EU transport policy in general, but have also kicked off reform efforts by increasing the costs of delayed non-transposition of the new EU legislation. The greater the costs of non-cooperation for the group in general, the more likely is an agreement, since these costs will erode the expected payoffs. External shocks add costs to the utility equation, resulting in an increase of general overall costs. Additional costs decrease the utility and increase the urgency of a settlement and, eventually, accelerate the settlement of a bargaining conflict. Consequently, the players are forced to settle earlier.

This study argues that a member state in the midst of transposing EU legislation, and in particular legislation in the transport sub-field, has an increased probability of reaching a settlement when an accident occurs.

> *Accidents matter – hypothesis:* An accident increases the probability of a timely settlement.

4.5 Summary of predictions

Table 4.6 summaries three groups of factors that affect the timeliness of national transposition processes across member states. It shows, as argued, that the EU directive's level of discretion may have a retarding effect on transposition timeliness. On the contrary, the more transposition time set in the directive,

21 Accidents probably also affect other policy areas, such as: food safety, banking, health and safety at work, protection from hazards, and border control.

the more swift and problem-free the national transposition process. Furthermore, the adoption of new legislative instruments should accumulate around the transposition deadline. At the national level, national forms and methods of transposition play an important role as well as the timing general elections. When more veto players are involved, the transposition process is slower. The package approach alters the pace of policy change by affecting the distribution of adjustment costs of a new European policy. General elections may have a either a retarding or an accelerating effect on transposition, depending on when they occur in the transposition process. Last but not least, external shocks increase the cost component in the cost/benefit equation. considerably. Transport related accidents push for fast implementation of the content of the new EU directive.

Table 4.6: Effects on transposition speed.

		Effect on transposition speed	
		Retarding	**Accelerating**
EU directive related factors	1. Level of discretion guaranteed by the directive	The more discretion in the text, the more difficult timely transposition.	
	2. Length of transposition deadline of the directive		The more transposition time set in directive, the more problem-free transposition. The more likely Member States are to comply.
Form and method of national transposition process	3. Number of veto players	The more veto players involved, the more delayed the transposition process.	
	4. Presence of national package	First European Directive in the national transposition package	Last European Directive in the national transposition package
	5. General elections	General elections scheduled at the beginning of transposition process	General elections scheduled at the end of the transposition process
Internal and external situational change	6. Transport related accidents		Accidents during the transposition period

4.6 Conclusion

In this chapter I have provided a theoretical framework to address the research question of why member states wait to adopt new legislation causing missed deadlines when transposing Internal Market directives in the field of transport. This framework is informed by findings of war of attrition models on the effect of costs and benefits on the settlement of bargaining problems. Assuming that a newly adopted EU directive affects the transposition actors' utilities, the national transposition process is not a zero-sum game. *Instead is understood as a bargaining between political and administrative groups of actors, who must reach an agreement about the distribution of cost and benefits.* Applying the logic of war of attrition models to the transposition problem, this study generated six hypotheses. In the remainder of the book, all six hypotheses will be tested. In the following chapter, which introduces the third part of the study, I present and discuss the data and methods used to test the hypotheses on the timeliness of national transposition processes.

Part III

Analysis within a combined research design

Chapter 5: EU 1995-2004 transport transposition data set:

'Who is Afraid of Cumulative Research?' (Title of the article by M. Gabel, S. Hix and G. Schneider published in European Union Politics 3(4): 481-500.

5.1 Introduction

After reviewing the rich scholarly discussion on implementation and transposition in the European Union (EU), I assessed the characteristics of the historical development of the EU transport policy field. Results from this review further supported my theoretical framework, which explains why member states miss deadlines for transposing EU transport directives. In this chapter, to test the six hypotheses quantitatively, I present a new data set of the second round that covers almost two-thirds of the full population of the EU transport *acquis* from 1995 to 2004. Before I operationalize and test the hypotheses in the subsequent chapters, here, I deal with methodological issues. First, I address my motivation of the selection of the policy field, the member states, and the time period of investigation. I then present the sources of information and assess the completeness of the data set, while devoting particular attention to missing values and other important choices.

5.2 Policy field selection

While the research focus is to understand the reasons and mechanisms behind member states' transposition delay of EU Internal Market legislation, directives are of particular interest. They are not immediately applicable at the national level, but must first be incorporated into national law. Therefore, this book's focus is the transposition of European directives. It is difficult, however, to analyze all European policy fields in which directives are issued within the context of the proposed study. Whereas the amount of 'legislation in force' in general has more than doubled from 4,566 legal acts in 1983 to 9,767 in 1998 (Wessels, Maurer and Mittag, 2003), the occurrences of EU directives in particular was 2,285 in 1998 and 2,674 (European Commission, 2006) on 8 March 2006.

The policy area selected for the study was guided by four considerations: Because the study's focus is on the timeliness of national transposition processes, I will not consider areas in which the EU primarily issues regulations, such as in the field of cohesion policy, international trade and the common agricultural policy (Alesina, Angeloni and Schuknecht, 2005). Second, I will focus on a core policy area of the Union established by the Treaty of Rome (Franchino, 2005). Furthermore, a classic way of distinguishing between policy types, which I will use, is in terms of regulatory, re-distributive and distributive policies (Lowi, 1964). Typically, EU policies have a strong regulatory emphasis (Nugent, 2003: 324), and Majone even argues that the EU can be thought of as a regulatory state (1991; 1994; 1996). In order to facilitate the generalization of my findings at a later point, the second consideration is whether the policy area in question fit well into the dominant EU regulatory category. And fourth, to be able to produce empirical regularities for research on transposition of EU directives, I present areas with a sufficiently large number of cases and sufficient variety between the cases (for concise overview of EU legislative output, see: Alesina, Angeloni and Schuknecht, 2005).

On the basis of these four criteria this current study opted for the transport sector. Transport has a strong regulatory component, and furthermore, is one of the crucial enabling technologies for civilization. Since transport had played a longstanding and key role in people's everyday lives and was a major factor in economic competitiveness and employment, the creation of the single market for intra-Community transport was judged as one of the necessary conditions for achieving the 'four freedoms' enshrined in articles 74-84 of the Treaty of Rome. Transport contributes to social and territorial cohesion and by its very nature is fundamental to the achievement of freedom of movement across the EU, satisfying a primary objective of EU policy. Furthermore, permitting quantitative research, the transport *acquis* includes a sufficient number of directives (106).

5.3 EU transport transposition data set 1995-2004

While the selection of the policy area was primarily guided by four analytical reasons, in the following sections, this study argues that we must make additional choices about which member states to include in the data set, what time period to cover, sources of information, what information to garner and what to do with missing values.

5.3.1 Selection of member states:

For analytical reasons this study opted for nine member states: France, Germany, Greece, Italy, Ireland, Spain, Sweden, the Netherlands and the UK. These states were selected to cover most of the important dimensions of variation on the national level independent variables: centralized versus decentralized states variation in legal traditions and practices, and variation in the number of veto players across and within member states. Here, institutional aspects of the member states' political system play a role, since they are part of the explanatory factors. Whereas some governments tend to be more stable than others, also included are member states with clear preferences for a limited number of transport sub-sectors, such as the Netherlands for inland waterwayss. In contrast, Germany considers all five modes of transport equally important. In addition, the study highlights a pair of notorious transposition laggards – Greece and Italy. Conversely, Spain and Sweden have often led the Commission's scoreboards on the notification of national measures of implementing directives (European Commission, 2005). Eventually, also included are France, Greece, Sweden and Ireland, a group on which little implementation research work has been done to date.

5.3.2 *Time period: 1995-2004*

This study opted to focus on only recent cases (1995-2004) of EU national implementation instruments in the area of transport covering almost ten years for three reasons. First, EU history experienced a new level of quality with the adoption of the Single Market in the early 1990s. It was the Single Market idea that triggered important new policy developments in more general areas.[22] The Transport Chapter illustrates that it was not until the 1990s that all sub-sectors were covered by EU legislation. The Internal Market Project entailed the first ever legislative efforts in the railway sector, an area that had not previously attracted considerable attention. Second, rounds of enlargement widened the group of member states. With Sweden, the study includes a country that became member of the EU as late as 1995. Another consideration is Schulz and König (2000) finding that data sources on EU legislation and national legal instruments such as Celex, are biased toward the period before the late 1980s, i.e. the Celex data base is complte only as of late 1980s. There is a considerable delay before the Celex database is fully updated by the Commission, as national data is transferred sporadically. To maintain the effect of right censoring controllable (with regard to those directives for which the transposition process as not been concluded yet), I ignored directives with transposition deadlines set for after 2004.

Overall, the EU transport transposition data set 1995-2004 covers almost ten years of crucial EU transport history while representing 63 percent of the full transport *acquis*, which had to be adopted by the member states of the last round of enlargement in 2004. The data covers all transport sub sectors. The distribution of policy sub-sectors in the transport *acquis* is summarized in Figure 5.5.

Road and shipping directives account for almost two-thirds of the transport *acquis*, whereas air and rail represent 12% each, general framework directives constitute 8% while inland waterways are used for 4%.

---

22 See also Alesina, Angeloni and Schuknecht (2005) for a breakdown of EU legislation by policy domain.

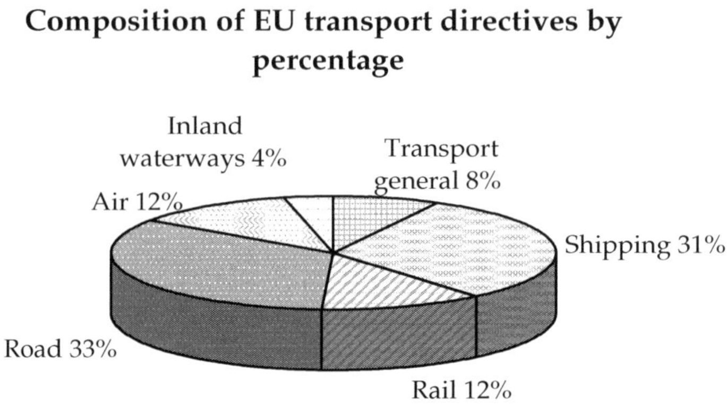

Figure 5.5: Composition of EU transport directives by percentage.

5.3.3 *Sources of information:*

Information on the EU transport directives is taken from the official legal database of the European Union – Celex (*Communitatis Europeae Lex*) which covers all Community legislation, preparatory acts, case-law of the European Court of Justice (ECJ) and parliamentary questions. Celex also aids the interaction between community law and national law by providing publication references regarding member states' national provisions to enact community directives. Almost 70% of all national implementing measures for Germany, Spain, the Netherlands, the UK, Sweden, Ireland, Italy, France and Greece have been reported in Celex and other Commission sources.[23] However, the official legal databases of the European Union are not the only accessible source to report national implementing measures (or an overview, see Hudson, 2005).

To compare and control for the quality of Celex, I contacted each Transport Ministry in the nine Member States and received a full list from their national transposition databases dating back to the very first directive of the transport *acquis*.[24] Interestingly, 80% of the data that was often referred to as 'unreliable' (Börzel, 2001; Mbaye, 2001; Mastenbroek, 2003) matched the national data. In only 20% of the cases I added further information on the national implementing instrument derived from the national databases. There was

23 See Steunenberg and Rhinard (2005) for an overview of Commission's efforts to gather reliable compliance data.

24 www.boe.es/g/es (Spain); www.gazzette.comune.jesi.an.it (Italy); www.jura.uni-sb.de/BGB1/suche.html (Germany); www.legifrance.gouv.fr (France); www.online-law.co.uk/lawsearch/lawsearch/html (UK); www.opmaat.sdu.nl (The Netherlands); www.swedengov.se/sb/d/3288 , www.infotorg.sema.se and www.rixlex.riksdagen.se/ntbin/thw?%24% (Sweden). I would like to thank Panagiota Massouridou to assist me in getting access to the secured data base for the Greek legal professions.

no biased lack of information across member states or transport sub-sectors worth mentioning. However, I did add information for all modes of transport within each member state following the efforts in line with transposition data of the second generation.

5.3.4 *Missing data:*

When considering the detailed information for each transport directive from the first national implementing measure, missing values became apparent. However, incomplete data on the EU directives or the national implementing measures seems unrelated to member states or transport sub-sectors.[25] Since these missing values are random noise, they are not expected to affect the findings in a systematic manner. Consequently, I took the following steps to improve the quality of data. First, in cases where a date of publication was not recorded, I used their date of adoption. Second, I excluded missing values for which I had not found a date of transposition. Third, I deleted two EU directives portions from the transport acquis which only dealt with transport in the broadest sense, namely: summer time provisions. Fourth, I excluded all cases in which member states had already complied before the EU directive was adopted. Finally, I deleted all transposition cases of consolidating directives that combined existing directives, repealed directives or corrected directives. The last information added on pending cases was February 1, 2004.[26]

5.3.5 *Recording the first national transposing instrument:*

Member states sometimes translate EU legislation by using more than one national transposing instrument. When they do this, they necessarily notify the Commission of all to-be-used measures. For the purpose of this research, it was not feasible to record all the transposing instruments that were notified to the Commission. Therefore, in order to calculate transposition delay at a later stage of this analysis, a decision had to be made with regard to which national implementing measure is recorded. It is an important question, not in the least because whatever legal instrument is recorded will be used to calculate the dependent variable, timeliness. Three primary considerations denote the first national legal instrument as the prudent choice: practical, conceptual and legal.

First, from a practical point of view, recording the first national implementing measure makes sense because the Commission considers the first national legal instrument notified as sufficient (IP15). It is sufficient with respect to

25 See Kaeding (2006).

26 Please see Steunenberg and Rhinard (2005) for additional information on the Transposition Group data set.

complying with the requirement of timely notification. That is not to say that timely notification is an appropriate measure to explain the completeness of implementation. Nonetheless, timeliness is the dependent variable of this study and, moreover, a necessary first step for full compliance with the EU Treaty obligations. Only after the Commission has been notified of the first instrument does the 'clock start ticking' to measure an instrument's appropriateness and correctness for transposing a particular EU directive.

From a conceptual point of view, opting for the alternative 'last' implementing measure would have been problematic. Since there is always the possibility that new measures will be added later on, due to the transposition of new EU legislation in the area, it is rather difficult to identify the last instrument, especially in a large-n study. [27] Conceptually, then, there is not such thing such as a last instrument (see Berglund, Gange and van Waarden, 2006 for detailed discussion). When is an instrument the last one? When is a national implementing process finalised?

From a legalistc point of view, opting to record the first national transposition instrument is prudent because the instrument normally represents the key legislative measure in the national transposition process. Moreover, it often clears the way for additional pieces of legislation, if required, to be implemented.

In summary, the first recorded measure might not indicate whether the national transposition process is complete. However, by using this indicator we can confidently ascertain whether there has been a delay. Focusing on the timeliness of national transposition processes, furthermore, taking for record the first instrument also diminishes the possibility of exaggeration of delays.

5.3.5 Data set:

The EU transport transposition data set covers the period of 1995-2004 and includes information on the first 367 national implementing measures in nine member states covering 67 EU transport directives and representing 63% of the total transposition *acquis* that member states had to transpose before the last enlargement round in 2004. To increase the quality of the Celex data (and thereby satisfy the recent efforts of the implementation data of the second generation), this study controlled for and added national data sources and tidied up the data set for analysis purposes.

27 I will return to this argument when presenting the case studies. When presenting them, I have the advantage of hindsight to accurately account for all legislative instruments, since all four cases had been concluded.

Chapter 6: EU transposition deficit – statistical illusion or reality?

'Failure to apply European legislation on the ground damages the effectiveness of Union policy and undermines the trust on which the Union depends. The perception that 'we stick to the rules but others don't', wherever it occurs, is deeply damaging to a sense of European solidarity... Prompt and adequate transposition and vigorous pursuit of infringements are critical to the credibility of European legislation and the effectiveness of policies.' (European Commission's Strategic Objectives 2005-2009, COM(2005) 12 final, p.5).

6.1 Introduction

There has long been a vague supposition that the EU has a transposition problem. The study first demonstrates that, indeed, the EU does have a serious transposition problem among member states and different modes of transport. Based on information from 367 national implementing measures covering nine member states during 1995-2004, indeed it is shown that that the EU transposition deficit is more than just a statistical illusion. While only 50 percent of national transposition instruments are completed on time, cross-country variance is respectable pinpointing to laggards and leaders among member states.

6.2 The European transposition deficit further specified

Calculating the difference between the transposition deadline set in the EU directive and the date of publication of the first national transposing instrument, Figure 6.6 shows that the EU faces a serious transposition deficit in the transport sector. Figure 6.6 displays the delays in weeks for the 367 national implementing measures in the transport data set. A *negative* delay, as indicated on the horizontal axis of the figure, indicates that a national implementing instrument was adopted early, i.e. before the official deadline set by the Council of Transport Ministers.

During 1995-2004, the nine member states under investigation notified 53 percent of the national instruments on time. In addition, we find cases that were transposed up to 2,4 years earlier than demanded by the directive (see index, No. 367 and 366). However, 47 percent were transposed late, varying between just a few days tardy to 251 weeks (almost 5 years) overdue, as it is the case for Greece's national transposing measure for the EU directive *on the harmonization of boatmasters' cerficates* (index No. 11). The mean transposition time in the transport sector was 26 weeks (six months) late, whereas the median was zero weeks, i.e. on time.

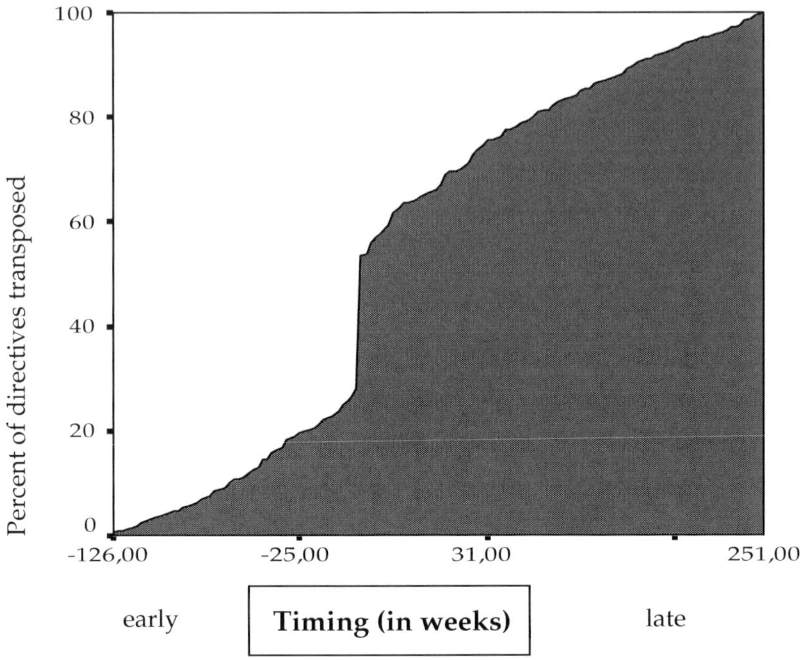

Figure 6.6: Transposition of transport directives in Germany, Spain, the Netherlands, UK, Greece, Ireland, France, Italy, and Sweden: Delay in weeks.

6.2.1 *Mean/median discrepancy:*

Before additional results are addressed a more detailed discussion of the discovered mean and median values is prudent to address first. The recorded discrepancy between median/mean values uncovers the following, which is crucial for the remainder of the book. One the one hand, we see that about half of the national transposition measures were notified on time, while the remaining half were late (median). On the other hand, the standard average (artithmetic mean) indicates that the average transposition delay was about six months. With a discrepancy between the mean and median of 26 weeks (half a year), we notice that a considerable number of national legal instruments must record a remarkably long delay. The distribution of the mean delay is skewed upwards so that the majority of national transposition processes have a delay lower than the mean. Indeed a closer look at the figures shows that *70 percent* of the delayed transpositions have a delay longer than six months (the mean), a circumstance that causes the discrepancy between median/mean values.

Looking at these patterns, we can identify three main groups of outcomes. The first (50 percent of cases) represents those national instruments notified on time. A second group of instruments had a transposition delay of less than six months (15 percent of cases), and finally, the third group of national measures were transposed more than six months late (35 percent of cases). I will return to this data characteristic when discussing the appropriate statistical method to test the theoretical framework.

6.2.2 *Variation across member states and policy areas:*

In line with Conant's findings (2002), which uncover delays upwards of 10 years, and also reveals a significant variation between both member states and policy areas, Table 6.7 shows that the nine member states can be clustered into three groups with Sweden (SE) and the UK performing the best, having an average transposition delay of less than two months. Germany (DE), France (FR), Spain (ES) and Ireland (IE) performance range below 30 weeks delay. The Netherlands (NL), Greece (EL) and Italy (IT) represent a group of their own, performing worst among the nine member states with an average transposition delay beyond 35 weeks. The independent sample of t-tests for the five member states indicate that the groups differ significantly in their average level of the dependent variable.
Interestingly, the patterns shift slightly if we consider the median value of

Table 6.7: National differences in transposition delays in weeks.

Delay (in weeks)	SE	UK	DE	FR	ES	IE	EL	NL	IT
Mean	3	7	25	25	28	29	35	37	42
Median	0	0	8	20	0	10	10	22	13

delay across member states. The transport data set reveals that the mean and median delays differ considerably between member states. Whereas the champions such as Sweden, Spain and the UK have a median transposition delay of zero weeks, the laggards of Dutch and French implementing instruments have a median transposition delay of 22 and 20 weeks respectively. In the Netherlands, approximately half of the population has values less than 22 weeks and the remaining half has values greater than the median.

Despite the problematic records for Italy, the Netherlands and France, transposition also varies across the different transport sub-sectors, namely: maritime, road, rail, air and inland waterways. Whereas maritime and general transport directives perform best with an average delay of 20 weeks or less, Table 6.8 illustrates that air directives are delayed an average of one year. Road and rail directives range in-between with eight and nine months of delay. Inland waterwayss directives take the most time. Here, the average transposition delay is 27 months (2,25 years). [28]

28 Testing the similarity of means for the differences of transport subsectors in transposition delays, similar conclusions can be drawn. Only inland waterways does not differ systematically from the average means of the other modes of transport despite its extreme value of an average transposition delay of 27 months.

Again we find slight changes when looking at the median values. Rail and inland waterways seem to be the transport sub-sectors with considerable transposition delays (32-98 weeks) across all member states.

Table 6.8: Different transposition delays of modes in weeks.

Mode of transport	Transport general	Maritime	Road	Rail	Air	Inland waterwayss
Mean	-17	20	31	38	49	109
Median	0	6	12	32	23	98

6.3 CONCLUSION:

Whereas the nature of the Commission's scoreboards has raised some questions about its quality in general and the existence of a serious EU transposition problem in particular, the analysis of the EU transport transposition data set from 1995-2004 *uncovers a noticeable transposition deficit*. The EU transposition deficit is more than just a statistical illusion; it is a sad reality. In line with the recent findings of Falkner, Treib, Hartlapp and Leiber (2005), the study uncovered evidence that the EU suffers from a serious transposition deficit. Falkner et al. (2005) maintain that in more than two-third of all cases (63 out of 91), the adaptation requirements were delayed by two years or more before full implementation. The data corroborate their findings. Almost 50 percent of the national transposing instruments are reported late.

Furthermore, the figures show that member states failed to meet the Barcelona (2002) Zero Tolerance Objective (2002) in case of directives whose transposition is more than two years overdue. According to the EU 1957-2004 transport transposition data set still 8 percent of national transposition processes were delayed for more than 2 years amounting to almost 5 years of transposition delay. *The EU transposition problem appears to be a epidemic problem and not a problem of 'statistical artifact'.*

In addition, the difference in mean and median values, which vary significantly across member states and policy sub-sectors, uncover three groups, namely: national transposition measures transposed *on time, delayed by less than six months and delayed by more than six months.* Especially in the Netherlands, France, Italy, Ireland, Greece and Germany, there exists a transposition problem with regard to transport directives.

While the Commission data seem to seriously underestimate the transposition deficit in terms of timeliness across all member states and policy sectors, the next chapter tests empirically the theoretical framework addressing the central question of why member states miss the deadlines when transposing EU transport directives.

Chapter 7: Determinants of transposition delay

'Wir brauchen Zeit!' (Staatssekretär im Bundeswirtschaftsministerium, Georg Wilhelm Adamowitsch in Frankfurter Allgemeine Zeitung, 16 March 2004).

7.1 Introduction

The focus of this chapter is to understand the correlational effects of the explanatory variables for timeliness of national transposition processes. In this chapter, I first operationalise the complementary variables. The subsequent sections present the research methods and the results. Herein, the existing arguments in the literature are confirmed, challenged, and extended. Finally, I summarise and discuss the findings and conclude with some comments that bridge to a second step of analysis.

7.2 Operationalization Of Theoretical Framework

7.2.1 *EU directive specific features:*

Transposition deadline set in directive

It is not problematic to test the argument that a comfortable transposition timeframe increases the positive probability of the adoption of the national implementing measure around the deadline. The lengths of granted transposition time, i.e. the time set in the EU directive fixing the period for notification of the national implementing measure to the Commission, are calculated by subtracting the deadline, set in the directive, from the date of publication of the EU directive in the Council of Ministers. The more time a member state has to transpose a directive, the lower the perceived costs of transposition, and therefore, the less likely that transposition delay will occur. Celex provides the full texts of the directives where the last but one article always includes the reference to the deadline, phrased as follows: 'Member States shall bring into force the laws, regulations and administrative provisions necessary to comply with this Directive by … '. The timeliness for transposition deadlines set in the directives varies. In some exceptional cases, like the Council Directive 97/26/EC *on driving licenses*, the EU directive enters immediately into force (time to transpose equals zero). In other rare cases, transposition deadlines are much more generous. For example, the Council Directive 96/35/EC *on the appointment and vocational qualification of safety adviser for the transport of dangerous goods by road, rail and inland waterways* provided 3.5 years for the complete transposition.

Amount of discretion
In principle, directives should specify, in the words of Article 249 of the Treaty, 'the result to be achieved' but leave 'to the national authorities the choice of form and methods.' The leeway of interpretation, hence, represents a core characteristic of a directive. Over the last decade, however, directives have become more and more detailed, to the point where they could be viewed as regulations (Bellis, 2003: 3-12). The Maritime Directive 2001/53/EC, for example, consists of only 4 articles printed on 1 page, but its Annexes include a full 26 pages. The Annexes cover 184 equipments, for which detailed international testing standards already exist, and leave little room for interpretation.

To test the '*discretion-matters*' hypothesis, this study relies on the *discretion ratio*, that is defined as the number of major provisions in a legislative act that grant discretionary executive powers to member states, divided by the total number of major provisions in the act. In line with Franchino (2004) and Thomson et al. (2005), who also identify the number of major provisions of each legislative act that grant discretionary executive power, I rely on the information provided by Celex and Eurlex. Coding every provision according to whether member states may be left with some sort of discretion, the rate varies in principle on a scale from 0 (no discretion) to 1 (full discretion). The rate for all 67 directives including all articles but the first (purpose) and the last (addresses) ranges between 0 and 0.7 accordingly. Note that I substracted the first and last articles from the denominator. This was because they, by definition, serve the formalities of a directive only; furthermore, I wanted to minimize the potential inclusion of any discretion given to member states.

7.2.2 National level specific features

Number of veto players
When fewer actors are involved in the making of a legal instrument, the transposition process is faster. This is because there is less discussion about the allocation of the perceived costs and benefits of the adoption of new national legislation. Hence, the number of transposition actors is linked to the selected national transposing measure. Information on the national legal instruments for all member states is drawn from the list of measures notified to the Commission, Celex, and the national legal databases. For example, the Greek legal system is composed of a number of legislative instruments: legislative acts (Νόμος), presidential decrees (Προεδρικό Διάταγμα) and ministerial orders (Κοινὴ Υπουργικὴ Απόφαση). In Germany, the EC directives are either implemented as legislative acts (*Gesetze*) or ministerial orders (*Rechtsverordnungen*). Note that until the mid-1990s, circulars (*Εγκύκλιος, Verwaltungsvorschrift, Circulaire, Resolución, Instrucción, Circular, Föreskrift*) were also widely used to transpose EU legislation into national law in a lot of member states.

Table 7.9: Categorization of national legal instruments in 9 member states.

	Legislative act	**Government decree**	**Ministerial order**	**Circular**
Germany	Gesetz	-	Verordnung	Verwaltungs-vorschrift
UK	Act of Parliament	Order in Council	Ministerial Order	-
France	Loi, DDAC, Ordonnance	Décret	Arrêté ministériel	Circulaire
Italy	Legge, legge communitaria, decreto legge, decreto legislativo	-	Decreto ministeriale	-
Spain	Ley ordinaria, real decreto-ley, real decreto-legislativo	Real decreto	Orden	Resolución, Instrucción, Circular
The Netherlands	Wet	Algemene Maatregel van Bestuur	Ministeriële regeling	-
Greece	*Νόμος* (Nomos)	*Προεδρικό Διάταγμα* (Proädriko diatagma)	*Κοτνή Υπουργική Απόφαση* (Kini ipurgiki apofasi)	*Εγκύκλιος* (Egiklios)
Ireland	Act of Parliament	-	Order	-
Sweden	Lag	-	Förordning	Föreskrift

Source: Steunenberg and Voermans (2005) endorsed with additional information on Italy, Sweden, Greece, Ireland and Sweden.

Compared to a government decree, a ministerial order, and a circular a legislative act involves more transposition actors. Table 7.9 summarizes the hierarchical ordering of national legal instruments for every member state under investigation according to these four categories.

Member states typically transpose EU legislation via non-legislative measures, in which the parliament is not involved.[29] This study goes one step further than the normal veto-player indexes (Tsebelis, 2001) by building its own

29 Spain 80%, the Netherlands 69%, France 60% and Denmark 28% (Steunenberg and Rhinard, 2005; Steunenberg and Voermans, 2005)

veto-player index varying for each directive and member state respectively (Steunenberg and Rhinard, 2005: 15). It will account for legal instrument specific veto player configurations.[30] If transposition requires a ministerial order, the number of ministries involved is counted, with the assumption that they may have different agendas. In the event that we come across an additional junior minister (Müller and Strom, 2004) who represents a different party group than the minister, we add this junior minister to the number. [31] If transposition is decided by the national government, a score that is based on the autonomy of the prime minister is added to the index (Strom, Müller and Bergman; 2003). Finally if transposition is handled by adopting a bill, the national legislative veto player index, by Tsebelis, is added.[32] The veto player index ranges on a scale from 0 to 16. In the end, this index accounts for potential veto players in non-legislative national transposition processes, such as ministerial orders. The veto player index can account for the number of ministries involved and the role played by junior ministers. Furthermore, it better differentiates among legislative acts. For example, in one case, France notified the Commission of a Legislative Act in 2001 (Tsebelis veto player index = 5) with the signature of 'eight' different ministries to transpose Directive 99/62/EC *on charging heavy goods vehicles for use of certain infrastructures* during a period of cohabitation. In addition, in this case, there was a relatively high political autonomy by the then French Prime Minister Lionel Jospin under the French President Jacques Chirac. This more nuanced measurement of potential veto players in the national transposition context resulted in a veto index of 16 instead of 5.

National transposition package approach

To recall through a transposition package a number of EU directives are grouped together for transposition purposes because they cover similar policy issues. In a transposition package, a number of directives, with varying deadlines are transposed at once. The so-called first directive in the package is the one with the earliest deadline, and the so-called last directive in the package is the one with the deadline furthest into the future. Due to the perceived transposition costs of directives yet to be transposed, the national package approach increases the probability of a delayed settlement of the first directive to be transposed, but accelerates a settlement for the last directive in the national transposition package to be transposed. Member states dif-

30 Tsebelis legislative veto player index would be a very crude measure since only few national implementing instruments are legislative acts.

31 In Germany, for example, the most important actors at the federal level in transport are the Minister of Transport and the Minister of Economic Affairs. The two ministries, however, hold diverging conceptions regarding sectoral regulations. Whereas the Ministry of Transport has often taken a pro-regulatory stand, the head of the transport division in the Ministry of Economic Affairs defined its role through ensuring that liberal views about transport counterbalanced those of the Ministry of Transport (Teutsch, 2001: 139).

32 For the missing data on Greece, I am grateful to Frank Häge who provided me with the necessary figures.

fer in applying package approach. Whereas Germany (39%), France (31%), and Spain (26%) often use this method in the transport sector, Greece hardly transposes EU transport directive in form of packages (2%). Furthermore, we see also differences in terms of transport sub-sectors. Regarding inland waterways, we hardly find transposition packages across the member states. But maritime, rail, and road directives account for 75% of the data set that were grouped in packages including 2 to 8 EU directives.

On the European level, on occasion, the Commission decides upon directives by also using the package approach, as in the transport sector (air and railway packages, Erika I and II (see Transport Chapter). These events may have facilitated member states to transpose those same directives in packages accordingly covering similar policy issues. Dinstinct from the EU packages of directives, however, in most cases, national transposition packages are the result of member states deciding to transpose a number of single EU directives with one national implementing measure. In Germany, for example, the *Seeschifffahrtsanpassungsgesetz*, on 18 September 1998, transposed eight maritime directives that had been adopted in the Council of Ministers between 1996 and 1998. Italy, on the other hand, used the package approach four times to transpose maritime directives between 1995 and 2004; these packages ranged in size from two directives to four directives. The information on 82 packages of the 367 notified national implementing measures, which represents 23% of all cases, was derived from Celex and the national databases. Controlling for decelerating and accelerating effects, we introduce dummies for those EU directives that represent the first or last directive in national transposition package.

Timing of national general elections

General elections may accelerate or delay national transposition records, depending on when they occur. If a general election falls within the last six months of a set transposition period, it has an accelerating effect. But a general election scheduled within the first six months of the official transposition period invariably slows the national transposition process. The argument is that a policy that is not adopted before the end of the legislative terms must be reintroduced, and by this reintroduction, raises the costs to the extent that transposition becomes more opportune. An overview of all national parliamentary elections can be accessed through the website on parties and elections in Europe by Wolfram Nordsieck.[33] I coded the variables with the number 1 for the occurrence of a general election, otherwise 0. Fifty-one percent (189) of the 367 national transposition processes were affected by general elections during the national transposition process. Only a few transposition processes experienced general elections both at the beginning as well as at the end of the transposition process (2%).

33 http://www.parties-and-elections.de/

7.2.3 *Transport related accidents:*

The previous Transport Chapter in this book highlighted the accident-driven approach behind EU transport policy. Driven by European transport accidents the Commission, member states and the Parliament have adopted new European transport legislation in the different sub-sectors by addressing the reasons for often devastating ecological disasters. The *'accident-matters-hypothesis'* in the context of EU implementation argues two points. First, transport related accidents that occur during the national transposition period increase the perceived costs of non-transposition of the new EU legislation. Second, accidents facilitate problem-free and timely settlements in the transposition bargaining. A summary of transport related accidents in Europe from 1995-2004 can be found in the Transport Chapter of this book. In the end, I assigned a '1' for the occurrence of an accident and 0 for no accident in the years during of the national transposition process. In 25% (94 out of 367) of the cases, mode-specific accidents are recorded.

7.2.4 *Summary of descriptives:*

Data limitations- notably missing data on key variables- reduce the effective sample to 361. Table 7.10 presents descriptive statistics of all the variables, and provides means, standard deviations, and min/max values for all the independent variables in the sample. (See appendix for correlation tables).

Table 7.10: Descriptive statistics: Min/max, means and standard deviations (n=361).

Variable	Minimum/ Maximum	Mean	Standard deviation
Discretion rate	0/.7	0.07	0.13
Transposition time set in the directive (in weeks)	6/184	46.57	36.71
Number of veto players	0/16	2.59	2.98
First directive in national transposition package	0/1	0.08	0.27
Last directive in national transposition package	0/1	0.11	0.32
Start of transposition in election year	0/1	0.28	0.45
End of transposition in election year	0/1	0.31	0.46
Transport related accidents	0/1	0.35	0.48

7.3 Method

As mentioned previsouly, almost 70% of the data set was transposed using only one national implementing measure. This fact, taken with other earlier considerations, induced me to use the first implementing measure to calculate *delay*.[34] Bearing in mind that only a few time-varying variables are present in the transposition data set, I checked for the likely amount of directives that would be eliminated by a potential binary dependent variable. This research would lose only 5% of its complete information. In the analysis of the missing values I could not find any significant pattern.

Ordered multinomial logistic model

This study runs an ordered multinomial logistic model. Two considerations were in mind when running it. First, the model was run in order not to lose a lot of information by collapsing the dependent variable to a dichotomous measure that merely indicates if the transposition was timely or not – a very legalistic concept of delay. Second, the earlier recorded discrepancy between mean/median in the previous chapter hints at the necessity to account for different groups of transposition outcomes. Whereas the mean transposition delay in the transport sector was 26 weeks (six months), the median was zero weeks, i.e. on time. In addition, interview partners and scholars (Falkner et al., 2005: 267)) dealing with transposition on a day-to-day basis agree that a 'psychological' threshold lies at six months. Delays within six-month margin occur regularly. The Commission does not normally take any formal infringement procedure with regard to delays in this time period, due in part to its lack of resources to allow an examination of all national implementing measures for timeliness and correctness (IP15). Consequently, the study identifies three ordered outcomes: *non-delayed transposition, transposition delay less than 6 months, transposition delay more than six months.* Whereas 50 per cent fall under category 1 (on time), 15 per cent fall under category 2 (less than 6 months delay) and 35 per cent fall under the last category (more than 6 months delay). An ordered multinomial logistic model can account best for the three groups of outcome. Long (1997), Long & Freese (2003) and Borooah (2002) provide the reference points of nominal data with multiple outcomes and the interpretation of multinomial coefficients.

34 Normally, this study would be predestinated to apply a hazard rate model to test the hypotheses about delay in the transposition process of EU directives. Alas, this is not the case. One of the advantages of event history over standard ordinary last squares (OLS) regresion is its ability to handle what is referred to as censoring (Box-Steffensmeier and Bradford, 1997; 2004; Golub, 1999: 747; Schulz and König, 2000; Schimmelpfennig, 2000; Box-Steffensmeier, Reiter and Zorn, 2003; Collier, Hoeffler and Soderbom, 2004; Fearon, 2004). A duration model, for example, allowed Mastenbroek (2003) to treat the not yet transposed directives as right-censored avoiding selection bias by eliminating directives on which the member states have taken no final action yet (see also Borghetto et al., 2006). Specifying the baseline hazard rate, however, is very time-consuming and cumbersome because it involves speculation about the effect of the passage of time on the probability that an event will occur. Especially with time-varying covariates, the calculation of the survival functions is quite complicated because one needs to specify a path or trajectory for each variable.

7.4 Results

Before calculating a statistical model for transposition delay, I conducted three tests to assess collinearity. I visually inspected the matrix of correlations amongst the independent variables (see Annex). I checked the tolerance and the variance inflation factors, the second of which relates to the amount that the standard error of the variable has been increased because of collinearity, but found no evidence of major concern.

Ordered multinomial logistic regression
Based on earlier findings of this study, I assume that the conditions that lead to long delays are likely to be different from those that lead to relatively short delays. The results of the analysis are presented in Table 7.11. In the first column, the coefficients for timely transposition, which also represent the baseline model, are displayed. Furthermore, table 7.11 distinguishes between two different kinds of transposition delay: short and long delay. In the second column, I look at the factors that predict delay of *less than 6 months*. In the third column, the study focuses on the more serious delays: those that take *longer than 6 months*. The multinomial coefficients must be interpreted in the context of the base category (timely transposition), and in the context of the other coefficients for that variable, as well.

The model fit of the ordered multinomial logit regression, with a R^2 of 0.35 is relative satisfactory. All factors in either column indicate in the predicted direction. The results in table 7.11 hint that there are some potentially important differences between the three types of transposition delays.

Transposition delays of more than six months were apparently more of a problem in national transposition settings with numerous veto players. On the other hand, there are certain indicators that matter more for shorter delays, such as the discretion ratio and the transposition time guaranteed in the directive. The strongest predictors of transposition performance are, again, the timing of general elections and the external shock related indicator. Whereas transport-related accidents are the most highly significant in explaining longer delays, it is the timing of general elections that can either slow or accelerate national transposition processes significantly. Depending on whether national general elections fall at the beginning or the end of a national transposition process, the procedure is slowed or accelerated respectively.

7.5 Discussion and summary

In summary, most findings of both analyses are in accordance with our expectations, and support the theoretical framework. All indicators are related in ways that were expected, and most of the explanatory variables are significant. Furthermore, the findings of the ordered multinomial logit regression

Table 7.11: Determinants of transposition delay: Ordered multinominal logit 1995-2004.

	Outcomes		
Variable	**On time**	**< 6 months delay**	**> 6 months delay**
EU LEVEL VARIABLES			
Discretion ratio	-1.83 *	3.58 **	2.11
	(1.39)	(1.21)	(1.37)
Transposition time	0.02 *	-0.02 **	-0.02
	(0.00)	(0.00)	(0.00)
NATIONAL LEVEL VARIABLES			
Number of veto players	-0.27 ***	-0.05	0.27 ***
	(0.06)	(0.07)	(0.06)
Package approach			
First directive in transposition package	-1.50 *	1.79 *	1.53 *
	(0.72)	(0.71)	(0.72)
Last directive in transposition package	2.24 **	-2.56 *	-2.15 **
	(0.80)	(1.03)	(0.79)
General elections			
At the beginning of transposition process	-4.67 ***	1.39 ***	4.07 ***
	(0.83)	(0.39)	(0.84)
At the end of the transposition process	2.88 ***	-0.85 *	-2.92 ***
	(0.41)	(0.40)	(0.41)
Transport related accidents	1.46 ***	-0.11	-1.41 ***
	(0.41)	(0.33)	(0.40)
N		361	
Prob>chi2		0.0000	
Pseudo R2		0.35	

Multinomial logistic regression. Firgures and coefficients with standard errors in parentheses. *p< .10, **p< .05, ***p< .01, ****p< .001 Timely transposition is the comparison group. Source : EU transport transposition data set 1957-2004.

show that there are specific sets of variables that explain shorter delays better than longer delays, and vice versa. Interestingly, it is the *EU directive specific characteristics* that explain *short delays*, and *national level explanatory variables* best account for *delays of more than 6 months*. Very long transposition delays may be ascribed to two factors: the selection of the transposing legal instrument, and the decision of whether to use the national transposition package approach or not.

EU directive characteristics that determine delays of less than six months
The findings uncover *that member states face more problems when transpositing EU directives with a limited transposition time set in the directive*, in general – it accounts significantly for short delays. Consequently, sufficient transposition time is important, especially as the number of directives increase. Despite the growing number of directives to be transposed over the years (+84%), however, the mean transposition time agreed upon in the Council has decreased by 24%. Whereas the average guaranteed transposition time in the 1970s was 11 months, it increased to 17 months in the early 1980s. Then, it steadily decreased over the late 1980s and late 1990s (from 15 to 13 months). Only recently, this trend has been reversed. A directive adopted after 2000 guaranteed, on average, 18 months for full transposition. In periods of high legislative output, thus, short-term transposition delays seem inevitable.

Furthermore, the *amount of discretion* provided by the EU directive is a significant determinant of short transposition delays. The more discretion the more likely delay.

It is only a small conceptual step from the amount of discretion to to the *level of detail* in the directive. Normally, the higher the level of detail, the smaller the amount of discretion. The amount of discretion provided decreases with the complexity of a directive. Bellis (2003) argues that because the definitions, specified conditions, and specified services were extremely detailed, they were obviously intended to be applicable in their own terms in all member states. In this respect Kaeding (2006) tested the EU directive's level of detail, as embodied by the *number of recitals*. He finds that the number of recitals has a considerable negative effect on transposition delay. The higher the amount of recitals, the more likely transposition delay. In line with Bellis (2003), it seems that the several recitals used by the member states or the Commission to add a number of points, that were not agreed upon during the negotiations, interferes with a swift transposition. They further increase the detail of the directive, which is strongly linked to the level of discretion allowed in a directive's interpretation. The more detail a provision has, the less discretionary power the member states have in transposing the directive.

National level factors that determine delay of more than six months
At the national level are explanatory factors of long transposition delays. The *veto player* coefficient indicates that the fewer actors involved in the making of the legal measure, the faster the transposition process, which is in line with research by Haverland (2001), Giuliani (2003) and Franchino (2004). To a large extent, the number of actors involved in the transposition process depends on which type of transposition instrument is selected by the member states. Types of national legal instrument differ in the amount of relevant actors involved. In the Netherlands, for example, Mastenbroek (2003) argues that directives often fall between the jurisdictions of more than one ministry,

resulting in communication and coordination problems, conflicts of interests, and competence issues that may cause problems. Dimitrakopoulos (2001: 616) also links differences in tradition, structures, and culture in the transposition process within the ministries to member states' transposition performance.

Furthermore, the selection of a *national package approach* may also have a considerable delaying effect on the first EU directive in the transposition package to be transposed. Different institutions decide which national legal instrument to use and whether the use of a transposition package is called for; it is worth noting that both these decisions affect the timeliness of national transposition processes. Note that such problems arising from these two explanatory factors are *homemade*, and therefore can only be solved at the national level.

Timing of general elections

Indeed the *timing of general elections* in a member state play strong. At the end of a legislative term, the costs of continued inefficient policies increase dramatically. Future payoffs shadow on the bargaining and the benefits from new policy are comparatively higher than the costs of delay. The opposite effect happens when general elections occur in the beginning of a transposition process. Here, the coefficient highlights the retarding effect of a general election. In this case, future payoffs are valued less. In addition, a change in domestic political setting lead government leaders to see new potential gains from alternative policy options. This could happen when, for example, a political party with stronger commitments to liberalizing railway undertakings come to power or the implementation of the new drivers' licenses generates new domestic political pressures.

Transport-related accidents

Situational changes in the internal and external environment require responsive decisions by the incumbent decision-makers. They are also strong determinants of transposition delay, in general, and longer delays, in particular. While transport policy itself is a crisis-driven EU policy area, *transport-related accidents* accelerate national transposition processes significantly. Consequently, crises and emergencies affect the decision making situation, leading to a different equilibrium. When continuous bargaining conflicts imply that a member state has settled in a *pareto-inferior* equilibrium, radical changes are often needed to break the stalemate and put the existing national policy on a welfare-superior path. The extreme welfare losses (by devastating ecological disaster and numerous fatalities in car, train, and aircraft accidents) dwarfs the costs associated with a major policy change.

7.6 Limitations and conclusion

What are the concluding implications of these findings? While the previous chapter clearly hinted at a serious transposition problem across EU member states, the first set of analysis shows, that, first, *delay is a multifaceted event*. The results of the model provide strong support for the assertion that distinguishing between the outcomes of transposition process (*on time, short, and long delay*) is a useful method of investigation. Second, *the study identified European level and national level factors that have different affects on the length of delay*, but which overshadow each other. If governments perceive that transposition is complex and may require the introduction of a legislative act, for example, they must take this into account while negotiating with the Council of Minister. Furthermore, the timing of general elections in a member state and transport-related accidents influence the timeliness of national transposition processes.

All in all, we identified 'effecs of a cause', i.e. factors that determine delays when transposing EU internal market directives. However, even with the most complex techniques 'correlation is not causation' (though causation is only possible with correlation). The statistical analysis has uncovered relationships between variables: to explain a dependent variable from a range of possible independent variables.

To identify 'causes of the effect' there is a strong argument in favour of case study analysis. Following a clear comparative logic it allows for the development of a more detailed analyses and possible theoretical innovation (if focusing on well-predicted and deviant cases derived from the statistical analysis) (Yin, 1993; George and Bennett, 2005). Here, especially comparative case studies are useful. Compared to a single case study, a comparative approach can overcome some of the single case study problems, such as inference and representativeness.

But, the comparative logic is contested. In fact, there is disagreement as to which type of comparisons are the most relevant. There are, two main types of comparison in the field of comparative politics: the most similar and the most different case design (Przeworski and Teune, 1970). Based on the ordered multinomial logistic regression, the following chapter will be entirely devoted to the case selection in order to, then, analyse well-predicted and outlying cases accounting for robustness and possible slight refinements of the theoretical model on the timeliness of national transposition process across member states.

Chapter 8: Cae selection of on- and off- liners[35]

'The use of mixed strategy helps to overcome potential sources of bias and to sort out spurious findings that might be produced in either small-n or large-n analysis when carried out in isolation' (Lieberman, 2005: 450).

8.1 Introduction

In the following pages, I demonstrate that the statistical findings must include case studies for two main reasons: First, they help further test the robustness of the statistical results that address the second sub-question of the study, specifically: What are the empirical effects of the factors? How do the determinants and the occurrence of these factors influence the timeliness of the national transposition processes? A 'causal-process' observation will provide information about mechanisms and context (Collier, Brady and Seawright, 2004: 253). Case study research allows a close examination of the hypothesized role of causal mechanisms in the context of the individual case. The in-depth analysis will make cases more easily comparable and causal mechanisms more clearly elucidated through, for instance, process-tracing and pattern-matching (Franchino, 2005: 250). The second main reason for choosing case studies is to further improve the model fit. Standard assessments about the strength of parameter estimates show that the goodness-of-fit between the specified model and the empirical data is improvable (R^2=.35). Since a case study is 'an intensive study of a single unit for the purpose of understanding a larger class of similar units' (Gerring, 2004: 342), in the end, it will achieve higher conceptual validity of timeliness and the independent variables in the transposition context.

In line with Lieberman (2005), this study will show that there are specific benefits of systematically combining both, quantitative and qualitative, in one design. Quantitative and qualitative research methods can share a symbiotic relationship. The large-n and small-n research designs provide different and complementary bases for causal inference (George and Bennett, 2005: 208). To provide an absolute criterion for answering the question about robustness and improvement one important tool is central: the actual scores of the cases should be plotted graphically relative to the predicted scores from the statis-tical estimate (so-called identification of outliers) (Lieberman, 2005: 439). Especially deviant cases are frequently encountered in large-n studies and usually noted as such without an effort to explain why they are deviant. Cases with large positive or negative residuals will be examined in the study to determine why these points fit so poorly. Next to pattern matching, process-tracing

35 I am grateful to Ingo Rohlfing who suggested the term 'on- and off-liner' (see also Rohlfing, 2005).

is particularly useful for obtaining an explanation for deviant cases- those whose outcomes are not predicted or explained adequately by the existing statistical model (Achen and Snidal, 1989: 167-168).

To succeed case selection is of utmost importance. In line with combined research designs the large-n studies will guide case selection for in-depth case studies. The case selection chapter is structured as follows. First, in line with Lieberman (2005), two criteria for case selection are presented. These criteria depend on whether the fit of the statistical model is relatively satisfying or, in contrast, is considered not sufficient based on the calculated deviant residuals. While this study opts for carrying out a model-testing and improving approach, so it then plots the deviance residuals for the statistical model against the transposition delay. Next, a most-similar/most-different design guides the selection of four national implementing measures. In the subsequent chapter the case studies are thencarried out.

8.2 Case selection criteria:

As a point of departure, the entire design of the case study, as well as its potential theoretical significance, is 'heavily influenced by the way the unit of analysis is defined' (Yin, 1993: 10). To answer the question what the empirical effects of the determinants of transposition delay are and how these factors influence the timeliness of the national transposition process, the unit of analysis is the national legal instrument. Furthermore, the primary criterion for case selection should be the relevance to the research objective of the study (Haverland, 2006), regardless of whether the case includes theory testing or theory improving. The problem of systematic error of case selection, however, is the recurrent trade-off in case studies. Since the research will require a comparison of several cases, they should be selected to provide the kind of control and variation by the research problem.

In order to assess model fit and to identify aberrant observations, plots of residuals are useful. Residuals are the difference between a model's predicted and observed outcomes for each observation in the sample. Cases that fit poorly have large residuals, known as outliers. Regardless of which method is used, further analysis of the deviant cases may reveal either incorrectly coded data or some inadequacy in the specification of the model. Deviant cases are frequently encountered in large-n studies, and they are met too.

8.2.1 Model-testing and improving:

Scholars differentiate between theory testing and theory improving depending on the fit of the statistical model (George and Bennet, 2005: 109-124). If the researcher is satisfied with the model's specifications fit, then, the main goal of the in-depth component of the mixed-method design is to further test robustness of those findings (model testing). If, however, the researcher believes that the model fit could be further improved (for example because quantifiable indicators or statistical estimators are weak, or because not all causal mechanisms and causal paths are satisfactory) then case studies can investigate why deviant cases are deviant, perhaps leading to the identification of omitted variables (model improving) (Lieberman, 2005).

From the study's research objective point of view, we intend to test *and* further improve theory: For researchers with an eye toward theoretical parsimony and clarity a model-testing approach compels the gathering of evidence that allows them to analyze the statistically significant results. For example, researchers 'gather evidence that allows us to write a detailed narrative from the vantage point of the preferred model' (Lieberman, 2005: 442). For theory-building purposes, another powerful advantage of case studies is in the further improving of concepts such as timeliness by focusing on deviant cases. The case study can focus on accounting for estimated differences between cases. The outcome in a deviant case may prove to have been caused by variables that had been previously overlooked, but whose effects are well known in other areas of research (George and Bennett, 2005: 111). In contrast to the model-testing case selection, which is based on the widest degree of variation of the independent variables that are central to the model, the model–improving approach involves selection of cases based on initial scores on the dependent variable (Liebermann, 2005: 11). Here, plotting graphically the actual scores of the cases relative to the predicted scores from the statistical estimates is helpful.

The literature identifies two relevant variants for model building (Rohlfing, 2005): first, a selection for most likely and least likely designs; and second, a comparison of onliers and offliers. In the first version, cases are assigned to the categories on the basis of whether they are expected to be most-likely or least-likely. In a least-likely design, a case warrants closer attention if it is found where it is not expected—in a category where the case is least likely expected to occur. Therefore, case 1 should be chosen for closer inspection and compared with case 2 exhibiting the expected result. In the second variant, cases are selected on basis of their extremeness on the dependent variable. Cases that belong to a different type should be matched with respect to their scores on the dependent variable so that process-tracing takes place on basis of most-similar and most-different designs (Przeworski and Teune, 1970) with typical and deviant-on-X cases (Rohlfing, 2005) and variation on the independent variables. [36] For the study's purpose, the second variant for model-improving design will further guide this study.

36 Most similar cases are ideally cases that are comparable in all respects except for the independent variable, whose variance may account of the cases having different outcomes on the dependent variable (George and Bennett, 2005: 81).

8.3 Assessing the model's fit

With a logit model design, the normal procedure in examining model accuracy and identifying outliers is to examine the martingale residuals (Stata, 2001: 292-298 and 369-375). But because martingale residuals are sometimes difficult to interpret (because the residuals are skewed, taking values in (−~, 1), deviance residuals are preferred here for examining model accuracy and outlier identification. They are a rescaling of the martingale residuals so that they are symmetric around the value of zero, and thus more like residuals obtained from linear regression. Deviance residuals can be interpreted as the difference between the observed logistic values minus that predicted by the model. If the model fits, one expects to see the cases to cluster smoothly around zero.

Plotting the deviance residuals for the statistical model against the transposition delay for all 361 national implementing cases, we can see that they differ according to the two categories of the dependent variable: namely non-delay and delay.

Figure 8.7 shows that the deviance residuals are smaller for national implementing measures that were notified to the Commission on time, and then increase the closer they approach the deadline (0). For the second category

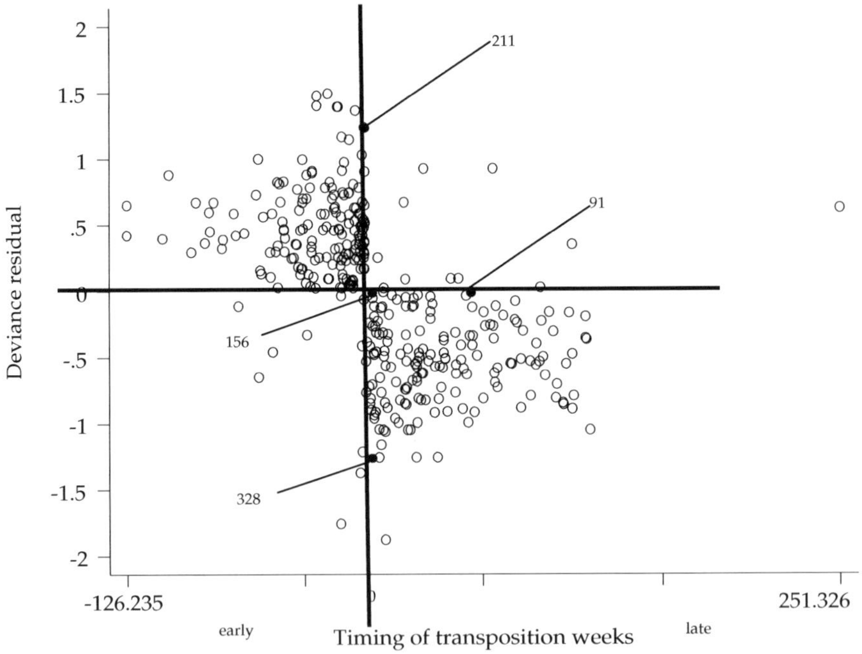

Figure 8.7: Deviance residuals for timely transposition of EU directives between 1995-2004.

(delayed), we find the reverse trend. Whereas the deviance residuals for cases closer to the deadline score high, the longer the delay lasts, the smaller the deviance residuals.

These patterns suggest three phenomena. First, the logistic model fits particularly poorly for cases around the deadline. Whereas almost all residuals for very early and very late transposition processes score below '1', cases around the transposition deadline approach the 'magic' threshold of '2'. Second, the logistic model underestimates the probability of delay for instruments transposed in time and overestimates the probability of delay for national implementing measures with long delays. Third, in the plot, several residuals stand out as being large relative to the others. In such cases, it is important to identify the specific observations with large residuals for further inspection (Long and Freese, 2003: 126). Actually, there is no rule for what counts as a 'large' residual. Despite Hosmer and Lemeshow's (1999: 176) caution that it is impossible to provide any *absolute* standard, a deviation of more than '+/– 2' is considered to be 'large' (Long and Freese, 2003: 127).

8.4 Selection of two on- and off-liners for timely transposition of EU directives

Following the idea of most-similar and most-different designs with typical and deviant on-X-cases, this study selects four cases on basis of their extremeness on the dependent variable. From a practical point of view, I decided to disregard national implementing measures that had been notified to the Commission before 1998. I chose two on-the-line cases, namely: 91 and 156. Two off-the-line cases were also selected, namely: 211 and 328. The four cases were chosen for the following methodological reasons:

In order to find on-the-X line cases, this study applies a most-different systems design. I consulted the deviance residuals and found that only 22 cases lay exactly on the 0-line. For comparison purposes, I chose two on-the-line cases with deviation residuals of 0, but that differed in the amount of transposition delay. Whereas case No. 156 was only three weeks delayed, case No. 91 was more than 8 months (32 weeks) late. But both were well predicted by the model since they had the same residual (zero). In addition, guided by a most-different design, I selected cases varying on the independent variables. While both cases represent different transport-subfields (maritime and rail), and the national legal instruments originate from different Member States (France and Spain), they vary considerable in the transposition times set in the directives, the discretion ratio, the number of veto players and in the application of a national transposition package and the occurrence of national general elections. Since cases fit the predictions of the theoretical framework, then examining them in detail will give an additional in-depth testing of the microfoundations of the framework when it is working correctly (Lieberman, 2005).

Table 8.12: Case selection of four on-and off-liners.

	Most different design		Most similar design	
Index	156	91	328	211
Case number	31-98-0055-9-311298	34-01-0014-4-150303	31-02-0059-2-050204	31-01-0053-9-170202
Member State	France	Spain	Germany	France
Transport sub-sector	Maritime	Rail	Maritime	Maritime
Name of the directive	Amending minimum require-ments for vessels bound for or leaving Com ports	Allocation of rail-way infrastructure capacity and the levying of char-ges for the use of railway infra-structure and safety certification	Establishing a Community vessel traffic monitoring and information system	Amending marine equipment 96/98
Deviation residual	0.04	-0.05	-1.23	1.21
Delay in weeks	3	32	1	2
Transposition time set in the directive (months)	6	24	18	6
Discretion ratio	0	0.6	0	0
Number of veto players	4	11	1	2
Package approach	yes	no	yes	no
General elections	no	yes	yes	yes
Transport related accidents	no	no	yes	no

For the two off-liner cases, I deliberately selected cases No. 211 and 328. Whereas the model fit for the selected on-the-line cases was good, the following cases are both poorly explained by the logistic model. Case No. 211 has a positive deviance residual of 1.2 (underestimated), while case No. 328 a negative deviance residual of (–1.2) (overestimated). Following a most-similar research design, both cases have similar values on the dependent variable; they are non-problematic cases in terms of delay. Similarly, the two national implementing measures used represent one mode of transport (maritime), but originate from different member states, namely: France and Germany. Compared to the earlier to on-the-line cases, here, the independent variables are more similar. While neither directive provides any level of discretion, the national implementing measures required only a low number of transposition actors. Since the two off-the-line cases passed the deadline by only few weeks, they will be helpful in improving the existing logistic model by comparing them to the on-liners. Comparing them to case No. 156, which is also almost transposed in time, but is, to the contrary, well-predicted by the theoretical model, will be especially helpful.

Table 8.12 summarizes the characteristics of the cases selected for further in depth investigation.

8.5 Summary

Informed by the research question, the unit of analysis, and the goodness-of-fit between the specified model and the empirical data, this study deliberately chose the four aforementioned cases. This study opted for a model-testing and improving case selection approach following a most-similar and most-different design with typical and deviant-on-X-cases. The two on-the-line cases (1,2) will help further assess the causal impact of six variables, namely: amount of discretion, transposition time set in directive, number of veto players, package approach, general election, and transport-related accidents. The two off-the-line cases (3,4) may help refine the existing model and guide this current study in particular and scholars of EU implementation in new directions more generally. In the following, I carry out the case studies.

Chapter 9: Tracing the process of four national transposition cases

'Les obligations de transposition pesant sur l'Etat découlent tant de la Constitution du 4 octobre 1958 que des traités européens. Un manquement à ces obligations n'affecte pas seulement notre crédit au sein de l'Union. Il expose la France à des sanctions contentieuses, y compris pécuniaires. Il entrave le bon fonctionnement du marché intérieur, affectant aussi bien la concurrence entre entreprises que la protection des consommateurs.' (Circulaire du Premier ministre, Jean-Pierre Raffarin, Paris, 27 septembre 2004).

9.1 Introduction

In the previous chapter, detailed explanations of the selection process in adopting four national legal instruments to transpose EU transport directives were provided. Namely, the sample of 1998/55/EC, 2001/14/EC, 2001/53/EC, and the 2002/59/EC was discussed. Two important sub-sectors in the transport field – maritime and rail which represent 43% of the overall EU transport *acquis* – are the focus of this chapter, as they have been crucial departments for the EU's economic and regional development.

With coastlines running virtually uninterrupted from the Aegean Sea across the Mediterranean, and along the Atlantic Ocean and the North Sea to the Baltic, the maritime sector is very important. Roughly 40% of the contemporary world fleet is European, and around 4% of the EU's gross domestic product (GDP) comes from maritime industries and services. Around 90% of global cargo is transported by sea, with 3.5 million tonnes of goods cruising through EU waters every year. More than 40% of the EU's internal trade goes by sea. Each year, nearly two billion tonnes of freight is loaded and unloaded at EU ports. Another indicator, if an unfortunate one, of the importance of EU waters is the fact that out of the world's 23 major oils spill incidents in the past 40 years, 11 occurred in European waters (WMU, 2006). Based on its economic importance, as well as the risks to the environment EU maritime legislation has attracted a lot of attention, and represents about 31% of the full EU transport *acquis*.

Railways in the EU, on the contrary, have been declining in economic importance over the last almost four decades. Though it currently represents about 12 % of the full EU transport *acquis*, its decline in market share is considerable, and probably irreversible. This is despite the railway's achievements of both a steady passenger flow, and a freight transport growth. Between 1970 and 2001, the rail's market share collapsed, falling from 21% to 7.8% (Di Pietrantonio and Pelkmans, 2004: 2). In the case of freight transport, railways lost market share, not only in relative terms, but even in absolute terms. It is estimated that between 1990 and 2001, the market share of general freight transport rose by 25%, whereas the respective shares of road transport (-35%) and rail freight transport (-6%) actually decreased. The current challenge of the European rail industry is to develop maximum passenger/customer value. Trains have to be safe, clean, reliable, and prompt, both for passengers and stock. Improved services may give rail transport a enormous competitive edge, making it the best way to combine low travel time with easy accessibility to both leisure and professional hubs.

Methodology

So far, the determinants of transposition delay have been identified. This chapter addresses the second sub-question how the identified determinants influence the timliness of the national transposition processes. The causal mechanisms underlying the correlations between the timeliness of national transposition processes and the individual components of the theoretical framework will be further elucidated through process-tracing. Qualitative research focusing on four case studies will further explain the ambivalent statistical results produced by the data and displayed, in the previous chapter, by the deviant residuals. George and Bennett (2005: 206-207), explain the process-tracing method as follows:

> 'The process-tracing method attempts to identify the intervening causal process – the causal chain and the causal mechanism – between an independent variable (or variables) and the outcome of the dependent variable. [...] Process-tracing forces the investigator to take equifinality into account, that is, to consider the alternative paths through which the outcome could have occurred, and it offers the possibility of mapping out one or more potential causal paths that are consistent with the outcome and the process-tracing evidence in a single case.'

I will trace the operation of the causal mechanisms at work in the transposition process, and infer the essence of the cognitive processes that accompany these mechanisms.[37] Consequently, this method calls for a theoretically informed, and very specific trace of the four national transposition processes. I will carefully map this process, 'exploring the extent to which it coincides with prior, theoretically derived expectations about the workings of the mechanisms' (Checkel, 2005: 6).

Data

The causal mechanisms that explain why member states miss transposition deadlines will be clearly elucidated through process-tracing. The required data for process tracing is qualitative in nature and includes official documents, EU legal databases, press accounts, and interviews. Information about the negotiation phase can be found in *Prelex*[38], which follows all Commis-

---

37 Process tracing is synonymous with a mechanism-based approach to theory development (Checkel, 2005: 17).

38 http://ec.europa.eu/prelex

sion proposals and communications from their transmission to the Council or the European Parliament. Links allow users to access directly the electronic texts available (COM documents, Official Journal, Bulletin of the EU, documents of the EP, press releases). The largest documentary databases on EU law (Eurlex and Celex) and national legal databases provide information on the national implementing measures. Information on the timing of national elections and the change of transport ministers were found in the annual political data provided by the *European Journal of Political Research.* Information on national-level transport related accidents were stidoed by content analysis (Krippendorf, 2004) of newspapers. For cross-checking purposes and the procurement of additional data for these theoretical informed case studies, I conducted 15 interviews in Brussels and in different member states between January 2005 and January 2006 (see Appendix for overview).

Structure of the four case studies

The structure of the four case studies is as follows. The analysis is grouped into two *on-the-line* and two *off-the-line* cases. On-the-line incidents represent those that are well explained by the theoretical model for apt transposition with residual deviants of around '0', and off-the-line incidents describe those that are poorly explained by the statistical model and the fuzzy set. To begin, a short introduction about the directive's relation with the full transport *acquis* is given. Then, analysis addresses the European level factors that account for transposition delay, namely: the European negotiation process in general, and the content of the European directive in particular. Following this is a closer look at the national transposition practices, and the transposition actors involved at the national level. Last but not least, the effects of past crises in the national transposition process are examined. These four cases are later used to generalize subsequent conclusions of this chapter.

9.2 On-the-Line Case Studies

9.2.1 *Case 1 – 1998/55: French transposition of the Council Directive 98/55/EC of 17 July 1998 amending Council Directive 93/75/EEC concerning minimum requirements for vessels bound for or leaving Community port and carrying dangerous or polluting goods.*

In order to sketch the overall scope of Directive 98/55/EC, the purpose of the amended Directive 93/75/EEC is crucial to understand. After the 1978 Amoco Cadiz accident yielded environmentally devastating consequences, and especially after the 1987 Herald of Free Enterprise accident claimed the lives of 193 people, the EU legislative bodies adopted *Directive 93/75/EEC concerning minimum requirements for ships bound for or leaving Community ports and carrying dangerous or polluting goods*. The idea was to oblige vessels bound for Community ports to notify the national authorities of the nature of the dangerous and polluting goods they were carrying, and to make available to those authorities a plan indicating the location of such goods on board. In addition, vessels were to immediately inform authorities in the case of accidents. In accordance with International Maritime Organisation (IMO) regulations, authorities were then to forward information about the accident to other shipping vessels in the area, and also to other affected member states.

9.2.1.1. European level characteristics:

Six months transposition deadline
The Commission proposal for the Council directive amending Directive 93/75/EEC was introduced on 23 September 1996, and was finally adopted in the second reading during the first days of the Austrian Presidency on 17 July 1998. Hence, it took almost two years to adopt the new EU legislation in the field of maritime safety. In light of developments in international legislation on maritime safety, the purpose of the Commission's proposal was to update the annexes to the 93/75 Directive and to facilitate their subsequent amendments. In the first reading, the European Parliament (EP), headed by the EP's rapporteur, Alfonso Novo Belenguer (Radicals, ES), was quite complementary to the Commission's text. The EP urged the Council to extend the scope of Directive 98/55/EC to include the carriage by sea of irradiated nuclear fuel, plutonium, and high-level radioactive waste in flasks. In total, the European directive has six recitals, it was just two pages long, containing two annexes, each of which were one page long. In the end, the transposition deadline was set at six months (31 December 1998), which is the normal timeframe for the implementation of an amendment that will replace, foremost, the annexes of already existing EU legislation. In the meantime, Directive 98/55/EC has been repealed by Directive 2002/59/EC.

Table 9.13: Policy cycle timetable of 98/55/EC.

98/55/EC	Initiated	Adopted	Deadline	French Notification to Commission
Date	23 September 96	17 July 98	7 November 99	19 February 99; 17 March 99

No discretion for interpretation
Amending Directive 93/75/EEC, Directive 1998/55/EC had two main objectives. First, it specified that the Directive 93/75/EEC covered nuclear transport, i.e. irradiated nuclear fuel, plutonium, and high-level radioactive waste. These radioactive materials (RAM), of natural or artificial origin, are of widespread use in developed societies all over the world. They are used in medicine, research, industrial manufacturing, agriculture, electric power generation, and in other applications that assist our daily lives. The handling, use, and management of RAM, including their transport gives rise to potential

radiological hazards. Directive 1998/55/EC was designed to include RAM. Second, Directive 1998/55/EC emphasised the search for harmonization of EU member states' legal instruments on the basis of already existing international standards, conventions, and agreements. Hence, the two objectives of Directive 1998/55/EC were to maintain the scope of Directive 93/75/EEC, and to facilitate the adaptation of those annexes to developments in international law through the committee procedure. It added relevant INF codes (International code for the Safe Carriage of packaged irradiated nuclear fuel, plutonium and high-level radioactive wastes on board ships) to the content of the accident information that was to be reported to the authorities of the Community port's member state. Therefore, the duty of notifying authorities of accidents was extended to include all ships, regardless of their date of construction or size. Directive 1998/55/EC specified how RAM should be carried on each kind of ship.

After all these adjustments, member states were left with little discretion as to how to interpret the provisions on RAM, a fact confirmed by all interview partners. Although one article was adopted to amend Directive 93/75/EEC's annexes I and II, they include a clear and straightforward checklist for vessels, and permit no discretion.

9.2.1.2. The national transposition process: France

With the exception of the UK, member states transposed Directive 1998/55/EC before the deadline, or else notified the Commission of a short delay of between one and five months. Table 9.14 illustrates that most member states did not encounter considerable transposition delays. This is despite the fact that no member state was able to refer to already existing national legislation, but instead had to actively adopt new legal instrument(s) to transpose the Directive (IP2).

Table 9.14: Transposition delays in months of Directive 1998/55/EC.

Member State EU15	BE	DK	DE	EL	ES	FR	IE	IT	LU	NL	AU	PT	FI	SE	UK
Transposition delay in months for 1998/55/EC	1	0	-3	0	4	3	5	-3	n.r.	4	n.r.	n.r.	3	0	21

Source: Eurlex and national databases; n.r. = no reference (16.9.04), Legend: BE (Belgium), DK (Denmark), DE (Germany), EL (Greece), ES (Spain), FR (France), IE (Ireland), IT (Italy), LU (Luxembourg), NL (the Netherlands), AU (Austria), PT (Portugal), FI (Finland), SE (Sweden), UK (United Kingdom).

France belongs to the group of member states that did not encounter serious transposition delay while transposing Directive 1998/55/EC. With a notification to the Commission of the first national instrument on 19 February 1999, France had a short delay of three months.

Relatively large numbers of transposition actors
In the end, France notified the Commission of two measures belonging to the 'lowest' level instrument in the French hierarchy of legal measures[39], namely, the ministerial order (*arrêté ministeriel*). The first order[40] was adopted almost three months after the transposition deadline set in the Directive, and the second one was 14 weeks after this deadline (17 March 1999)[41]. Both ministerial orders were signed by the director for maritime transport, M. Gressier, and three ministries were directly involved in the transposition process, namely: the Ministry of Economics, the Ministry of Environment, and the Ministry of Transport. An interview partner of Transport ministry stressed the three dimensionality of the Directive – it covered boat, harbour, and circulation – which required the extraordinary involvement of more than just the Ministry of Transport. Despite the fact that lowest national instrument was chosen, the number of veto players (4) was consequently relatively high.

Transposition package with 98/55/EC and 98/74/EC
Whereas Directive 98/55/EC was one among four directives to be transposed in the maritime units, it was the first Directive in a transposition package with Directive 98/74/EC. It was the State Council (*Conseil d'Etat*) that was responsible for determining whether the text would require legislative action, or else could be dealt with by government regulation. Furthermore, in accordance with the State Council and the SGG *(Secrétariat Général du Gouvernement*), the SGCI (*Secrétariat Général du Comité Interministériel pour les questions economiques européennes*) decided on the application of the package approach.

Adopted on 1 October 1998, the last Directive in the package, however, had a transposition deadline set for 2 November 1999—almost one year later than that of Directive 98/55/EC. Considering the time difference, one can see that the package approach matters. While the latest transposition measure in the package was adopted almost eight months in advance, this packaging method had a delaying effect for the transposition of Directive 98/55/EC. Adopted three months later in the Council of Transport Ministers, but having double the transposition time guaranteed by the EU Transport Ministers, the transposition of Directive 98/74/EC was combined with the Directive 98/55/EC (that covered minimum requirements for vessels bound for or leaving Community port and carrying dangerous goods) which had a delaying effect on the transposition process of Directive 98/55/EC.

---

39 Consult chapter 8 for an overview of all types of national implementing measures in the nine member states covered by this study.

40 *Arreté du 19 février 1999 portant modification du règlement annexé à l árreté du 23 novembre 1987 modifié relatif à la sécurité des navires.*

41 *Arreté du 17 mars 1999 pris en application de l'article 3 du décret du 14 décembre 1929 modifié relatif au reglement général du pilotage. JORF du 20/03/1999, p. 5256.*

Third French cohabitation (1997-2002)
During the transposition period, 17 July 1998 to 17 March 1999, the political climate in France was not tense, and no general election took place. Instead, between 4 June 1997 and 7 May 2002, France experienced its third cohabitation. Whereas Jacques Chirac of the liberal-conservative Union for a Popular Movement (UMP) was the president of the French Republic, Lionel Jospin, from the Socialist Party (PS), was Prime Minister. 'It was a relatively stable five-year term of government' (IP1). During these five years, Jean-Claude Gayssot, of the French Communist Party (PCF), was the only transport minister under Lionel Jospin, a fact that guaranteed the prospect of continuity and 'business as usual.' (IP1).

9.2.1.3. Crises:

No maritime accident
During the eight months of the transposition period, no maritime accident occurred. An accident would have had an effect on the implementation process in France. The next ecological disaster, however, was not far off. On 12 December 1999, the oil tanker Erika sank 40 miles off the coast of Brittany, releasing more than 10,000 tonnes of heavy fuel oil. The ecological disaster was devastating, polluting 400 kilometres of the French coast line. Only a few months later, the next European maritime directives were adopted under the highest political priority during the Portuguese Presidency (January-June 2000).

9.2.1.4. Preliminary findings:

The knowledge gleaned by following the French transposing of EU maritime Directive 1998/55/EC, from the Commission's initiative to the final adoption of the last ministerial order corroborates the study's theoretical framework (see table 9.15). Whereas the six-month deadline set in the Directive, which is very formal in character and leaves no room for interpretation, would have been sufficient time for transposition. However, the extraordinary number of transposition actors and the national transposition packaging caused some delay in the end.

Three French ministries had to agree on a national instrument that would be used in transposing 1998/55/EC, a directive that covered three issues: boat, harbour, and circulation. This lead to some coordination efforts between the SGCI and the head of the Ministry of Transport, efforts that would ultimately risk a problem-free procedure. Furthermore, the SGCI had agreed to set up a transposition package for two maritime Directives adopted by the EU ministers of transport in 1998, whose transposition deadlines, however, differed by almost one year. Consequently, this approach caused a three-month delay for the first Directive in the package (98/55/EC), but accelerated the transposition process of the second Directive (98/74/EC) by almost eight months. Next, I address the second on-the-line case whose implementation record is less convincing.

Table 9.15: Results of case study no. 1.

		Transposition of 1998/55/EC in France
European directive related factors	*Transposition time set in the directive*	6 months
	Amount of discretion granted by the directive	No discretion for interpretation
Form and method of national transposition process	*Number of veto players*	Relatively large numbers of transposition actors
	Package approach	Transposition package with 98/55/EC and 98/74/EC
Situational change of internal and external environment	*General elections*	No election; Third French cohabitation
	Transport related accidents	No maritime accident

9.2.2 *Case 2 – 2001/14: Spanish transposition of Directive 2001/14/EC of the European Parliament and the Council of 26 February 2001 on the allocation of railway infrastructure capacity and the levying of charges for the use of railway infrastructure and safety certification*

The EU has had the goal of revitalizing its railways on the agenda since the early nineties. Three railway packages have, meanwhile, been adopted amounting to a series of directives. This all started in 1991, with the adoption of single directives, like *Directive 91/440/EEC on the development of European railways*. The intention of this Directive was to improve the legal framework for railways, and to halt the ongoing decline in their market share. Directive 91/440/EEC was complemented by a follow-up in 1995, *Council Directive 95/18/EC on the licensing of railway undertakings* and one on *allocation of railway infrastructure capacity and the levying of charges* (95/19/EC). A second step of reforms at EU level, which were adopted on 26 February 2001, goes under the name '*first railway package*.' Referring to rail freight only, it represented an attempt at liberalizing the sector through the introduction of open access and forms of head-on competition—at least on the Trans-European Rail Freight Network (TERFN). The TERFN is responsible for 50% of EU railway networks and 80% of traffic. Open access and head-on competition will extend to the whole network by 2006, according to the 2004 adopted '*second railway package*'. On 3 March 2004, the Commission adopted its third railway package. This package contained four legislative measures, which are still being negotiated in the Council's working groups. Directive 2001/14/EC, which is part of first railway package, will be the focus of the second case study of this chapter.

9.2.2.1. European level characteristics:

Two years transposition deadline

The EU negotiations for the first railway package, containing Directives 2001/12, 2001/13, and 2001/14, were concluded in February, 2001. The Commission proposal was introduced during the Austrian Council Presidency on 22 July 1998. On 25 August 2000, the Council declared that it could not accept all the EP's amendments that were drafted by EP's rapporteur, Johannes Swoboda (PSE, Austria). Subsequently, the Council convened the Conciliation Committee, which met for the first time on 11 October 2000. Meanwhile, several meetings of EP's delegation and in trialogues (Farell and Hértier, 2003; Häge and Kaeding, 2007) took place before and after that date. On 22 November 2000, the Conciliation Committee reached its final agreement on the entire railway package. Ultimately, the first railway package was signed by the EP after its third reading and by the Council after two and a half years of bargaining. The date of the signing was 26 February 2001.

Regarding infrastructure access, Directive 2001/14/EC superseded and repealed Directive 95/19/EC. Strongly inspired by the 1998 *White paper on infrastructure access pricing*, Articles 7 and 8 of Directive 2001/14/EC inject new, essential, and detailed principles of charging. The deadline for transposition was set at two years (15 March 2003)[42]. Compared to the average 18 month transposition time of other transport directives in 2000 to 2005, the 24 month deadline was considerably above average (IP5).

While Directive 2001/14/EC was in transposition, Article 30 of Directive 2004/49/EC (in the second railway package) amended the title of Directive 2001/14/EC, as well as the contents of Articles 30.2., 32, and 34 to remove provisions on safety.

Table 9.16: Policy cycle timetable of 2001/14/EC.

2001/14/EC	Initiated	Adopted	deadline	Spanish Notification to Commission
Date	22 February 98	26 February 01	15 March 03	17 November 2003; 30 December 04; 7 April 2005

42 There are derogations in respect of the implementation of certain provisions of the Capacity Directive for Ireland, the UK and Greece, and those provisions do not have to be implemented until 15 March 2008.

Relatively high level of discretion
Directive 2001/14/EC is a 17 page document with 40 articles and 3 short annexes. It deals with potentially applicable principles and procedures for the setting of railway infrastructure charges, both international and domestic, and the allocation of railway infrastructure capacity[43], i.e. each Member State has to designate the allocation body which should be informed of all train paths available, and has to ensure that the railway infrastructure capacity is allocated on a fair and non-discriminatory basis. The existing directives had not prevented major disparities in the structure of railway infrastructure charges, nor the levels of such charges, nor the form or length of capacity-allocation procedures. Thereupon, Directive 2001/14/EC provides much detail necessary to describe the general character of the infrastructure manager's[44] monopoly regulation. It addresses the following questions explicity: Who is entitled to access the network? Who allocates access? What is the allocation process? How long is an allocated access period? How is access priced? What are the other terms of access? What if the network is congested? The directive is considered a 'rather complicated document' (IP5), with 50[45] recitals that state the scope of the legislation. Although they are not legally binding, they clearly indicate the Directive's complexity. In the end, however, Directive 2001/14/EC does allow for a certain degree of flexibility (IP5). It entails a considerable amount of discretion in the interpretation and application of its requirements. All interview partners confirmed that it provides infrastructure managers and train operators with appropriate incentives and flexibility in capacity allocation, and in performing allocation procedures fairly (Article 7.2.; 8.1.; 10.1.; 14.1.; 16; 19; 29).

9.2.2.2. National transposition process:

Member states had different points of departure after the adoption of the first liberalizing directives in the early 1990s. Whereas most member states had not foreseen any separation in the railway sector administration, Sweden was the first European country that provided the legal framework for non-discriminatory competition on the rail network, remarkably, even before its official membership to the EU. Sweden's railway reform of 1988 separated the infrastructure and the operator completely. The separation in administration had also already been accomplished in the UK. The British railway system had been divided into a number of different entities, including infrastructure, passenger and freight operators, rolling stock companies, and regulator. In Spain, too, the railway system also had been divided into different admin-

43 'Allocation'means the allocation of railway infrastructure capacity by an allocation body (2002/14/EC Article 2 e)

44 'Infrastructure manager' means any public body or undertaking responsible in particular for establishing and maintaining railway infrastructure, as well as for operating the control and safety systems (Directive 2001/14/EC Article 2c)

45 Directive 2001/14/EC is the transport directive with the most recitals in history.

istrative entities, in the 1990s, following the British model, but all entities still fell under the umbrella organization RENFE (*Red Nacional de los Ferrocarriles Espanoles, empresa pública operadora*).

Table 9.17: Transposition time in months of Directive 2001/14/EC.

Member states EU 15	BE	DK	DE	EL	ES	FR	IE	IT	LU	NL	AT	PT	FI	SE	UK
Transposition delay in months for 2001/14/EC	19	-3	25	n.r.	8	23	n.r.	4	n.r.	21	9	8	0	Already existing legislation	Already existing legislation

Source: Eurlex and national databases (16.9.04); n.r.= no reference, Legend: BE (Belgium), DK (Denmark), DE (Germany), EL (Greece), ES (Spain), FR (France), IE (Ireland), IT (Italy), LU (Luxembourg), NL (the Netherlands), AT (Austria), PT (Portugal), FI (Finland), SE (Sweden), UK (United Kingdom).

Table 9.17 illstrates that, all in all, member states had difficulties in transposing the directive by the deadline. Whereas initially Sweden, the UK, Denmark, Finland, and Italy notified the national measures to the Commission on time, in the end, only Denmark and Finland complied with EU legislation to the Commission's satisfaction. Infringement proceedings were started against the UK and Sweden because their existing legislation was not sufficient in scope (IP5). On the other hand, most member states experienced more considerable transposition delays, including Germany, France, the Netherlands, and Belgium. After months of intensive legislative activity, Belgium, for example, needed 24 national implementing measures. At first, Spain notified the Commission that its first instruments would be only moderately late, estimating implementation on 17 November 2003. The adopted legislative act, however, was to come into force six month later, on 18 May 2004, which is referred to as the so-called *vacatio legis*[46]. *Even then, it was not enforced before 31 December 2004, accumulating almost two years of delay.*

Large number of transposition actors:

After the adoption of the first railway package in 2001, Spain initially waited before taking any action. Since Directive 2001/14/EC gave considerable leeway to the member states, Spain watched and consulted with other member states 'to see which interpretation was pursued' by them (IP6). Apparently, RENFE (*Red Nacional de los Ferrocarriles Españoles*) had steady contact with

46 The period between the publication of a statute in the Official Journal of Laws and the beginning of the tax year. The official Spanish text in the legislative act reads as follows (Ley39/2003, BOE 276/40561): *'La presente ley entrará en vigor a los seis meses desde su publicación en el boletín oficiál del estado.'*

its French and German counterparts for these reasons, and also because it became clear that not all Spanish political forces would agree with their government's approach in the transposition process. Therefore, Spain hoped to watch and learn from other states so as to develop a measure that would please the most people.

On 17 November 2003, the Spanish parliament adopted a legislative act[47] opting for the 'radical division' between the new public administration, ADIF (*Administrador de Infraestructuras Ferroviarias*) and the RENFE-Operator. Although this legislative act was 'again a good example for Spain's radical transposition style' (IP7), there was still a pending issue to be solved. Before the legislative act could come into force, the questions about the umbrella organization (RENFE)'s debt had to be solved, leading to a provisional *vacatio legis* of six months (IP4). Two ministries were involved in the Spanish transposition process. The Ministry of Transport (*Fomento*) lead the process of transpostion, while the Ministry of Economics (*Ministerio de Economía y Hacienda*) tackled the debt of 7,200 million Euros (El País, 2004: 60; Goméz, 2005)

A legislative act (*ley ordinaria*), which is the highest legal instrument in the hierarchy of Spanish legal measures, involves a considerable number of veto players in the policy-making process. Legislative acts represent only about 12% of the total legal instruments used for the transposition of EU directives in Spain (Steunenberg and Voermans, 2005: 132), yet the adoption of a *ley ordinaria* requires parliamentary approval as well as the advice of the State Council. The additional role played by the Ministry of Economics made a six months *vacatio legis* indispensable.

Furthermore, the 'gladiator style' (IP4) separation[48] incited extensive discussions between the conservative Aznar government and left opposition parties in the parliament and, consequently, delayed the drafting of complementary regulations, which were considered necessary. Although the administrative separation of units (infrastructure and circulation) had been already taken place in the early 1990s, the discussion now was more about the physical separation of persons and the threat of licensing third contractors to the national infrastructure due to rationalizing means (IP7).

Transposition package without relevance

The first railway package was being transposed concomitantly with eight other ongoing transposition processes in the railway sectors units of the Ministry of Transport. Despite the massive workload, Spain transposed all

47 Ley 39/2003, de 17 de noviembre, del Sector Ferroviario BOE no 276 de 18/11/2003 p. 40532.

48 Whereas Germany and France opted for a middle way, Spain decided to separate infrastructure manager and railway understaking from each other, not only legally, but also in terms of buildings and human resources.

three directives of the first railway package through one legislative act (*ley*) 39/2003 on 17 November 2003, amending the already existing legislation of 30 July 1987. Although Spanish authorities applied a transposition package for the entire first railway package, the timeliness of the transposition process was not improved. This was because all three EU directives were not only adopted by the EU Ministers of Transport on the same day (26 February 2001), but they also had the same transposition time guaranteed—a final date fixed for two years later (15 March 2003). Consequently, it is not possible to differentiate between the first or the last Directive in this particular Spanish transposition package, nor would the theoretical model foresee any effect on the timeliness of transposition.

Spanish general election of 14 March 2004

The aforementioned conflicting discussions between the conservative Aznar government and the left opposition in parliament were further augmented by the campaigning for the general elections of 14 March 2004. With these discussions now came an interruption in the transposition process. Over time, the clear division between *ADIF* and *RENFE-Operador* became an election campaign issue (IP4). Although less ideological than the French counterparts, the Spanish unions UJT (*Transistors Uniunión*) and SEMAF (*Sindicado de Maquinistas y Ayudantes Ferroviarios*) demonstrated against the legislative act. The autonomous regions in Spain, CCAA (*Comunidas Autónomas*), especially those governed by the opposition party groups – Aragón, Asturias, Castilla-La Mancha and Cataluña – initiated a constitutional proceeding concerning their regional transport competence (Articles 79d and 31). Their goal was to carry out their full regional competences in the railway sector in general and the infrastructure in particular, since they would be responsible for the practical application of the legislative act, as well as its three related regulations. Although their constitutional proceeding was eventually dropped, all interview partners confirmed that it served to irritate the national situation for some time.

Despite the overall displeasure about the conservative government's radical approach, a few weeks before the general election, the conservative government seemed very likely to keep their positions after the election. But then something unforeseen happened, traumatising Spain and the Spanish voters. After the fatal Atocha Central Station bombings on 11 March 2004, the centre-left party, PSOE, lead by Zapatero won the elections. Those who had criticized the legislative act in parliament were now (surprisingly) in power. They assigned a new transport minister, Magdalena Álvarez. Her first action as transport minister was to postpone the coming into force of the transposing legal instrument. She added another year to the *vacatio legis* in order to facilitate discussions between the trade unions (UJT and SEMAF) and the autonomous regions (CCAA), which had supported the new government fiercely in opposition during the election campaigns.

This self-imposed year of reflection (14 March 2004 to 30 December 2004) concluded with three additional implementing measures (*real decreto*) adopted on 30 December 2004 [49] – one year after the publication of the legislative act 39/2003. Based on Article 86 of the Spanish Constitution, the government may issue this special type of decree in regards to the status of the law in case of extraordinary and urgent need (Steunenberg and Voermans, 2005: 131). The provisions of the *real decreto-ley* are directly applicable, but they must be immediately submitted to parliament. Although the Spanish government considered the speediest Spanish legal instrument urgently necessary (IP4), the Commission, considered it to be insufficient. The Commission started an infringement procedure for non-compliance, leading to two additional ministerial orders (*orden*) adopted on 7 April 2005[50], which are provisions issued by the minister without explicit authorization through law. Thereupon, the Commission closed the infringement proceedings against Spain.

Ultimately, Spain adopted six national instruments covering almost all different types of instruments, whereas most of the other member states – with the exception of Belgium – remained in the margin of between one and four. The Spanish Ministry of Transport, Magdalena Álvarez, stands still in contact with the Commission to further improve the transposition of the first railway package in Spain (IP4).

9.2.2.3 Crises:

No major railway accidents on Spanish territory

Whereas the UK is 'sadly famous' for its fatal railway accidents, Spain has not experienced any major train crashes, in general; nor did any occur during the transposition period. The Atocha bombings during the election campaign had a delaying effect on the proceedings of Spanish policy-making. However, since they were not directly related to transport or railway liberalization, no accelerating effect could be expected.

9.2.2.4 Preliminary findings:

In the end, the Spanish authorities notified the European Commission of six legal instruments that would be used to transpose the first railway package, including Directive 2001/14/EC. The preconditions for a swift transposition process were already null because of the high degree of discretion given to the member states. This flexibility resulted in a time-consuming 'wait and

49 Real decreto 2395/2004, de 30 de diciembre, *por el que se aprueba el Estatuto de la entidad pública empresarial Administrador de Infraestructuras Ferroviarias*. Real decreto 2396/2004, de 30 de diciembre, *por el que se aprueba el Estatuto de la entidad pública empresarial RENFE-Operadora*. Real decreto 2387/2004, de 30 de diciembre, *por el que se aprueba el Reglamento del Sector Ferroviario*.

50 Orden 5754 FOM 12324/2005 and orden 5755 FOM 12331/2005.

see' situation right after the EU Ministers of Transport had adopted Directive 2001/14/EC. After the Spanish authorities had deliberated on the different approaches envisioned by Germany and France, they decided to go for the 'gladiator style' of separation between ADIF and RENFE-Operador. The *potestad reglementaria* opted for the highest Spanish instrument, the *ley ordinaria,* involving large numbers of transposition actors (State Council, parliament, autonomous regions etc.). However, before transposition could begin, the ADIF's debt of 7,200 million Euros had to be tackled by the Ministry of Transport and the Ministry of Economics. This situation resulted in one additional agency's involvement, the Ministry of Economics, and required the introduction of the so-called *vacatio legis*. Furthermore, the radical Spanish approach caused considerable agitation within the country. Unions protested in the streets of Madrid, autonomous regions began legal proceedings, and the opposition antagonized the draft legislation in parliament.

Table 9.18: Results of the second case study.

		Transposition of 2001/14/EC in Spain
European directive related factors	*Amount of discretion granted by the directive*	Relatively high amount of discretion
	Transposition time set in the directive	2 years transposition deadline
Form and method of national transposition process	*Number of veto players*	Relatively large numbers of transposition actors
	Package approach	Transposition package without relevance
Situational change of internal and external environment	*General elections*	Spanish general election of 14 March 2004
	Transport related accidents	No railway accident

The hostile response by unions, autonomous regions, and the opposition was further harassed by the general elections, which were scheduled in the last month before the Directive's transposition deadline (15 March 2004 – *17.11.03 plus 6 months*). The fatal Atocha Central Station bombings of 11 March 2004 were likely responsible not only for preventing the Aznar's from winning the elections, but also for further delaying the transposition process of 2001/14/EC. The Directive was set to the side, as other issues, such as terrorism and security, earned priority status. After the bombings and the unexpected electoral victory of the centre-left, however, Spain needed a general period of reflection. A new centre-left government assigned a new transport minister, whose first action was to proclaim this year of reflection. Furthermore, by postponing the final adoption of Direct 2001/14/EC by one year, the Spanish government also honoured the trade unions' and the autonomous regions for their strong support during the election campaigns.

9.3 Off-the-line case studies

While the first two cases corroborate to great extent the theoretical framework on apt transposition, the following off-the-line studies will help to further improve our understanding of timely transposition.

9.3.1 *Case 3 – 2002/59: German transposition of Directive 2002/59/EC of the European Parliament and of the Council of 27 June 2002 establishing a Community vessel traffic monitoring and information system, and repealing Council Directive 93/75/EEC*

9.3.1.1 European level characteristics:

The sinking of the oil tanker Erika off the French coast in December, 1999 spurred new developments in Europe's maritime safety policies. The 'Erika I' package included two Directives that would update existing Directives on classification societies, Port State Control, also update a Regulation on the phasing out of single-hull tankers. 'Erika II' aimed to bring about lasting improvements in the protection of European waters, and spoke to accidents and marine pollution. This second set of measures was presented on 6 December 2000 by the Commission. It contained two proposals for Regulations and one proposal for a Directive. This final proposal will be the focus of this case study.

18 months of transposition time

As is the case for 95% of all transport directives,]Directive 2002/59/EC was a European Parliament and Council directive. Repealing Directive 93/75/EEC, the only one in the Erika II package, Directive 2002/59/EC was adopted by the EU Ministers of Transport and the EP relatively quickly. Initiated on 6 December 2000, Directive 2002/59/EC was mainly the EP's issuing of stricter provisions. In the first reading, on 13 June 2001, the EP's transport committee, and especially the rapporteur, Dirk Sterckx (ELDR, Belgium),urged the Commission and the member states to broaden the scope of their objectives. The hope was that new objectives would include all types of ships as well as the development of a working relationship with the international maritime community to promote a culture of safety in all transport sectors. Furthermore, the Committee accussed the Commission's proposal of ignoring the 'human element and over-emphasizing technological solutions' (IP14). In the second reading, the EP asked for additional measures. It suggested the introduction of an adequate compensation scheme[51] for EU ports accommodating a ship in distress, and also suggested the possibility of requiring that ships to come to a Community port to be adequately insured. On 12 June 2002, the Commission modified its proposal to include almost all the amendments proposed by

51 Addressing of who has to pay for the salvage costs of a ships on national waters?

Parliament. Just two weeks later, on 27 June 2002, the Council finally adopted Directive 2002/59/EC repealing 93/75/EEC. In the end, the EU negotiations took only 18 months. The process is probably best explained by the high political priority assigned to the maritime safety dossier by the member states after the Erika accident in 1999 (IP14).

Member states, the Commission, and the EP agreed on a 18 months transposition deadline (5 February 2004), which was the average transposition time guaranteed to all EU transport directives in that period (2000-2004). However, compared to the average 13 month transposition time for maritime directives in the *acquis*, 18 months is quite long. Interview partners confirmed the extraordinary timeframe set for this Directive, which they ascribed to 'the Commission's colloquial approach towards member states.' In the pre-negotiation phase, member states were already allowed to raise their concerns and influence the content of the Directive as well as the transposition deadline, which they considered to be crucial (IP12 and IP13).

Table 9.19: Policy cycle timetable of 2002/59/EC.

2002/59/EC	Initiated	Adopted	Deadline	German Notification to Commission
Date	6 December 2000	27 June 02	5 February 04	27 February 04

Almost no leeway for national interpretation
As mentioned before, this Directive is to be viewed in the context of the second package on maritime safety (Erika II), and as a direct response to the sinking of the Erika in 1999. In general, it applied to ships of 300 gross tonnages, and was to improve maritime safety and reduce the possible environmental consequences of accidents at sea. The Directive, in particular, foresaw the improvement of accident prevention measures. It also called for the monitoring of ships sailing in European waters, an action that would also cover ships not calling at European ports. The Directive expressly provided for the installation of a notification system that would include vessels not calling at Community ports. Before entering member States territories, ships must be equipped with EDI (electronic data interchanges), the automatic vessel identification system (AIS system), and a voyage data recorder (VDR) system ('black box') to facilitate investigations following accidents (IP4). The Directive also called for increased cooperation among member states and a closer monitoring of vessels that present specific risks to maritime safety and the environment.

Ultimately, Directive 2002/59/EC strengthens the power of coastal member states to take action in the event of accident or pollution risks off their coasts, and even outside their territorial waters. The directive enables them to order a potentially threatening ship to change route; member states also have the options of sending aboard a risk evaluation team, as well as piloting or towing the ship. Finally, the directive requires each member state to designate ports of refuge where vessels in distress can seek shelter.

In total, Directive 2002/59/EC is 16 pages long, including 4 annexes of about 1 page each. Additionally, the Directive lists 22 recitals compared to the median number of recitals in transport directives (8), which may indicate its complexity and may also explain the atypical amount of time for transposition set in the Directive in the first place.

Furthermore, the 32 articles guarantee little leeway for interpretation. The exceptions to this are Articles 15 and 16. Whereas Article 15 introduces an exemption for services performed between ports on one member state's territory, the remaining ones do not include any amount of discretion in this regard. Concerning Article 16, interview partners spoke of the highly technical nature of the Directive 2002/59/EC, and this article in particular. Repeatedly they underscored the German efforts to keep Länder competences out of the directive, a feat that could only be accomplished by a restrictive interpretation of Article 16 II. It reads as follows:

> 'Costal stations holding relevant information on the ships referred to in paragraph 1 shall communicate it to the coastal stations concerned in the other Member states located along the planned route of the ship.' (Article 16 of Directive 2002/59/EC)

In order to guarantee a centralised coordination along the German coastlines, the federal ministry insisted that this task was to be taken over by a federal body and would not fall under the responsibility of the bordering *Länder*.

9.3.1.2 National transposition process:

Directive 2002/59/EC encountered timeliness problems across the member states. Whereas only Denmark and Spain notified the Commission of their instruments on time, all the other member states experienced delays in notification, ranging from 1 month in Germany to 10 months in the Netherlands, and 19 months in Belgium.

In comparison to the other member states, Germany performed rather well. Notifying its ministerial order [52] (*Verordnung*) on the 27 February 2004, it surpassed the deadline by only three weeks.

52 *Elfte Verordnung zur Änderung seeverkehrsrechtlicher Vorschriften vom 18/02/2004 BGBl*. Teil I no 8 vom 27/02/2004 p. 300.

Table 9.20: Transposition delay in months for Directive 2002/59/EC.

Member State EU15	BE	DK	DE	EL	ES	FR	IE	IT	LU	NL	AT	PT	FI	SE	UK
Transposition delay in months for 2002/59/EC	19	-4	1	n.r.	0	5	n.r.	n.r.	7	10	n.r.	5	n.r.	Already existing legislation	5

Source: Eurlex and national databases (16.9.04); n.r.= no reference, Legend: BE (Belgium), DK (Denmark), DE (Germany), EL (Greece), ES (Spain), FR (France), IE (Ireland), IT (Italy), LU (Luxembourg), NL (the Netherlands), AT (Austria), PT (Portugal), FI (Finland), SE (Sweden), UK (United Kingdom).

Small number of national transposition actors

The goodness of fit between the pre-existing German legislation and Directive 2002/59/EC seems evident. Despite the considerable workload for the drafters of new maritime legislationcaused by the subsequent accidents on European sea[53], German legislation had to include relatively small number (12) of newly introduced articles by the ministerial order. All interview partners confirmed the Directive's harmony with pre-existing German legislation. Out of seven issues covered in the EU directives, four had been already discussed in Germany, namely: Article 5 (monitoring of ships entering the area of mandatory ship reporting systems), Article 9 (infrastructure for ships' reporting systems, ships' routing systems, and vessel traffic services), Article 12 (obligation on the shipper), and Article 20 (places of refuge). Moreover, the transposition team explicitly chose *not* to introduce new legislation. Instead, the German ministerial order changed already existing annexes to legislative acts, and altered the content of ministerial orders, without introducing new instruments [54]

The German interpretation of Article 16 of the Directive was a practical one (IP12). Germany adopted a ministerial order (*Verordnung*) in maritime transport. Normally, Länder competencies are involved in maritime transport legislation, being that six *Länder* have access to the sea, namely: Mecklemburg-Western Pomerania, Schleswig- Holstein, North Rhine-Westphalia, Lower Saxony, Bremen and Hamburg. However, *Länder* involvement in Article 16 would have made the transposition procedure much more complicated by

53 Between 2000 and 2003, sixteen EU maritime legislations had been adopted. The maritime unit in the German Ministry of Transport had a considerable number of ongoing transposition processes (7) right after the start of the national transposition processes.

54 *Änderung der Anlage zum Schiffssicherheitsgesetz; Änderung der Schiffssicherheitsverordnung; Änderung der Anlaufsbedingungsverordnung; Verordnung über die Sicherung der Seefahrt und die Änderung der Sportbootführerscheinverordnung-See.*

requiring all six governments to adopt implementing measures. Instead of involving *Länder*, Germany used an adopted ministerial order on the federal, not local, level. This kind of order is the fastest German transposition instrument. It ranks lowest in the set of implementation measures in Germany, requiring only a very small number of compulsory actors (Steunenberg and Voermans, 2005: 174-188). The ministerial order was signed only by the Minister of Transport, a fact that underscores the relatively small number of actors involved. After all, the provisions are issued by one minister with explicit authorization through law (*Ermächtigungsgrundlage*), and do not require the signatures of other actors.

Package approach with 2000/59/EC, 2001/106/EC and 2003/75/EC

The German Ministry of Transport decided to apply a transposition package including four EU directives, namely: 2000/59/EC, 2001/106/EC, 2002/59/EC, and 2003/75/EC. The deadlines of the four directives differed by 14 months. Whereas the first directive's 2000/59/EC deadline was set for 28 December 2002, the last directive's deadline (2002/59) was 5 February 2004. In the end, the German ministerial order transposed all four EU directives at once, causing a considerable overdue for the first measures in the package. The first directive, 2000/59/EC, was transposed with a delay of almost 15 months. Consequently, the hypothesis in this book about the delaying effect of the package approach for the first directive is corroborated. The package approach's affect on the last directive in the package, however, is less straightforward. The last two directives in the package, with similar transposition deadlines, were transposed three weeks late. This can be considered a very short delay; however, a clear accelerating effect is certainly not confirmed in this case.

German general elections of 22 October 2002

During the adoption period of the German ministerial order transposing EU directive 2000/59/EC, between 25 September 2002 and 18 February 2004, there was indeed one general election, scheduled for 22 October 2002. Falling only one month after the adoption of the EU transport directive, it might have had a delaying effect on the German policy-making process. The interview partners confirmed that the fiercely fought election campaign created a near standstill in national politics. 'Ministers had to campaign [and] mobilize their electorate, which did not leave sufficient time for day-to-day politics.'(IP13).

However, as it happened, the electoral outcome did not cause a change of government; the ruling Schröder red-green coalition achieved a marginal win. Yet, even if the constellation of the government did not change, with the Social Democrats and the Green Party still in power, the portfolios were indeed reshuffled, and the Ministry of Transport was taken over by Manfred Stolpe[55]. This reshuffle paralyzed German policy-making the following

55 Formerly held by Kurt Bodewig.

months. Since a new minister and with him personal assistants, and so forth, had to become acquainted to their new positions, it took some time before 'the Berlin republic could move on with politics as usual' (IP12).

9.3.1.3 Crises:

Accidents in the North Sea, the Baltic Sea and the Atlantic
From the early EU negotiations onwards, Germany had been one of the member states pushing for stricter legislation in the field of maritime safety. Although not directly affected by the Erika accident in 1999, it was already sensitized by three earlier accidents in its own waters, both of which had caught a lot of media attention. The Clement sank in the Bermuda Triangle in the Baltic Sea on 6 March 2000, and the Baltic Carrier caused an ecological disaster in the Baltic Sea on 29 March 2001. Foremost in influence, however, was the Pallas accident in late 1998, which was by all accounts, been very present in people's minds. 'Pallas should be not possible in the future anymore,' a common statement went (IP12). What had happened?

It was on 25 October 1998 that the wood cargo ship Pallas caught fire near the Danish coastline. During four days the cargo ship floated in the North Sea, while attempts of extinguishing the fire and sending out tugboats had failed. Finally, the Pallas floated to and grounded on the German island Amrum, in the North Sea. When it landed, it caused the deaths of one crew member[56] (von Wecheln, 1999) and more than 16,000 birds, and devastated the wading sea by dumping into it 60,000 tonnes of heavy fuel oil.[57] Later investigations revealed that the responsible classification society, and several others, had not noticed the chain cable's exceeding amount of rust. The chain cable's deplorable state was left at 80% of its original weight, which precluded any attempts of anchoring. Furthermore, the lifeboat on the ship was not serviceable, which dissented with the regulations (von Wecheln, 1999). Last but not least, the cooperation between the Danish and the German bodies was not good. Given the fact that a burning, disassembled ship was floating towards Germany's coast, Denmark should have alarmed the German coast guard immediately.

The lessons learned from the Pallas accidents in the North Sea and the Erika accident shortly thereafter before the French coast were taken very seriously by Germany and the European Commission. Next to the salvage operation of the Pallas in the North Sea, which cost about 14 million DM (7,16 million EUR) it was an ecological disaster for the North Sea in general and the small island, Amrum, in particular due to reasons which are addressed by the provisions of the directive.

56 The others had been rescued under severe weather conditions by helicopter.
57 See other case study on Directive 98/55/EC where Germany, probably due to this accident in own waters, transposed the Directive very fast.

The transposition process in Germany was overshadowed by another ecological disaster, albeit one far from the German coastline. On the 13 November 2002, five months after the adoption of the Directive 2002/59/EC, the oil tanker Prestige broke in two off Galicia in Spain. It released a considerable amount of the 70,000 tonnes of heavy fuel oil onboard. This maritime catastrophe caught a lot of media attention, in Germany too (IP12). It illustrated, once again, the importance of improved enforcement of existing EU legislation in the field of maritime safety.

9.3.1.4 Preliminary findings:

Circumstances seemed ideal for Germany to notify the Commission of its transposition measures in a timely fashion. Directive 2002/59/EC came with an ample deadline. It also contained rather strict provisions. Leaving almost no leeway for interpretation, Germany decided to apply its lowest level instrument to transpose the Directive, an instrument that allowed few veto players. Moreover, Directive 2002/59/EC was the last in transposition package. In addition, despite the situational changes in the external environment caused by three maritime accidents that directly affected Germany's coastline and the Prestige accident which too place in the first months after the adoption of the directive, Germany passed the deadline by a mere three weeks. Note that in comparison to other member states, Germany performed quite well.

Table 9.21: Results of case study number three.

		Transposition of 2002/59/EC in Germany
European directive related factors	*Amount of discretion granted by the directive*	Almost no leeway for national interpretation
	Transposition time set in the directive	18 months of transposition time
Form and method of national transposition process	*Number of veto players*	Small number of transposition actors
	Package approach	Package approach with 2000/59/EC, 2001/106/EC and 2003/75/EC
Situational change of internal and external environment	*General elections*	German general election from 22 October 2002
	Transport related accidents	Earlier and actual accidents in the North Sea (Prestige, 1998), the Baltic Sea and the Atlantic (Erika, 1999)

Two issues may reasonably be pointed to as causes for the short delay. They both indicate that the level of political priority assigned to the transposition process may play an important role. While the German parliamentary elections in 2002 did not result in a change of government, they did require a lot of resources. As it happened, then, resources became unavailable for day-to-day policy-making. Until election day, polls forecasted a close run between the two alternative party group blocs, a situation that called for the full engagement in the electoral campaign by every member of the cabinet. The German government remained in place after the election. This was, largely because of the strong performance of the smaller coalition party, headed by Joschka Fischer. Another strong influence of the victory was that of the Eastern German electorate. The electorate gave strong support to the ruling government that had just promised emergency funds for recovery after the devastating hundred year flood in Eastern Germany which had occurred in late summer 2002. Despite the maintenance of power, however, the minister posts were reshuffled. The minister of transport was replaced and endorsed with a new portfolio. Manfred Stolpe was not only Minister of Transport, but was, from then onwards, special appointee for the new federal *Länder* whre the general election, in the end, had been won. During the first months after the election, it was this new portfolio that attracted most of the minister's attention, thereby granting a rather unassertive start for the transposition of Directive 2002/59/EC (IP12). Political priority attached to the transposition process was low.

With regard to the maritime accidents in German waters, the Erika I package demonstrates that people forget quickly. Despite the fact that the ecological disaster caused by the Erika tanker was by far the worst in EU history, the first Erika package was not at all rapidly transposed into national law. In fact, by 23 September 2003 (the transposition deadline), only five EU countries had transposed both of the Directives relating to the Erika I package. The Commission even initiated legal proceedings against Austria, Belgium, Finland, Greece, Ireland, Italy, Luxembourg, the Netherlands, Portugal and Sweden for failing to implement one or both of the Erika I Directives (IP14). This example indicates that the priority assigned to transposition by the transposition actors is crucial, and it must be reinforced on a regular basis. Accidents have a brief impact. They only affect the perceived costs and benefits of new EU legislation when they occur within the national transposition process itself on national territory.

9.3.2 *Case 4 – 2001/53: French transposition of Commission Directive 2001/53/EC of 10 July 2001 amending Council Directive 96/98/EC on marine equipment*

9.3.2.1 European level characteristics:

International conventions, such as the 1974 International Convention for the Safety of Life at Sea (SOLAS), require that marine equipment onboard ships conform to certain safety regulations. The Marine Equipment Directive (MED) seeks to enhance safety at sea and prevent marine pollution through the uniform application of relevant international instruments. These instruments establish common rules about equipment and eliminate differences in the implementation of international standards in the member states. The MED 1996/98/EC, as amended by Directives 98/85/EC, 2001/53/EC, and 2002/75/EC, began a two-year transition period on 1 January 1999, and became mandatory on 1 January 2001. In general, Directive 1996/98/EC applies to marine equipment on both new and existing vessels that are registered in the EU/European Free Trade Agreement (EFTA) area. In particular, the Directive covers life-saving appliances, marine pollution prevention, fire protection. It also refers to fire-fighting equipment, navigational equipment, and radio-communication equipment.

Six months transposition time

The Commission Directive 2001/53/EC, amending Directive 1996/98/EC, was adopted by regulatory comitology procedure involving the Committee on Safe Seas and the Prevention of Pollution from Ships (COSS), which was set up by Council Directive 93/75/EC of 13 September 1993. Falling under regulatory procedure (Steunenberg, Koboldt and Schmidtchen, 1996), the Commission was obliged to consult the COSS, whose opinions were binding on the Commission. Chaired by the Commission, the COSS meetings always counted among its attendees representatives of old member states which were very active. Whereas France, Germany, and the Netherlands were very involved in the meetings, the Spanish representative, for example, hardly participated in the negotiations. After several months of weekly discussions, the Commission directive was adopted by a qualified majority during the first days of the Belgium Council Presidency, on 10 July 2001.

The typical transposition deadline for amending directives that fall under the comitology procedure was six months. The deadline for Directive 2001/53/EC was also set for six months, to be completed by 31 January 2002. The length of time afforded here was, however, considerably less than the average transposition time for transport directives (18 months) in general.

Table 9.22: Policy cycle timetable of 2001/53/EC.

2001/53/EC	Initiated	Adopted	Deadline	French Notification to the Commission
Date		10 July 01	31 January 02	29 January 02

Little discretion allowed in interpretation

The MED 2001/53/EC is very technical. It covers certain statutory equipment carried and used on ships registered under the flags of the EU member states which are required to meet the international conventions (SOLAS, MARPOL[58]

58 International Convention for the Prevention of Pollution from Ships

etc.). The aim of the MED is to ensure that equipment meets common standards of safety and performance acceptable to each member state through the harmonization of states' approval requirements. The equipment categories covered are listed in Annex A of the Directive. [59] Annex A is divided into two sections, A.1. and A.2., and equipment can fall under either or both sections. Only equipment listed under A.1 is required to be certified in accordance with the MED. Those items listed in A.2. must comply with national requirements (IP10). Each member state, or the organizations acting on their behalf (notified bodies), must ensure, when issuing or renewing the relevant safety certificates, that the equipment onboard complies with the requirements of the Directive.

The MED's high level of technicality did not leave any room to manoeuvre in interpreting it. On the one hand, its sternness is reflected in the high number of appendix pages. Whereas the directive includes only 4 articles on 2 pages, the annexes consist of 26 pages. On these 26 pages are tables on equipment for which detailed testing standards either exist or do not yet exist on the international stage. On the other hand, the number of recitals is relatively small, which reflects a low degree of complexity (Kaeding, 2006). Furthermore, the comitology procedure set a six month transposition time that underscores the rather technical issue of the MED. Technical amendments normally grant a transposition deadline of not more than six months. Last but not least, interview partners confirm that there seemed to be only limited possibilities of interpretation for member states while transposing the Directive into national law. 'It was rather a 'copy-and-paste' job' (IP11).

9.3.2.2 National transposition process:

Table 23 illustrates the timelines in which member states transposed the MED into national legislation. Whereas some member states – Italy, Denmark, Luxembourg, Portugal – had considerable problems and delays of more than one year, other member states – Sweden, Spain, the UK, Ireland, and the Netherlands – did not encounter delay- causing problems in the transposition process (IP8 and IP9).

Table 9.23: Transposition delay in months for Directive 2001/53/EC.

Member State EU15	BE	DK	DE	EL	ES	FR	IE	IT	LU	NL	AT	PT	FI	SE	UK
Transposition delay in months for 2001/53/EC	7	13	8	3	-1	0	1	21	13	1	5	12	9	-1	0

Source: Eurlex and national databases (16.3.04); n.r.= no reference, Legend: BE (Belgium), DK (Denmark), DE (Germany), EL (Greece), ES (Spain), FR (France), IE (Ireland), IT (Italy), LU (Luxembourg), NL (the Netherlands), AT (Austria), PT (Portugal), FI (Finland), SE (Sweden), UK (United Kingdom).

59 Life-saving appliances, marine pollution prevention fire protection, navigation equipment, radio communication equipment, COLREG 72 and bulk carrier safety equipment.

France, too, did not encounter any problems in notifying its national instrument [60] to the Commission on time. Whereas the transposition deadline was set for 31 January 2002, the French transposing instrument was adopted 29 January 2002 and published on 8 February 2002.

Comparatively 'high' number of French transposition actors

France transposed the MED with the lowest ranking instrument in the hierarchy of French national implementing measures, namely: ministerial order (*arrêté ministériel*). It required and obtained only the signature of the Ministry of Transport, at a time when five other transposition processes in the field of maritime transport were also underway. In total, the French ministerial order includes six articles on two pages, and refers to two already existing legislative texts from the mid-1980s. [61] According to the interview partner, the goodness-of-fit was extraordinarily high. '*On n'a rien créé*' ('We did not create anything') (IP11).

Despite the fact that the national implementing measure required only one minister's signature, another institution was actively involved in drafting the French national legal instrument. As mentioned before, the key players in carrying out the transposition of a directive are the national notified bodies. They are in charge of assessing member states' conformity to the applicable directive. Member states are responsible for their notification to the Commission. They select the institutions they will notify from the bodies falling under their jurisdiction which comply with the requirements of the directive and the principles laid down in Decision 93/465/EEC. But not every member state has a notified body for the MED. Whereas Italy has three, Germany does not have any, but uses the one in Luxembourg. [62] In France, there is one notified body, namely: *Bureau Veritas* (BV). Normally, the manufacturers have to contact the notified bodies and arrange for the equipment to be type examined. Once a production-control phase module is deemed appropriate the equipment is affixed with the mark of conformity, indicating that it complies with the Directive. From the date of its entry into force, only equipment complying with 2001/53/EC is allowed to be placed onboard sea-going vessels. This means that the Directive is a very powerful economic weapon for the industry deciding on provision of certifications. Herein lies the interest and the necessity of involvement of the notified body in the policy-making process since they have to carry out the licensing task. With the involvement of these notified bodies, the national implementing measure, in practice, calls for two actors: the minister, and the respective notified body.

---

60 *Arrêté du 29 janvier 2002 modifiant l'arrêté du 23 novembre 1987 relatif à la sécurité des navires JORF no 33 du 08/02/2002 p. 2595.*

61 *Décret no 84-810 du 30 aout 1984 modifié relatif à la sauvegarde de la vie humaine en mer, à l'habitabilité à bord des navires et à la prévention de la pollution ; arrêté du 23 novembre 1987 modifié relatif à la sécurité des navires.*

62 For further details please consult: http://www.mared.org/

No package approach
Whereas the French administration uses transposition packages in the field of transport, and especially in maritime policy, the MED was not part of one. In fact, only Denmark set up a transposition package for Directives 2001/53/EC and 2002/75/EC.

French general elections shortly after the transposition deadline
During the French transposition process, between 10 July 2001 and 29 January 2002, no general elections were scheduled. Neither did the Minister of Transport change. However, 2002 was a super-election year in France with presidential elections on 21 April and 4 May, with elections for the French National Assembly on 9 June and 16 June 2002. The final date of elections was almost one year away in the quite distant future, from a transposition actor's point of view. However, the first half of 2002, which included the last months of transposition process, was considered characterized by a paralysis of France decision-making. Due to the numerous elections and predicted change of government, French policy-making was slowing down (IP11). With regard to Directive 2001/53/EC, the adoption of the French legal instrument occurred within the last months of the electoral campaigning, which could have fostered a timely transpose. The general election was set for spring 2002, and all draft legislation from the old parliamentary term had to be adopted by then. The principle of discontinuity states that all non-adopted legislative proposals have to be re-introduced at the beginning of the new legislative term. Therefore, according to this principle, the drafts had to be passed within the last months before the new, post-election government formation. In the end, President Chirac was elected, and the opposition centre-right coalition held majority in the parliament. The former Prime Minister Lionel Jospin left and with his resignation, the government reshuffled. On 7 May 2002, Gilles de Robien became new Transport Minister of France.

9.3.2.3 Crises:

No transport related accidents:
Between the six month period of the French transposition process of Directive 2001/53/EC (10 July 2001 to 29 January 2002), there was no maritime transport related accident taking place on French territory.

9.3.2.4 Preliminary findings:

Whereas the theoretical model would have predicted a longer delay for this case, the findings are ambiguous. The transposition time was only 6 months, which is short compared to the average 18 month deadlines set in transport directives, but on the other hand, normal for technical amendments agreed in comitology. The number of transposition actors was even higher than reported in the statistical data, including next to the ministry of transport the French notified body (BV). Hence, the number of actors was comparatively high, including the Ministry of Transport and the *Bureau Veritas* (French notified body). Moreover, the Directive left meagre room for member states to exercise discretion in interpreting its provisions.

Table 9.24: Results of case study number four.

		Transposition of 2002/59/EC in France
European directive related factors	*Amount of discretion granted by the directive*	No discretion of interpretation
	Transposition time set in the directive	6 months transposition time
Form and method of national transposition process	*Number of veto players*	Relatively high number of transposition actors
	Package approach	No package approach
Situational change of internal and external environment	*General elections*	General election three months after deadline (21.4.-16.6.2002)
	Transport related accidents	No maritime accident

Again in this case, the political priority attached to the Directive may help explain the timeliness of transposition across the member states. The political priority assigned to Directive 2002/59/EC was high. Two clear indications of its deemed importance are the role played by the French notified body (BV), and the specialization of the department in charge of implementing the Directive.

Although it is considered a second actor in the French transposition process, the Bureau Vertias (BV) has always had a considerable interest in extending its market share, and consequently its influence, on French policy-making in the field of maritime transport (IP10). Since the mid-1980s, BV had been preparing a text for a possible European directive, which, however, was not adopted until 1996. However, BV considered the certification of marine equipment '*une arme terrible pour l'industrie*' ('a terrible weapon for the industry') (IP10) because the assessment of the body seeking notification determines if it is technically competent and capable of carrying out the conformity assessment procedures in question. Furthermore, the notified body must also demonstrate the necessary level of independence, impartiality, and integrity. The notified body earns a lot of money with assigning certificates. It controls the certification of marine equipment for France. This is why BV has always had a strong interest in global maritime industry. Moreover, according to the interview partners, BV has always been very commercially aware, and has had strong relations with the government in order to guarantee its profits in the big maritime market. In former times, it was the BV that controlled the policy making process.

Mr. Pinog, who had been the director for marine merchant in the Ministry of Transport, took over the head BV position in the mid- 1990s. His promotion to this seat granted informed communications between the government and the industry. Over the last few years, however, BV's influence has diminished from being actively involved in all decisions in the area of marine equipment to equally shared competences among the ministry and BV. Currently, in marine equipment, a division of labour between the ministry and the BV is practiced. Whereas the safety matters are handled by the Ministry of Transport, BV deals with the commercial aspects of the directive. All interview partners confirm that this coordination among the two institutions work very well by guaranteeing short communication tracks and immediate coordination in a policy area which is both strategically powerful and profitable.

Another indicator of the high priority France assigned to maritime equipment is the special civil servant assigned for the dossier. Whereas in the UK, for example, different departments are involved in the transposition of the MED (IP10) – which involves more time-consuming coordination among the actors – in France, there is only one person responsible for all aspects of the MED. Here, one finds '*une addresse email spécialisée*' ('a special email address') set up for maritime equipment issues only (IP10). This specialization is also a rather unique phenomenon in French administration. All in all, it was the high priority attached to the marine merchant in French policy-making exemplified by the special civil servant post and the considerable involvement of BV in French marine merchant policy-making that facilitated the MED's problem-free and timely transposition.

9.4 CONCLUSION

The study has shown that the process tracing method is a helpful research tool. It uncovers the correlational findings and elucidates the causal mechanisms explaining why member states miss their deadlines when transposing EU Internal Market directives. Moreover, it helps to clarify and correct for measurement errors and concept overstretch committed in large-n statistical analysis. It, for example, allowed controlling for first and last national implementing measures since all four cases had been concluded by the end of this study. Representing two major transport sub-fields which account for over 43% of the EU transport acquis, liberalizing and harmonizing types of directives alike, the four maritime and railway cases in this chapter advance our understanding of national transposition processes across member states in the EU. Based on official documents, EU legal data bases, press accounts, and interviews with stakeholders in the European and national policy-making procedures, the process tracing method directed this study to trace the four national transposition processes in three different member states in a very specific and, most importantly, theoretically informed way.

Tracing back the processes of the French (98/55/EC) and Spanish (2001/1/EC) *on-the-line cases corroborates earlier findings and illustrates that the statistical model has some explanatory power*. While both cases have been explained well by the statistical model, the case studies in this chapter clarify how the different factors in rather complex national transposition processes work can cause delays of varying lengths.

On the other hand, process tracing further elucidates those cases that are *off-the-line*, i.e. show higher values of deviance residuals. Focusing on the German (2002/59/EC) and the French (2001/53/EC) cases, *we obtained an additional explanation for those deviant cases*. The case studies uncover an additional important factor in explaining transposition delay. We found that the political priority assigned to the transposition process seems to matter and might be a missing component causing the outliers.

In particular, for the German case, we found that despite a handful of crises – three maritime related accidents in German waters some years before the start of the transposition process, and one ecologically devastating accident on the Atlantic during the 20 months of the German transposition process – Germany's notification to the Commission was still one month delayed. Interview partners confirm that a maritime accident beyond German waters would not attract Germany's attention or, thereby, accelerate the transposition procedures. Those three examples of loss at sea with a direct effect on Germany, however, had occurred too long ago to influence the German transposition process of 2002/59/EC. However, the Pallas accident in 1998 did influence the process. Interview partners confirm that, due to this accident in Germany's own waters, another related Directive (1998/55/EC) was transposed three months before the expiry of the deadline. However, in terms of time, the Pallas disaster was too distant in the public memory to have a direct impact on the German transposition process of Directive 2002/59/EC.

Furthermore, the general election of 22 October 2002 affected the priorities of the transport ministers' political agendas. The election did not put a new ruling party in change the government. However, the minister for transport was replaced, and the position was enriched with an additional portfolio that attracted the new minister's full attention and delayed the start of the transposition process at the beginning of his term. The elections had been won in the 'east' of Germany, after the hundred year flood and the government actions it aroused. The electorate in the east had given strong support to the ruling government. This same government had just promised emergency funds for recovery after the devastating flood that lead to the evacuation of 37 towns and resulted in the largest natural-disaster mission in history of the German Armed Forces and the Technical Relief (*Technisches Hilfswerk*). Therefore, during his first months in office, the new minister of transport, and special appointee for the new Länder, rather unassertively start the German transport policy, in general, and the implementation of EU directives, in particular.

The second outlying case further elucidates the importance of political priority for a swift and problem-free transposition process across member states. The high priority France priority assigned to merchant marine affairs can be viewed in two ways. On the one hand, we see the ministry of transport and the industry working together in a very productive way. While the assigning of certificates is seen as '*une arme terrible*' ('a powerful weapon') for the merchant industry, the notified body has been assisting in drafting French positions in EU negotiations and national policy-making. Helpful here was the exchange of high-level personnel between the two institutions. Also indicating the high priority of this directive was the uncommon setup of contact points for marine equipment within the notified body as well as the ministry's facilitating the exchange of information.

If political priority is indeed important for the timely transposition of EU directives and constitutes the missing component in explaining the unexplained variance in the two deviant cases, then we might have another look at the two well-explained cases to see how this factor plays out there. Whereas it is not so evident in the first French case, the Spanish case shows that political priority indeed mattered. Whereas the transposition process of Directive 2001/14/EC caused media-wide discussions (IP4) about the separation of the Spanish railway operator and railway infrastructure manager, the Atocha attack on 11 March 2004, left Spain in total paralysis for the subsequent months and condemned the transposition process to insignificance. Until the last week before the general elections, on 14 March 2004, the national implementing measure attracted considerable public attention, with unions demonstrating in the streets of Madrid, and autonomous regions filing a law case against the government. It is fair to argue that without the Atocha attacks, the government would have remained in power and would have adopted subsequent legislation faster. The fatal incident, however, resulted in additional Spanish measures on safety and security that further delayed the process. Therefore, Directive 2001/14/EC was adopted more than two years after the set transposition deadline.

However, the current study requires more than a simple cross-check with the two well-explained cases in order to generalize the importance of political priority for the timeliness of national transposition processes across member states. This will be the focus of the next chapter.

Chapter 10: Assessing the relative importance of necessity and sufficiency for timely transposition

'When a member state fails to implement laws on time, everyone looses out. The playing field remains from level. And real opportunity for growth and jobs are lost.' (Charlie McCreevy, European Commissoner for the Internal Market, 2006).

10.1 Introduction

Departing from the large-n statistical and supplementary small-n case study analyses this study argues that we still have to take one last step in order to round up the study on timeliness of EU transport directives. Furthermore, I argue that we need to address few remaining shortcomings of the four case studies. Two issues are of primary focus. First, the generalizabilty of the four case studies findings. Second, we do not yet know the relative importance of explanatory factors and combinations of variables in terms of necessity and sufficiency.

Having completed intensive study of the four case studies, the case study analyses identified political priority as an important missing variable. The *finding's Achilles' heel* is, however, that, for the moment, these four case studies are unable to support broad and well-bounded propositions. We must test whether the adjusted model is generalizable. Consequently, the final step requires an additional concluding quantitative analysis in order to generalize the findings to similar cases that focus on the same unit of analysis. However, political priority is a very difficult variable to measure, although it has been tossed around by many EU scholars. *It would surpass the study's resources to generate the variable for 365 cases. Moreover, doing so may not even be necessary.* Alternatively, a technique may help to deploy a reasonable test of the slightly adjusted model by using a smaller sample of cases; the technique should still apply binomial probability formula and calculating levels of significance. In short, the fuzzy set technique may be a prudent way to generalize findings.

Existing regression and case study analysis in the field of transposition is concerned only with either the effects of a cause *or* the causal mechanisms underlying compliance with EU law driven by *either* quantitative *or* qualitative research design. But fuzzy set takes an intermediate step. It addresses the question of importance of the effects of the variables by asking under which assumptions a given casual factor and/or combinations of factors might be *necessary* or *sufficient* for an outcome, in general, and transposition delay, in particular (third sub question). Fuzzy set enables researchers to evaluate set-theoretic relationships such as intersection and inclusion and, thereby, necessity and sufficiency (Ragin and Pennings, 2005: 425). It permits the identification of necessary and sufficient conditions by means of the subset principle (Ragin, 2000; Goertz and Starr, 2002; Braumoeller and Goertz, 2000; Rihoux, 2006) which represent a 'core part of social science theory' (Goertz, 2002: 65) such as the EU literature[63]. Finding factors to be necessary and/or sufficient for an outcome, the hypothesis under consideration assumes that it (or a combination of factors) will exert its effect independent of all other factors and are present in all instances of an outcome. Or to put it in regression terms, whether: Y= f(X1, X2, X3) or Y= f(X1*X2*X3) (or any combination of these three factors).

Hence, sitting directly between large-n and small-n studies, the fuzzy set technique provides a *set of new tools* for generalizing the case study findings. It also helps the analysis of the relative importance of the identified explanatory factors and configurations of conditions for timeliness of national transposition processes across member states. It is critically important to go this one step further, and undertake the two main challenges here.

In the following pages, this chapter represents the third main part of this study testing the adjusted theoretical framework on timeliness of national transposition models. After reviewing the fuzzy set literature in social sciences and a brief discussion about how the fuzzy set technique works, I present the data set and outline the 'calibration' of the outcome and the causal factors individually. The results suggest that the case study findings can be generalized on a broader sample of cases. Next to three other variables *political priority is indeed a usually necessary condition for timeliness*. In addition, the study finds a sufficient combination of conditions whose significance will be discussed in the chapter's concluding section.

10.2 The Fuzzy set technique

Although the fuzzy set technique originates in the mid-1960s [64], scholarly work in the field of social sciences has been scarce and not existent in EU studies at all. Instead methodological discussions about the advantages and pitfalls of correlational causation have dominated the field of research (for an overview see Smithson and Verkuilen, 2006).

---

63 Deutsch, Burrell and Kann (1957: 58) found necessary conditions for an amalgamated security community. Sandholtz identifies two necessary conditions for international collective action to emerge in telecoms liberalization in Europe. Schimmelfenning argues that 'sharing a community of values and norms with outside states is both necessary and sufficient for their admission to the organization.' Another dominating argument is that veto players are a necessary condition for policy change (Tsebelis, 2002). See Goertz (2002) for an overview of 150 examples in the social science literature.

64 There are three other related techniques namely QCA (Qualtiative Comparative Analysis), multi-value QCA (MVQCA) and MSDO/MDSO which are presented in brief in Rihoux (2006). For a critique see: Lieberson (1992); King, Keohane and Verba (1994); Mahoney (2000).

Only recent volumes and special issues in political science illustrate that the advantage of the fuzzy set technique is 'no longer a claim made by a particular small group of comparativists, but it has materialized into firm and unique empirical findings, which warrant further investigation and application' (Ragin and Pennings, 2005; Rihoux and Grimm, 2006). Ragin's (1987) discussion and his take on the causes of IMF riots (2000), in particular, have made a fundamental contribution to comparative social sciences. Cress and Snow (2000) stress the importance of organizational viability and framing activities for obtaining targeted outcomes by homeless social movement organizations while applying fuzzy set. When these conditions are present and occur in conjunction with political mediation, the particulars of which affect the types of tactics associated with successful outcome attainment, they find that the homeless SMOs are likely to have their greatest impact. Mahoney (2003; Katz, vom Hau, Mahoney, 2005) evaluates the relative strengths and weaknesses of fuzzy set analysis and regression analysis in explaining the 'great reversal' in Spanish America.[65] Whereas the fuzzy set analysis reaches substantively important conclusions about probabilistically necessary conditions for economic development, 'the regression analysis generates findings that are not meaningful' (Katz, vom Hau and Mahoney, 2005: 567). The coefficient estimates are unstable, and coefficient variances are high for several variables in almost every multivariate model specification. The explanation is in the advantage that fuzzy set techniques do not suffer from a small-n or degrees of feedom problem. Since each combination is reduced to a single value, each combination is, in effect, treated as a single case (Katz, vom Hau and Mahoney, 2005: 568).

Next to these sporadic empirical contributions applying fuzzy set technique, primarily two groups of scholars apply fuzzy set technique. Their particular focus within the field of social sciences is on either warfare or welfare. Whereas Goertz and Starr (2002), Levy (2002), and Schroeder (2002) focus on the outbreak of World War I, Goertz and Levy (forthcoming) edited a book including causal explanations and case studies on the end of the Cold War. The welfare literature is grouped around Kvist (1999; 2004; 2006) and Pennings (2002), who apply fuzzy set technique on comparative welfare state research. Surprisingly, no fuzzy set approach has yet been applied to EU studies in general or EU implementation studies in particular.

65 From 1750 to 1900, the most marginal colonial territories often became the region's wealthiest countries, whereas the most central colonial territories often became the region's poorest countries. To explain this reversal, their fuzzy set analysis finds that strong liberal factions are probabilistically necessary for economic development ad that dense indigenous populations are probabilistically necesary for social underdevelopment (Katz, vom Hau and Mahoney, 2005: 539). More studies applying the fuzzy set technique can be found at www.compass.org/WPshort.htm.

10.2.1 *Advantages of the fuzzy set technique:*

There are three additional benefits of using the fuzzy set. It reduces uncertainty, identifies causality; and, finally, reveals necessary and sufficient conditions and specific combinations, that might otherwise be hidden by the traditional correlational techniques (i.e. regression).

Verkuilen (2005) argues that the fuzzy set approach can help reduce the uncertainty in social science. Ambiguity sprouts from the multiple meanings of background concepts and from lack of firm concept boundaries. Furthermore, 'the fuzzy set logic presents a promising new tool for comparativists that can be used to reveal causalities' (Pennings, 2003: 541). Häge (2005) shows that Niemann's study (2004) on the conditions for communicative action can be improved by incuding precision and the validity of conclusions drawn from the empirical analysis. Finally, 'the fuzzy set logic presents a promising new tool for comparativists that can be used to reveal causalities' (Pennings, 2003: 541). Pennings (2003) assesses the main variations in the constitutional control of the executive in 45 parliamentary democracies and how these differences can be accounted for. He identifies necessary and sufficient conditions. But, only fuzzy set analysis shows that the degree of constitutional control can be explained solely by a specific combination of institutional conditions stemming from the four dichotomies and not by one single dimension.

These scholars further argue that fuzzy sets are useful for both qualitatively and quantitatively oriented researchers and that the qualities of fuzzy set theory warrant a more frequent use and application in social sciences. The fuzzy set technique constitutes a step away from large-n studies, and a step toward a more case study oriented research design. It shares one key characteristic of qualitative analysis: the ability to fully account for the richness and complexity of individual cases, as well as the diversity across cases (Ragin, 1987, 2000). The advocates of the fuzzy set technique argue that it maximizes the use of the scholar's analytical and case knowledge and helps to translate this knowledge into numerical values that, at least, approximate meaningful degrees of membership (so-called calibration). It facilitates the identification of necessary and sufficient conditions and specific combinations of conditions. Given the relatively small number of cases in existing studies (10-35), the advantage of the fuzzy set technique is that research using it can often achieve standard levels of statistical confidence (Lieberson, 1992; Pahre, 2005: 131; Smithson and Verkuilen, 2006). Hence, for the purpose of this study it will help to measure political priority in a 'bigger than four' sample of cases to generate concluding generalizable findings that explain the timeliness of national transposition processes.

But before I consider the fuzzy set technique's application to the transposition discussion, this study will devote a few lines to outline how this technique works. Discussed in the next section are the key issues that must be reported so as to guarantee validity and reliability in this diversity oriented technique.

10.2.2 *The fuzzy set technique- How does it work?*

In order to enable a multicausal explanation, the scores of the conditions (independent variables) and the outputs (dependent variables) have to be transformed into so-called 'fuzzy sets.' They are 'sets with elements whose membership grades can have any real value between 0 and 1' (Pennings, 2003: 542) – no member and full member. The following value sets in table 10.25, with six levels of membership, will be used in the analysis:

Table 10.25: Six levels of fuzzy set membership.

'1'	=	fully in
'0.8'	=	mostly but not fully in
'0.6'	=	more or less in
'0.4'	=	neither in nor out
'0.2'	=	more or less out
'0.0'	=	fully out

In this sense, a fuzzy set can be regarded as a 'continuous variable that has been purposefully calibrated to indicate degree of membership in a defined set' (Ragin and Pennings, 2005: 424). For example, Berlusconi's Italy might receive a membership score of 1 (full membership) in the set of rich countries, but a score of only .8 or .6 in the set of democratic countries. Determining whether it is .8 or .6 demands a very high degree of correspondence between the theory and the fuzzy set membership scores, in other words, precise boundaries between sets of memberships.

The direct and active involvement of the researcher in the act of calibration leaves him or her open to criticism for choosing the wrong aspects, empirical indicators, empirical evidence, or qualitative breakpoints. These are called problem of wrong qualifications of elements (Kvist, 1999). Consequently, this membership assignment exercise is one of the sensitive points of much of fuzzy set literature. There are two criteria that are crucial in empirical research, in general, and in calibration, more particularly. They are validity (measures must actually measure the concept), and reliability (measure must be reasonably reproducible). Fuzzy set studies have to devote time on a detailed justification of the 'calibration'. Fuzzy set technique outcomes can offer improvements to the reliability and validity of the correlational conclusions, even when there are no substantial changes made to the original quantitative results.

10.3 Constructing degrees of membership of causal factors for transposition delay

10.3.1 *Data set:*

To generate generalizable findings and to test for necessity and sufficiency the sample selection and the construction of degrees of membership are crucial. Necessary and sufficient conditions are special kinds of hypotheses that operate relative to a threshold. They are especially common in studies that relate dichotomous variables to one another (Pahre, 2005: 132). As outlined previously, all fuzzy sets must identify full membership, non-membership, and a mid-value or breakpoint. Since calibration of cross-national data is time-consuming and resource intensive, it was necessary in this study to determine which EU directives and member states to include in the current study, and which to defer for future research.

Case selection

The selection of cases is dependent on the substantive and theoretical interests of the researcher (Ragin, 2000: 122). So in terms of testing the generalizability of the earlier case study findings we should randomly select national transposition processes from the EU transport transposition data set (1995-2004) excluding the already four investigated cases. In terms of necessity and sufficiency, recent works argue that we should test necessary conditions by selecting cases by the dependent variable, but that the testing of sufficient conditions should be done by choosing cases based on the characteristics of the independent variables (Pahre, 2005: 131).

...of EU directives

This study opted for seven EU directives[66]. Covering all transport sub-sectors, the chosen directives were all relatively recent in helping to generate a measurement for political priority. The further away in time, the more difficult it will be to trace back information from media and interview partners.

66 The seven EU directives in include: 2000/30 Directive on the technical roadside inspection of the roadworthiness of commercial vehicles circulating in the Community; 1999/95 Directive concerning the enforcement of provisions in respect of seafarers' hours of work on board ships calling at Community ports; 1999/35 Council directive on a system of mandatory surveys for the safe operation of regular ro-ro ferry and high-speed passenger craft services; 1998/41 Directive on the registration of persons sailing on board passenger ships operating to or from ports of the Member States of the Community; 1996/67 Council Directive on access to the ground handling market at Community airports; 1996/50 Directive on the harmonization of the conditions for obtaining national boatmasters' certificates for the carriage of goods and passengers by inland waterways in the Community; and 1996/48 Council Directive on the interoperability of the trans-European high-speed rail system.

The four directives were adopted in 1996, two in 1999, one in 1998, and one in 2000. None of the chosen directives amend earlier EU directives. Instead, they represent a full set of new EU directives in the field of transport that control for the distorting effects of amending directives. New legislation represents an equal point of departure for all member states involved. While the cases vary on the outcome variables including political priority, the selected cases vary considerably on the outcome variable. They range from 67 weeks early transposition to 110 weeks delayed transposition, and reflect the overall percentage of statistical data set.

...of member states

While varying both in the outcomes as well as the causal factors, France, Germany, Italy, Spain, and the UK were selected because they represent the five biggest and most important economies and industrial bases in the EU. They prioritize different transport sub-sectors due to their geographical characteristics (see Transport Chapter). However, whereas Greece and the Netherlands would have a bias towards one particular mode of transport—maritime and inland waterwayss, respectively—it is in the large European economies that all five modes of transport have relatively similar shares, which makes the modes of transport more comparable in the seven selected cases. Four of these nations have housed leaders (Spain and UK) as well as notorious laggards (Italy and France) in the transposition of EU legislation before the last round of enlargement in 2005. Germany takes a middle position in terms of leadership.

In total, the data set represents a sample of the total population with 35 cases, which is a relatively big number compared to abovementioned fuzzy set applications in social sciences. Table 10.26 illustrates the crisp scores for the 35 cases, as they can be found in the mother data base, on which the pervious multinomial logistic regression results are based. In order to translate the crisp scores of the dependent and independent variables into fuzzy set partial membership scores, information was derived mainly from *Celex*, *Eurlex*, national transposition data bases, official government websites of the selected five Member States, I went back to the case study material based on the annual review of national politics by the *European Journal of Political Research*, and the five major national newspaper archives, namely: *The Guardian* (UK); *Le Monde* (France); *Frankfurter Allgemeine Zeitung* (Germany); *Corriere della Sera* (Italy) and *El País* (Spain). In addition, I placed phone calls with transport attachés from the Permanent Representatives of the five Member States in Brussles to finetune the membership scores and, in the special case of political priority, to gather additional information on the member states' salience devoted to particular EU transport dossiers.

Table 10.26: Crisp scores of the dependent and independent variables.

Transport directive	Mode of transport	Member states	Discretion ratio	Transposition time set in directive	Number of veto players	First directives in transposition package	Last directives in transposition package	General election at the beginning	General election at the end	Transport related accidents	Length of transposition Delay (in weeks)
2000/30 Directive on the technical roadside inspection of the roadworthiness of commercial vehicles circulating in the Community	Road	France	0.3	25	2	0	0	0	1	1	-16.1
		Germany	0.3	25	1	0	0	0	1	1	-10.3
		UK	0.3	25	5	0	0	0	0	1	-12.1
		Italy	0.3	25	1	0	0	1	0	1	66.6
		Spain	0.3	25	3	0	0	1	1	1	-10.7
1999/95 Directive on the enforcement of provisions in respect of seafarers' hours of work on board ships calling at Community ports	Maritime	France	0	26	2	1	0	0	1	1	-2.3
		Germany	0	26	1	1	0	0	1	1	-12.4
		UK	0	26	3	0	0	0	0	1	-6.3
		Italy	0	26	2	0	0	1	0	1	5.1
		Spain	0	26	3	1	0	0	0	1	2.3
1999/35 Council directive on a system of mandatory surveys for the safe operation of regular ro-ro ferry and high-speed passenger craft services	Maritime	France	0	78	1	0	0	0	0	0	-27.8
		Germany	0	78	8	0	0	0	1	0	-80.1
		UK	0	78	1	0	0	0	1	0	-7.7
		Italy	0	78	3	0	0	1	0	0	-18.9
		Spain	0	78	1	0	0	0	1	0	1.2
1998/41 Directive on the registration of persons sailing on board passenger ships operating to or from ports of the Member States of the Community	Maritime	France	0.1	23	2	0	1	0	0	0	-14.2
		Germany	0.1	23	1	0	0	1	1	0	15.0
		UK	0.1	23	1	0	0	0	0	0	-25.6
		Italy	0.1	23	0	0	0	1	0	0	0
		Spain	0.1	23	2	0	0	1	0	0	-100.2

Transport directive	Mode of transport	Member states	Discretion ratio	Transposition time set in directive	Number of veto players	First directives in transposition package	Last directives in transposition package	General election at the beginning	General election at the end	Transport related accidents	Length of transposition Delay (in weeks)
1996/67 Council Directive on access to the ground handling market at Community airports	Air	France	0.4	49	6	0	0	0	0	0	-109.8
		Germany	0.4	49	2	0	0	0	0	0	-2.4
		UK	0.4	49	0	0	0	0	1	0	3.0
		Italy	0.4	49	7	0	0	1	0	0	-68.9
		Spain	0.4	49	4	0	0	1	0	0	-83.0
1996/50 Directive on the harmonization of the conditions for obtaining national boatmasters' certificates for the carriage of goods and passengers by inland waterways in the Community	Inland waterways	France	0.1	25	0	0	0	0	1	0	-28.0
		Germany	0.1	25	4	0	0	0	0	0	16.0
		UK	0.1	25	1	0	0	0	0	0	-25.3
		Italy	0.1	25	2	0	0	1	1	0	-16.2
		Spain	0.1	25	0	0	0	1	0	0	-5.2
1996/48 Council Directive on the interoperability of the trans-European high-speed rail system	Rail	France	0.3	130	5	0	0	0	0	1	-95.6
		Germany	0.3	130	1	0	0	0	0	1	-6.0
		UK	0.3	130	1	0	0	0	0	1	0
		Italy	0.3	130	6	0	0	1	1	1	-110.6
		Spain	0.3	130	4	0	1	1	0	1	-96.0

10.3.2 Calibration:

... of the outcome

Starting with the outcome, we see that transposition delay is not just a measure with respect to the extent of transposition delay. Relying significantly on the interval data derived from the data set of the previous correlational tests presented in table 14, the fine-tuning of the membership scale for the dependent variable makes the diversity of the outcome visible. Assigning six membership scores to the total of 35 outcomes in the crisp set, I argued that a delay of less than two weeks can still be considered 'on time', whereas a membership score of 1 accounts for cases with delay of more than four years, which occurs in only 3.5 % of the total outcomes of the overall data set (13 out of 367). The crucial threshold lies in the period between six and twelve months, which occurs in 12.3 % of the total number of cases (45 out of 367). Although interview partners confirmed some of the membership thresholds, the distribution of cases plays some role. According to an outcome's distribution the overall assignment of membership scores for the outcome is as follows: 0 to delays of less than 2 weeks, 0.2 for delays of less than 2 months, 0.4 of delays less than 6 months, 0.6 for delays of less than 1 year, 0.8 for less than 3 years and, 1 for all values above one year. Table 27 illustrates the fuzzy set partial membership scores and highlights the considerable variation of the outcome values. Scores of 0 occur 5 times. Sscores of 0.2 and 0.4 occur 10 times each. There are 3 scores of 0.6, and 7 scores of 0.8. But there is no score of 1.

... of the causal factors

Discretion/transposition time/veto players

Fuzzy set membership scores had to be assigned to all causal factors. First, I determine the amount of discretion allowed in the transposition of a directive, the transposition time set in the directive, and the number of veto players in the 35 cases. To accomplish this, I started again from the crisp set data used for the ordered multinomial logistic regression. I crosschecked the number of ministries involved and the type of the national legislative instruments used in transposition in order to determine a number of veto players. The interval data that accounts for the amount of discretion was further enriched by controlling for specific terminology in the EU directive that granted room for interpretation, such as 'appropriate, sufficient, may, at last, if necessary ...'. All 367 national implementation measures vary between 0 and 0.7. The 35 measures that constitute the focus of this study were assigned to 1 of 6 fuzzy units. One is at 0, 1 is at 0.2, 10 are at 0.4, and 5 are at 0.6. As an example of how discretion influenced the fuzzy set values, consider Directive 1996/67/EC *on access to the ground handling market at Community airports*. This directive, which was valued at 0.6 in terms of discretion, leaves considerable amounts of discretion in 10 of its 25 provisions. Of the provisions, one makes the approval of ground handling activity at an airport, a job fulfilled by supplies of ground handling services, conditional. Approval in this matter is to be obtained from a public authority figure that is independent of the managing body of the airport (Article 14).

Furthermore,

> *'A Member State may, where appropriate on a proposal from the managing body of the airport, prohibit a supplier of ground handling services or an airport user from supplying ground handling services or self-handling if that supplier or user fails to comply with the rules imposed upon him to ensure the proper functioning of the airport. [...]'* (Article 15 of 1996/67/EC)

Both articles provide examples for the generous amount of discretion guaranteed to the member states in Directive 1996/67/EC).

In terms of transposition deadlines, I assigned 0.2 to directives with a set transposition time between two days and six months. A membership score of 0.4 was assigned to transposition deadlines between six months and one year. A score of 0.6 was assigned to deadlines between one and two years. The value 0.8 is attributed to, for example, Council Directive 1996/48 *on the interoperability of the trans-European high-speed rail system*, which provides the rare occasion of a transposition time of almost 3 years. In only a few cases, directives are in force immediately after the adoption by the Council of Ministers and are assigned, in this study, a score 0[67].

Packaging/elections/accidents/political priority
The full beauty of the diversity oriented calibration technique, however, can be best appreciated by the use of the remaining causal factors, namely: package approach, timing of general elections, the occurrence of transport related accidents and political priority assigned to the specific dossiers. Depending on a transposition package's *size* and the *diversity across transposition deadlines set in the EU directives*, the transposition method can have different effects on the process' timeliness. The fuzzy set technique can account for this diversity. Going back to the more limited number of cases enables me to compare the number of EU directives in a package and their respective transposition deadlines. Deadlines can vary between zero and two years making the fuzzy set technique a more refined measurement tool than statistical analysis.

As an example of the effects of the *national package approach* on directives, consider the German legislative act [68] transposing Directive 1998/41/EC. The crisp set for both categories is '0'. There was no effect in terms of delay for either categories; the first directive in the transposition package or the last one. A closer look at the transposition package reveals that the German legislative act transposed eight EU directives[69] at once. In addition, the transposition deadlines across the directives differ by 29 months (2.4 years). Whereas

67 Directive 99/48/EC: adapting to technical progress in approximation of law of transport of dangerous goods by rail.

68 *Gesetz zur Anpassung der technischen und steuerlichen Bedingungen der Seeschiffahrt an den internationalen Standards* (Seeschiffahrtsanpassungsgesetz) vom 09/09/1998, Bundesgesetzblatt Teil 1.

69 1996/40/EC, 1997/34/EC, 1997/58/EC, 1998/18/EC, 1998/35/EC, 1998/41/EC, 1998/42/EC and 1998/55/EC.

Table 10.27: Fuzzy set partial membership scores of the outcome and the causal factors (calibration).

Transport directive	Mode of transport	Member states	Discretion ratio	Transposition time set in directive	Number of veto players	First directives in transposition package	Last directives in transposition package	General election at the beginning	General election at the end	Transport related accidents	Political priority	Length of transposition Delay (in weeks)
2000/30 Directive on the technical roadside inspection of the roadworthiness of commercial vehicles circulating in the Community	Road	France	0.4	0.2	0.2	0	0	0	0.8	0.6	0.4	0.4
		Germany	0.4	0.2	0.2	0	0	0.2	1	0.6	0.8	0.2
		UK	0.4	0.2	0.4	0	0	0.2	0	0.6	0.8	0.2
		Italy	0.4	0.2	0.2	0	0	0.4	1	0.8	0.8	0
		Spain	0.4	0.2	0.2	0	0	0.2	0	1	0.8	0.2
1999/95 Directive on the enforcement of provisions in respect of seafarers' hours of work on board ships calling at Community ports	Maritime	France	0	0.2	0.2	1	0.2	0	1	1	0.6	0.2
		Germany	0	0.2	0.2	1	0.2	0.2	0.8	0.8	0.8	0.2
		UK	0	0.2	0.2	0	0	0	0.2	0.6	0.8	0.2
		Italy	0	0.2	0.2	0	0	1	0.4	0	0.4	0.4
		Spain	0	0.2	0.2	1	0.4	0.2	0	0.4	0.8	0.2
1999/35 Council directive on a system of mandatory surveys for the safe operation of regular ro-ro ferry and high-speed passenger craft services	Maritime	France	0	0.6	0.2	0	0	0	0	0.4	0.2	0.4
		Germany	0	0.6	0.8	0	0	0.2	1	0.8	0	0.6
		UK	0	0.6	0.2	0	0	0.4	0.8	0.8	0.6	0.2
		Italy	0	0.6	0.2	0	0	1	0.4	0	0.2	0.4
		Spain	0	0.6	0.2	0	0	0.4	0.8	0	0.8	0
1998/41 Directive on the registration of persons sailing on board passenger ships operating to or from ports of the Member States of the Community	Maritime	France	0.2	0.2	0.2	0.6	0.8	0	0	0.4	0.4	0.4
		Germany	0.2	0.2	0.2	0	0.6	1	0.8	0	0.8	0
		UK	0.2	0.2	0.2	0	0	0.2	0.4	0	0.4	0.4
		Italy	0.2	0.2	0	0	0	1	0.8	0	0.8	0
		Spain	0.2	0.2	0.2	0.2	0	0	0	0	0.2	0.8

Transport directive	Mode of transport	Member states	Discretion ratio	Transposition time set in directive	Number of veto players	First directives in transposition package	Last directives in transposition package	General election at the beginning	General election at the end	Transport related accidents	Political priority	Length of transposition Delay (in weeks)
1996/67 Council Directive on access to the ground handling market at Community airports	Air	France	0.6	0.4	0.6	0	0	0.4	0.2	0.8	0	0.8
		Germany	0.6	0.4	0.2	0	0	0	0	0.6	0.2	0.6
		UK	0.6	0.4	0	0	0	0.2	0.8	0	0.2	0.4
		Italy	0.6	0.4	0.6	0	0	0.8	0	0.4	0	0.8
		Spain	0.6	0.4	0.4	0	0	0.6	0.2	0	0	0.8
1996/50 Directive on the harmonization of the conditions for obtaining national boatmasters' certificates for the carriage of goods and passengers by inland waterways in the Community	Inland waterways	France	0.2	0.2	0	0	0	0.2	0.8	0.6	0.2	0.4
		Germany	0.2	0.2	0.4	0	0	0.4	0.4	0	0.4	0.4
		UK	0.2	0.2	0.2	0	0	0.2	0	0	0	0.6
		Italy	0.2	0.2	0.2	0	0	1	0.8	0.4	0.4	0.4
		Spain	0.2	0.2	0	0	0	1	0.2	0.2	0.2	0.2
1996/48 Council Directive on the interoperability of the trans-European high-speed rail system	Rail	France	0.4	0.8	0.4	0	0	0.4	0	0	0.2	0.8
		Germany	0.4	0.8	0.2	0	0	0.2	0.2	0.8	0.2	0.2
		UK	0.4	0.8	0.2	0	0	0.2	0.4	1	1	0
		Italy	0.4	0.8	0.6	0	0	1	0.4	0	0.2	0.8
		Spain	0.4	0.8	0.4	0.2	1	0.6	0.4	0	0.2	0.8

Directive 1996/40/EC had a deadline of 1 February 1997, Directive 1998/35/EC did not have to be transposed before 1 July 1999. Since the transposition deadline for Directive 1998/41/EC is next to last, but still with a considerable difference of six months after the deadline of the first? directive (1 January 1999), I assign a fuzzy set membership score of 0.6 in the category *last directive in transposition package* compared to a crisp set score of 0.

A look at the *general election* dates of the five member states assisted in the construction of fuzzy values that account for elections. Elections, in this study, are valued with consideration not only of the six months preceding or following a general election, but *throughout the whole national transposition periods* as well; the *change of transport ministers* is also figured into the membership score. A general election that results in an almost unchanged coalition government guarantees stability and continuity. But government change, and even a simple reallocation of portfolios within a legislative term, hampers stability and continuity. The lists of transport ministers for every member state helped identify those crucial mometns of minister change. For example, during the 19 months Spanish transposition process (29 April1999 to 25 November 2000) of Directive 1999/35/EC *on a system of mandatory surveys for the safe operation of regular ro-ro ferry and high-speed passenger craft services*, Spain had one general election in the last six months of the transposition process. In Spring 2000, the conservative ruling party (*Partido Popular*) won, as expected, with a 10% lead over the second ranked socialist party, PSOE (*Partido Sociolista Obrero Español*). Since the Aznar government stayed in power, I would have assigned a 0.8 instead of 1 to account for continuity and the high likelihood of Aznar´s second term. However, despite the stabilizing effects of the electoral outcome, the ruling government reshuffled the government portfolios. The transport ministry was assigned to the former Vice-Prime Minister and head of the Prime Minister's office (Ministerio de Presidencia), Álvarez-Cascos. This reshuffling lead me to assign the value '1'. Note, however, that in 1999, only a few weeks after the adoption of the EU directive in Brussels, an earlier reassignment of the Spanish government's portfolios had taken place, leaving the transport ministry with a new minister, Arias-Salgado. The reshuffle took place without a general election. Since there was no general election in the early months of Spanish transposition the crisp set value was set '0'. Accounting for the reassignment of the transport ministry during the early period of the legislative term, I assigned a membership score of 0.4, considering that a change in portfolio constituted a major break of continuity of Spanish transport policy-making, in general, and the starting of the transposition process for Directive 1999/35/EC, in particular.

In addition, the diversity oriented fuzzy set technique gives precision to the crisp set scores for the *transport related accident* variable. The large-n study allowed me to refer only to major accidents that were referred to in Commission communications, and lead to various sets of packages of directives in the different transport sub-sectors (see transport chapter). The fuzzy set technique, due to a smaller number (N=35) of cases, enables me to go back to the five major national newspapers and scan them in terms of major national accidents in the EU directives' related sub-fields that may have attracted only national attention, but had an impact on the national policy-making processes. One example is the Ievoli Sun disaster before the British coastline in 2000, in which the ship lost 4,000 tonnes of styrene and bunker oil off Alderney, in the English Channel. Although this ecological disaster did not make it to the front page of the Financial Times, it attracted considerable media coverage in British newspapers (Guardian, 2000 a, b). Considering its devastating consequences for the UK, in pariticular, this study assigned a fuzzy set membership score for that particular transport related accident of 0.4. Twenty-four other crisp set values were determined accordingly.

Last but not least, the fuzzy set technique makes the assignment of membership scores for *political priority* feasible. With a N=35, the number of cases is big enough to generalize its findings to the broader set of EU transport transposition process across member states. And at the same time, it is small enough to investigate for the salience attributed to EU directives in the national transposition contexts. Since this is the only conditions, which does not lean back on crisp set scores, I had to go start from scratch. Drawing on the findings of the Transport Chapter, feedback from the five national transport attachés guided the appreciation of membership assignments. While earlier findings of this study clearly shows that transport policy is characterized by national needs, shaped by the facts of economic geography, additional data provided by the European Commission will help to clarify and back up my decisions.

In case of the national implementing measures for Directive 2000/30/EC on *the technical roadside inspection of the road worthiness of commercial vehicles circulating in the Community*, for example, all five Member States scored relatively high. Whereas Germany, Italy, Spain and the UK score 0.8, only France's value of .4 is comparatively low. While this general pattern is confirmed by the transport attachés, the Commission's data complements this finding. Over the last ten years, international road haulage on national territory has increased considerably in almost all Member States, but France.

Table 10.28: International road haulage on member states' territories (1995-2005).

Member State	France	UK	Germany	Spain	Italy	EU average
Increase in %	+ 5%	+ 12%	+ 36%	+ 56%	+ 75%	+ 11%

Table 10.28 displays that international road haulage on French territory has only increased at a meager 5% (European Commission, 2006). To the contrary, the figures for the other four countries show a much stronger increase – scoring all above the EU average of (+11%). International road haulage has virtually boomed in Italy (75%), Spain (+56%), Germany (+36%) and to a lesser extent the UK (+11%).

Since the Directive's aim is to improve the safety and equipment of heavy commercial vehicles circulating in the Union by supplementing the annual roadworthiness inspections of a representative proportion of the heavy commercial vehicles on Member States' roads, it is evident that those countries experiencing a considerable increase in international road haulage give higher priority to this dossier. Vehicles that prove not to be roadworthy as a result of a random inspection, wherever they are registered, may be exempt from free circulation. The idea is that these random inspections would rapidly improve the maintenance of the Union's commercial vehicles and commercial vehicles from third countries that transit the Union.

But not only the considerable increase of international road haulage on Member States' territories, but also the relative number of accidents involving personal injury per year per 1000 population connects to the overall picture. Table 10.29 shows differences across the five Member States which confirm earlier findings on the different levels of political priority attributed to the roadworthiness of commercial vehicles.

Table 10.29: Number of accidents involving personal injury per year per 1000 population.

Member State	Germany	UK	Italy	Spain	France	Average EU 15
Nb. of accidents per 1000 population	4.7	4.1	3.7	3.6	2.0	3.4

Source: European Commission (2001: 197).

Similarly, it is specific Member States' interests in the field of safety operations of ro-ro ferry and high-speed passenger craft services that account for the varying scores for the five member states (Directive 1999/35/EC). Following two ship disasters of roll-on-roll-off passenger ships[70] (Estonia, 1994 and Express Samina, 2000) in the 1990s eight north European states immediately agreed to set up a higher standard for ship stability in what has become know s as the Stockholm Agreement. Specifically this agreement took into account the crucial effect of water accumulating on lower decks in the event of an accident which had caused a considerable number of fatalities in the Baltic and Aegean Sea. The eight states were, next to the Scandinavian countries, Germany and the United Kingdom, which score higher than the remaining three. Table 10.27 summarizes the fuzzy set partial membership scores for the outcomes and all causal factors.

70 Ro-ro describes a significant feature of a ship designed to carry wheeled cargo such as automobiles, trailers or railway carriages. This is in contrast to lo-lo (lift-on-lift-off) vessels which use a crane to load and unload cargo, i.e. cargo must be winched abroad.

10.4 Four necessary and one sufficient combination of conditions

The first step in testing necessary and sufficient conditions for timely transposition is to discriminate whether the dependent and independent conditions are present or absent in each of the cases (subset principle). Generally speaking, a condition is necessary if its membership scores are consistently lower than the degree of membership in outcome. X is a necessary condition for Y if Y is a subset of X. A condition is sufficient if its membership scores are consistently greater than the degree of membership in the outcome. Because necessity is not sufficient, the condition is not always present when the outcome has the same value.

10.4.1 Necessary conditions:

Normally it is important in any analysis to first test for necessary conditions before examining sufficiency, especially when there is 'limited diversity' (logically possible combinations of causal conditions lacking empirical instances) (Ragin, 2000: 131). There are two options: First, to visualize the scatter plots showing the distribution of the 35 cases along the output and all conditions individually and in combination; second, to run an analysis which calculates levels of significance for all nine conditions. Although, in our case, with a N=35 it makes sense to run a significance test, I would like to briefly lay out with an example how to visualize necessity.

Figure 10.8, for example, illustrates the distribution of cases in a two-dimensional plot with the outcome (length of transposition delay) on the y-axis and the necessary condition 'transposition time' on the x-axis. In a perfect plot for necessary conditions we would expect all cases to be on or below the diagonal. Cases in the lower right-hand corner of the plot are directives which have considerable time to transpose but, nevertheless, do not delay considerably. From the evidence in the figure, it is reasonable to conclude that membership in 'transposition time set in the directive' is not *fully* necessary and sufficient for membership in 'transposition delay'. Ten cases lie above the diagonal. The key is to understand that when fuzzy membership scores in the outcome are less than or equal to fuzzy membership in the cause, then it is possible to argue that instances of the outcome are a subset of instances of the cause (Ragin, 2000: 217).

While we are interested in finding necessary and sufficient conditions for transposition delay, the above-mentioned example indicates that the following confinement has to be acknowledged. Since 'fully necessary' or 'fully sufficient' causation is rather rare, i.e. all the cases together either lie above or below the diagonal, it is helpful to adopt a benchmark at which a given factor can be considered *usually necessary* or *usually sufficient*. In this study, I test causal factors and their combinations as 'almost always necessary' and 'almost

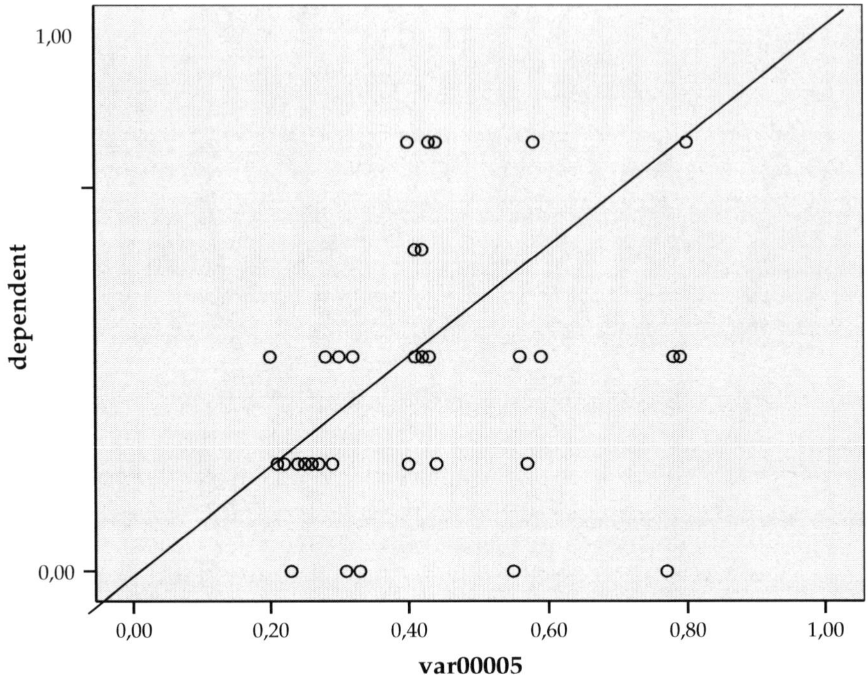

Figure 10.8: Scatter plot showing the distribution of the 35 cases along the condition 'transposition time' and the outcome 'length of transposition delay': Necessity.

always sufficient' conditions. This test requires a causal factor or combination of factors to be necessary or sufficient at a score above a 0.65 benchmark. Hence, this study seeks to specify factors that are necessary or sufficient for outcomes more than 65% of the time. Another procedure to address randomness is statistical significance. Given a relative large number of cases (35), the significance level is set at .05 for 29 and more cases, and .01 for 31 and more cases (Ragin, 2000: 114). As in the above-mentioned example, now, the length of the transposition time set in the EU directive appears to be *usually* necessary – with only four cases lying outside the diagonal range. In addition, I use a binomial probability formula to calculate levels of significance. To compute the abovementioned findings, this study relies on the FS/QCA software package (Ragin and Drass, 2002).[71] Table 10.30 shows the presence and absence of causal conditions and outputs for the 35 cases.

71 Due to the fact that I will use two procedures to account for randomness, I will not address the problem of imprecise measurement by adding an adjustment factor – even if this adjustment shifts the line separating consistent and inconsistent cases in a more lenient direction.

Table 10.30: Results of fuzzy set test: Necessary conditions.

	Proportion of cases	
Causal Factors	**Case >= Length of transposition delay**	**Case <= Length of transposition delay**
Granted transposition time	0.86 (**)	0.46
Amount of discretion	0.49	0.57
Veto player	0.46	0.54
First directive in package	0.34	0.74
Last directive in package	0.74	0.64
General election at the beginning	0.57	0.43
General election at the end	0.83 (*)	0.57
Transport related accident	0.83 (*)	0.51
Political priority	0.82 (*)	0.49

Note: The level of significance for all proportions > .65 is listed in parentheses. ** significant at the 0.01 level; * significant at the 0.05 level.

In total, table 10.30 identifies four significant 'usually necessary' conditions, but no single sufficient conditions:

The *transposition time set in the directive* adopted by the Council of Ministers is a 'usually necessary' condition but not a sufficient condition for membership in delayed transposition. Moreover, it is significant on the .01 significance level. This underlines, again, that a directive-specific feature helps to explain transposition delay. The transposition time set in a directive, which is agreed upon in Brussels, has an undeniable influence on the future transposition process. For example, whereas the 1996/48 Council directive *on the interoperability of the trans-European high-speed rail system* guaranteed about 2.5 years for the transposition, 1998/41 Directive *on the registration of persons sailing on board passenger ships operating to or from ports of the Member States of the Community* allowed only 6 months for implementation. Given that the average transposition time set in EU transport directives decreased until early 2000 (Kaeding, 2006), and afterwards increased continuously, it is possible to explain the better performance of member states in recent years– a trend which is referred to in the latest Commission scoreboards (2005)—in terms of increased deadlines.

General election at end of a transposition period is also a 'usually necessary' condition, but is significant only at the .05 level. Accounting for general elections, in general, and also for the change of transport ministers' portfolios, in particular, this study shows that in 83 % of the membership scores for this condition are consistently lower than the degree of membership in outcome.

Transport related accidents across member states are a 'usually necessary' condition for timely transposition. For example, during the transposition of the railway Directive 1996/48/EC *on the interoperability of the trans-European high-speed rail system*, Germany experienced a tragic ICE accident on 3 June 1998. A vessel caused the deaths of about 100 passengers in Enschede, an accident that was caused by lack of adequate controls and an overstressed wheel.[72] Although the Directive does not foresee any harmonization of security check standards, it does argue the necessity to ensure interoperability in the fields of infrastructure, energy, control-and-command, and signaling and rolling-stock (recital 12). Germany notified its ministerial order[73] on 20 May 1999, six weeks (fuzzy set membership score: 0.2) after the deadline set in the European directive (8 April 1999).

Last but not least, the level of *political priority* attributed to the legal dossier is an 'usually' necessary condition for timeliness of national transposition process across member states.

10.4.2 Sufficient combination of causal conditions:

Making an interim balance, the study identifies four usually necessary conditions, but no single sufficient ones. But when no single causal condition is sufficient, researchers anticipate the finding that different combinations of causal conditions are sufficient for the outcome (Ragin, 2000: 130). Sufficiency of a combination of causes reads that the cause in question *always* produces the outcome in question. To assess sufficiency of causal combination, the researcher examines the cases conforming to the combinations and evaluates whether they agree in displaying the outcome in question (Ragin, 2000: 132). Exploring any logically possible combination of causal factors this study discloses one usually sufficient combination of conditions: 'general election at the end', 'transport related accident' and 'political priority'. The evidence shows that membership scores in the combination of these causal conditions, not general election at the end, not transport related accident and not political priority, are less than or equal to membership scores in the outcome. The scatter plot showing the relationship between fuzzy membership in the causal combination and fuzzy membership in the outcome is presented in figure 10.9.

72 The steel tire of the wheel in question had been fragmented by stress. Before that happened, a fissure of the wheel from the center outward had occurred. This fissure could have been detected, had there been a control procedure, but such a procedure was not used by the Railway company (www.railfaneuope.net/ice/eschede.html).

73 *Verordnung über die Interoperabilität des transeuropäischen Hochgeschwindigkeitsbahnsystems (EIV), BGBl I 1072.*

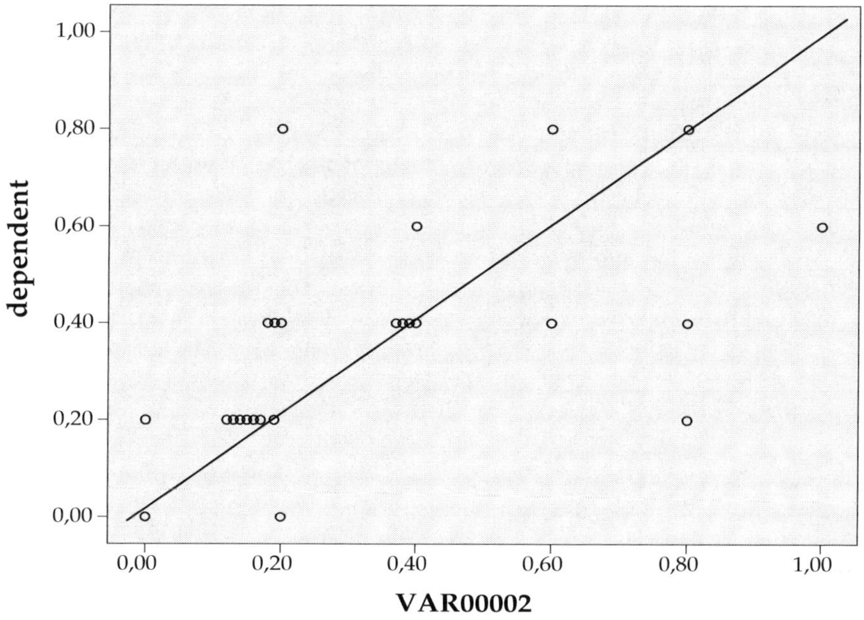

Figure 10.9: Scatter plot of 'timely transposition' against 'general election at the end/ transport related accident/political priority': Sufficiency.

The upper-triangular plot shown in Figure 10.9 is a direct reflection of the fact that membership scores in the fuzzy set' are less than or equal to membership scores in the fuzzy set 'timely transposition'. When membership scores for the combinations of conditions are high, membership scores for 'timely transposition' must also be high because the causal combination is sufficient for the outcome. To summarize, Figure 10.9 supports the argument that the combination of general election at the end/transport related accident/political priority is a usually sufficient for timely transposition.

10.5 Summary and discussion – To what extent does the fuzzy set technique improve the earlier findings?

To address the generalizability of empirical findings derived from the case study analysis in chapter nine the fuzzy set technique has proven very helpful. Next to the testing of the empirical model (including the political priority variable, with a broader sample (N=35) of cases), it allows the researcher to provide a clearer picture of national transposition processes. The fuzzy set technique also enables researchers to address questions of necessity and sufficiency for single variables and for combinations of conditions that are too often ignored in traditional analysis.

Clearly, the fuzzy set technique enriches the conclusions reached by prior regression and case study analyses. It is not only that the fuzzy set technique allows one to learn more out of the data; it sheds more light on the black box of the transposition processes in member states. Indeed, there is no single cause by itself capable of producing the outcome. It is neither election campaigns nor a change of government per se that even affects the possibility of a swift transposition. But, *general elections that are scheduled towards the end of a transposition process*, or the simple reshuffling of the ministers' portfolios on short notice do seem to delay transpositions. More nuanced measurements for transport-related accidents across member states further stressed that accidents require responsive decisions from the states' incumbent decision-makers. In addition, the political priority assigned to EU dossiers needs careful consideration. No priority hampers timely transposition, i.e. an issue given no priority will invariably be transposed late.

Furthermore, the fuzzy set approach clarifies transpositions by translating language into numbers. Timeliness which represents a source of vagueness has been very difficult to pin down to one concrete indicator. In addition to being vague, this term has important qualitative boundaries. We can recognize cases or definite problems of timeliness, between which there is continuous variation. So, eventually, the conception of variables in terms of fuzzy set membership provides a way to operationalize and typologize phenomena that sticks closer to theoretical discourse (Goertz and Mahoney, 2005; Rhioux, 2006: 691). This concluding analysis demonstrates how fuzzy sets can perform a more precise operationalization of theoretical concepts. The fuzzy set technique, for example, is well-equipped to manage the vagueness of the concept of timeliness ('*on time*') for a larger-n analysis. The statistical analysis has uncovered that delay seems not to be simply delay and that separating out the outcome between short and long delay seems to be a useful strategy. In turn, fuzzy set has permitted a 'more nuanced representation of categorical concepts by permitting degrees of membership in sets rather than binary in-or-out membership' (Ragin and Pennings, 2005: 425). Like terms such as democracy, support for political violence, poverty, national transposition processes can be timely to some degree, as could a nation be developed or unequal (Verkuilen, 2005: 463). One can generally recognise cases of definitive delay, between which there is continuous variation. If one's goal is to explain differing levels of development in a specific group of cases, 'fuzzy set analysis usually works best' (Katz, vom Hau, Mahoney, 2005: 569).

Lastly, the results of the fuzzy set analysis of the theoretical framework point to further empirical refinements. Following Verkuilen (2005) I agree that fuzzy set theory provides a useful and tractable way to address relationships that are too often ignored in traditional analysis: the relevance of single conditions and combinations of causes. While there is no significant single sufficient condition (which is not surprising since it is probably impossible to identify conditions sufficient for any social outcome), this study identifies four 'usually necessary' conditions: the transposition time set in the directive, the political priority assigned to the dossier, the occurrence of general elections at the end of the transposition process, and transport related accidents. According to the definition of necessity, these four factors exert their effects independent of all other factors, and are present in all instances of an outcome. Whereas transposition actors can influence the first two conditions on the European and national level, the scheduling of general elections and the occurrence of transport related accidents lie beyond their policy-making space. If political leaders can manipulate these first two conditions, then they may be able to minimize transposition problems. Furthermore, the combination of general elections at the end of a national transposition process with a transport-related accident on its territory, and high political priority attributed to the EU legislation by itself produces timely transposition. It represents a sufficient set of conditions for timeliness.

All in all, this concluding analysis has round up and underlined the advantages of a *combined approach*. Quantitative studies are needed in order to generalize, formulate hypotheses and identify outliers. Case studies help further to assess the plausibility and strength of observed statistical relationships between variables and unveil missing values. But it is the fuzzy set technique, in a third step of analysis, that can be best viewed as 'an additional item in the old kit bag we already own' (Verkuilen, 2005: 492). For the purpose of this study, the fuzzy set technique was valuable in generalizing the case study findings. Futhermore, it allowed us to ask under which assumption a given causal factor or a combination of conditions might be necessary or sufficient for the timeliness of national transposition processes across member states.

Last but not least, the final part of this study will begin with a summary and discussion of the findings of the different sets of analysis. It will address the question as to what extent this study addresses the shortcoming of the existing EU implementation literature. In a later step, the empirical and methodological implications for future studies in the field are assessed.

Part IV

Summary of findings, conclusions and outlook

Chapter 11: Summary of findings, conclusion and outlook

'The European Council underlines the importance it attaches to Better Regulation at national and European level as a core element in achieving the goals of the Partnership for jobs and growth and urges all institutions and the Member States to implement their respective commitments.[...] The European Council recalls that better regulation is also a matter for Member States to implement in their domestic law-making and in the transposition of Community law and reaffirms its commitment to making progress in all of these areas.' (Presidency Conclusions 23/24 March 2006, p.22 indent 61 and 62).

The purpose of this book was to find out why delays are so common in national transposition processes, where member states are supposed to configure ways to implement policies handed down by the European Commission. Toward this goal, it was necessary to comprehensively review current literature on EU implementation studies. A close look was given to the development of EU transport policy from 1957 to the 2006 mid-term review of the *White Paper on European transport policy for 2010*. Next, an actor-centered theoretical bargaining framework on the timeliness of national transposition processes of EU law was expounded upon. Then, aggregate data were presented and studied and endorsed by four, highly scrutinized, case studies. The fuzzy set technique closed the loop and completed the analysis, conceding equal space to large-n, small-n and fuzzy set methodologies.

My ambitious goal in this area was to contribute a meaningful and informative piece of work to the existing field of implementation literature. This final chapter draws together the most important elements of the study's academic relevance which are mainly twofold: empirical, and methodological. First, it summarizes the main empirical findings. Following this is a discussion of the generalisability of the data on national transposition processes of EU transport directives. And second, this chapter presents the methodological contribution of the book, focusing on the potential added value of mixed-method research designs in social science, more generally, and EU implementation studies, in particular. Moreover, it is argued that there is a strong necessity for cumulative data in EU studies, a relatively young field of research with considerable potential in terms of data triangulation. In completion, I summarize the findings below in the course of discussing their relevance for thinking about transposition processes and compliance issues specifically and its societal consequences more broadly. Implications for more thoroughly understanding the causal dynamics underlying the transposition outcome in light of broader national and European discourses are discussed.

11.1 Empirical contribution

11.1.1 The European Union has a serious transposition problem

Above all, the study illustrates that the EU has a serious transposition problem. The empirical findings suggest that problem in transposition processes occur in almost 66% of all national implementing measures. Furthermore, seven driving factors invariably influence the timeliness of national transposition processes of European legislation. They can be arranged into three groups: European-level, national-level, and crisis-related variables. Tardiness can result from particular circumstances in any of these groups.

- Transposition delay is common:

The EU 1995-2004 transport transposition data offers new evidence that the EU has a transposition problem. 47 percent of national implementing measures have been notified *late* to the Commission, of which 70 percent recorded delays of more than six months, with a maximum delay of 4.8 years. The time length of missed deadlines varies significantly between member states and between transport sub-sectors. Furthermore, the mean and median transposition delays across member states indicate that 'delay' is not a simple, but instead a complex entity. Whereas the median of the 367 national implementing measures lies with zero months, the mean is 6 months. This denotes that a number of national implementing measures have considerable transposition delays, a finding that was paramount in later analyses.

- Gold-plating is common:

Yet, it is not only the commonness of *tardy transposition* that raises major concerns about efficient and effective policy-making. Following the discussion of 'gold plated' EU legislation in EU member states which is embedded in the broader EU better regulation discourse (for example the Davidson Report in the UK, 2006), the picture is even worse.[74] *Not only late transposition but also early transposition is problematic.* Early transposition requires national businesses to adapt to new legislation before their European counterparts, an action that may lead to a competitive disadvantage in the Single Market (Stephen, 2004). The EU 1995- 2004 transport transposition data uncover that *20 percent of the national implementing measures had been in force more than six months before their deadlines.* In the end, not only a 47 percent of the national implementing measures jeopardize the effectiveness of the internal market because of its tardiness. No, in sum, *almost 70 percent of all national legal measures transposing the EU transport acquis in nine member states, cause problems,*

74 A gold plate is any burden placed on national businesses that is not strictly required by the original EU directive. In other words, anything beyond the minimum requirements necessary for meeting a directive can be considered gold plate (Bellis, 2003; Ambler, Clittenden and Obodovski, 2005).

either because they are transposed too late, risking the opening of an infringement proceeding, or because they are too early, risking warping effects on the regulatory environment for business and citizens in the EU alike.

All in all, the EU has a transposition problem, both in terms of delay and over-implementation – a problem which has yet not found its way into the scholarly debate. Next to the Commission scoreboards and the ECJ infringement data, both of which represent rather conservative measures of the transposition problematic in the EU (Börzel, 2003; Mbaye, 2001), this new data is much more reliable.

In line with the second round of implementation data in the field (Mastenbroek, 2003; Berglund et al., 2006; Haverland and Romeijn, 2007; Kaeding, 2006) this book has also provided some progress regarding the *conditions under which transposition performance of member states could be improved*. This progress is in the identification of seven potential European and national drivers and constrainers for timely transposition. These factors should especially interest those people in power, because some of the drivers and constrainers may have a bearing on underlining that better regulation is 'also a matter for Member States to implement their domestic law-making and in the transposition of Community law' (Council of the European Union, 2006: 22).

11.1.2 Driving and constraining forces for timely transposition in the EU:

- Policy design and implementation affect each other

Focusing on EU transposition delays, this study identifies three sets of catalysts for policy change (see table 11.31). In line with the implementation studies from the 1970s (Pressman and Wildavsky, 1973: 178), this study, in particular, shows that we must not separate policy design from implementation. That is, we consider European directive specific characteristics as well as national transposition instrument features; we also recognize the different effects on the timeliness of national transposition processes. Differentiating between policy design- related (European-level), policy implementation- related (national-level) and crises-related, the study argues that each set has a different impact on the dependent variable: timeliness. *It seems that serious delays, those longer than six months, are homemade in the capitals of member states. The specific features of European directives, on the other hand, especially their technical aspects, account for short term delays: those of six or less months. Crises,* which are understood as sudden situational changes of the internal or external environments, *account for both short and long delays.* In this sense, this study agrees that *'implementation should be part of design', suggesting that policy theory is formulated 'with a view toward execution'* (Pressman and Wildavsky, 1973: 189).

- Transposition delay is caused by legal, administrative and political factors

Furthermore, the study has illustrated that transposition is more than just a legal or administrative process run by civil servants in public administrations. *Next to legal and bureaucratic practices and procedures it is politics that matter.* To put it differently, this study has shown that 'implementation is the continuation of politics by other means' (1973: 189) (to paraphrase a famous Clausewitz dictum), so to say the continuation of 'who gets what, when, where, and how' (Lasswell).

Table 11.31: Driving and constraining forces for timely transposition in the EU.

	Factor	Effect
Policy design related (European-level)	Transposition time constraints	Delays < 6 months
	Problem of discretion	
Policy implementation related (National-level)	Political priority	Accelerating and retarding effect
	Election timing	
	Number of transposition actors	Delays > 6 months
	National transposition package	
Crisis related	Transport related accidents	Accelerating effect

EU-LEVEL FACTORS CAUSING SHORT DELAY (< 6 MONTHS) – POLICY DESIGN RELATED

– *Transposition time constraints*

Administrations must always act under time constraints, regardless of whether administrators like them. The fact that administrations are obliged to act within a legally fixed periods compels them to improve their co-ordination and organization to respect deadlines (Gil Ibánez, 1998: 165). From the equally important legal point of view, time constraints are required by the principle of legal certainty. This study has found that the transposition time set in the directive is significant and, moreover, the deadline is usually a necessary condition for apt transposition. Furthermore, the importance of a generously set transposition deadline is clear. In the German case (case study 3), it was discussed that the EU Directive 2002/59/EC guaranteed a comfortable 18 month deadline, compared to the average transposition time of 13 months for maritime directives. Interestingly, as interview partners have uncovered, apparently, the deadline could be traced back to the Commission. It was especially the 'Commission's colloquial approach towards member states' (IP12) that allowed member state's to raise concerns and thereby influence the content and the transposition deadline considerably. Substantial consultation efforts by the Commission, hence, guaranteed that the deadlines imposed on member states could sufficiently reflect the internal constraints of those states, i.e. decentralized political structures. The right to be heard in the national context means that the prescribed transposition time should be long enough to allow member states to: 'present an available defense, consult the central, regional, or local public entities involved, co-ordinate the administrative actions of the different entities involved, and confirm or rebut every piece of evidence presented by the Commission' (Gil Ibánez, 1998: 196).

More surprisingly, despite their great significance in national policy-making, there is no clear rule about how transposition deadlines should be determined. It is the Commission's job to set the transposition deadline in a proposal sent to the Council and Parliament. This starts the European legislative process. Here, however, much depends on an individual civil servant in the Commission to gather information about national member states' potential problems with the draft proposal. The transposition deadlines, then, are often integral parts of the negotiation process (Häge and Kaeding, 2007).[75]

Transposition deadlines receive different levels of consideration, varying from case to case. The Commission, being part of the recently valorized impact assessment studies (Renda, 2006), may first make an evaluation of the transposition's complexity by conducting a *tour d'Europe*. Then, after this tour, a deadline will be imposed. More complex cases require longer time-limits. Interestingly, this study's figures, covering the early 1980s until 2004, display, however, that since the mid-1980s to the late 1990s, the average guaranteed transposition time has steadily decreased from 18 to 13 months. Despite the 84 percent increase in numbers of directives to be transposed over the years (Wessels, Maurer and MIittag, 2003: 46-47), the average transposition time agreed upon in the Council has decreased by 24 percent (Kaeding, 2006). Thus, in periods of high legislative output, all things being equal, transposition delays seem inevitable.

– *Problem of discretion*

Discretion is a difficult concept to define in general terms. Discretionary power may be defined as the margin of freedom granted to an administration to take action; power is granted, explicitly or implicitly, by the law. Discretion depends on several factors, such as: types of rules, a member state's legal culture, and the social and personal values and traditions that surround the

75 The recently adopted energy efficiency directive illustrates this point nicely. Whereas the Commission proposal foresaw a one year transposition deadline, the member states drafted their common position with a deadline set for two years. The EP disapproved, contending that two years was too long a deadline for such an urgent issue. Ultimately, the Council and the EP agreed on a one year deadline, but added derogation arrangements for some of the directive's provisions.

relevant person or organization (Gil Ibánez, 1998: 199). The statistical analysis shows that the level of a member state's discretion in transposing an EU directive is a significant positive indicator for short delays. The Spanish case (case study 2) highlights the potential problem with a relatively high level of discretion. While European Directive 2001/14/EC left considerable leeway of interpretation to the member states, it resulted in a 'wait and see' attitude in the Spanish transport ministry and railway body. Before taking any transposition actions, the Spanish watched and consulted other member states' transport ministries and railway companies 'to see which interpretation was pursued' by them (IP6), and later to finally cut their own path.

Despite what EC law, and some ECJ case law, says, it is clear that some degree of national discretion is unavoidable. Since the Commission does not have enough resources to control them, member states have a lot of discretion in the day-to-day applications of transposition. In other words, member states *de facto* already have a wide discretion in enforcing EC law. It should be taken into account, however, that national enforcers can sometimes be better placed than Commission officials to assess the optimal level of discretion, and to recognize the problems of enforcement and application of Community law. In fact, it may be said that Commission action reduces the capacity of national governments to respond to divergent and changing problems with appropriate flexibility. On the other hand, if member states do not respect the goals of EC law, then they could risk future restraints in discretionary power (Gil Ibánez, 1998: 25). Whatever either side contributes, the Commission and member states must strike a balance of power to determine suitable levels of discretion.

National-level factors causing long delay (> 6 months) – Policy implementation related

– *Political priority*

When a directive is attributed with high political priority, timely transposition is a natural outcome. With the assumption that cabinet ministers behave as perfect agents of their parties and are able to act as virtual dictators in the policy areas they control (Laver and Shepsle, 1996), this analysis showed that it is the ministers who assign levels of priority to the transposition process. While coalition governments, which rule in 18 of the 25 member states, provide considerable discretion to ministers in drafting legislation (Gallagher, Laver and Mair, 2001; Laver and Shepsle, 1994; 1996),[76] it is the minister in charge of the relevant department who presents the policy proposal at cabinet, giving him or her a privileged position in the policy area in question (Gallagher, Laver and Mair, 2001: 56). Ministers set the government agenda in their policy (Mar-

76 One-party government in the EU-25 include: UK (*Labour Party*), Malta (*Partit Nazzjonalista*), Spain (*Partido Socialista Obrero Español*), Greece (*Nea Dimokratia*), Sweden (*Socialdemokratiska Arbetarepartiet*), France (*Union pour un Mouvement populaire*) and Portugal (*Partido Socialista*) (www.parties-and-elections.de).

tin, 2004; Martin and Vanberg, 2004; 2005; Jones and Baumgartner, 2005) and, consequently, ministers have considerable control over the length of the national transposition process and over the transposition outcome in particular.

Political priority represents a significant usually-necessary condition for timeliness because it denotes a change in the usual order of things in the political realm. That is, under special circumstances, the political priority of transposing a directive is unusually high, for any number of reasons. But, sometimes directives simply do not garner much priority – for electoral, economic and strategic reasons.

This analysis showed that the most important concern for ministers is pleasing their electorate. The Spanish and German cases showcased ministers who were involved with priorities other than transposing directives. The Spanish transport minister, Magdalena Alvarez, extended the reflection time needed after the Atocha bombings by one year, in order to also consult with the stakeholders affected by the railway reform. Because Álvarez was indebted to these stakeholders for helping her and her party group to win the elections, she prioritized their needs and put the transposition of Directive 2001/14/EC on the backburner. Ultimately, because it was not high in political priority, the directive was transposed two years late. In the German case, the 2002 elections gave the newly appointed minister of transport, Stolpe, an added portfolio – that of a special appointee for the new federal *Länder*. This new portfolio attracted most of his attention because it had special meaning on the heels of the devastating hundred-year flood. It was the flood afflicted new German *Länder* that tipped the scales in favor of the ruling socialist-green government. After efforts in this area, Stolpe had little time to focus on the transposition of Directive 2002/59/EC. Low in priority, the directive was ultimately transposed one month late, despite the Pallas accident on German waters that was still strong in sentimental and political presence at the transport ministry.

Besides electoral concerns, economic and strategic considerations also influence the priority assigned to a particular transposition procedure. This was evident in the second French case study. In 2002, Directive 2001/53/EC was set for transposition by a ministerial order, which called for the involvement of the transport ministry and the notified body (*Bureau Veritas*). This directive had the unwavering attention of both departments, for it was considered a 'terrible weapon for the industry' (IP10) of the marine equipment industry. The notified body controls the certification of marine equipment for France which makes it a powerful and profitable organization. For obvious reasons, Directive 2001/53/EC was given a very high political priority.

The third case study, however, illustrates how rapidly a political and economic issue can be buried in oblivion. Despite the ecological disaster caused by the tanker Erika in December 1999 breaking in two 40 miles off the coast of

Brittany (France) and spilling about 10,000 tones of heavy fuel, the Commission had to initiate legal proceedings against ten member states for failure of compliance with the Erika I package that had been adopted by the Ministers of transport in December 2001. Only Spain and France who had been directly affected by the ecological disaster adopted national implementing measures for the Erika I package ahead of time – six months and five months respectively. The reason for the delayed action by the other member states can be found in the lack of political priority attached to the dossiers by the administrative apparatus headed by the minister. *A minister's signature on a directive, however, 'should be a firm commitment' for a swift and problem-free transposition process and not just 'a vague aspiration' (McCreevy, 2005).*

– *Election timing and change of minister*

Election timing is another strong indicator, and a necessary condition, for the timeliness of national transposition processes. In line with Smith and Stam (2004: 125) who argue that election timing affects both the outcome of elections and the government's subsequent performance, this study sees a relationship between the timing of general elections and transposition performances of member states. Depending on whether an election falls at the beginning or end of the fixed transposition period, the national transposition process is either retarded or accelerated. The argument is that ministries and agencies are bound by the legislative program for the whole year, or sometimes even an entire legislative term. In Denmark, for example, because of the way the parliamentary year is organized, all bills must be dealt with within one and the same parliamentary year. All outstanding bills must be withdrawn, and then submitted again in the new year (Mandrup, Raudi and Pennings, 2002: 6).

Furthermore, the fuzzy set techniques unveiled that it is not simply the timing of general elections but specifically the reshuffle of minister portfolios that matter because electoral campaigns or major government crises affect the national transposition records. Linking ministers' resignations with transposition performance, this study showed that before a minister resigns, open files are sought to be closed. Alternatively, a new minister and his or her entourage require a period of vocational adjustment before business-as-usual can take off.

So, elections, in general, and government reshuffles[77], in particular, accelerate transposition processes that are already in their last months. However, for transposition processes that have only just begun, elections and government reshuffles actually yield a delaying effect. For example, the Spanish legislative act transposing Directive 2001/14/EC was introduced near the end of the

---

77 For push and pulls of ministerial resignation see, for example, Fischer, Kaiser and Rohlfing (2006).

Aznar government on 17 November 2003. However, the national transposing instrument was not to come into force before 18 May 2004 – six months later – which is referred to as the so-called *vacatio legis*. Hence, the Aznar government never got around to enforcing the instrument before the general elections in March 2004. With the change of government, it was the responsibility of the newly elected party, and specifically of the newly appointed transport minister, to transpose the directive. By the time the new minister learned the ropes, Directive 2001/14/EC had been on the backburner for a long time. In the end, the national transposing instrument for Directive 2001/14/EC was selected on 18 May 2004, two years after the deadline.

– *Coordination problem (Number of veto players)*

The analysis corroborates earlier findings in the field (Haverland, 2000; Giuliani, 2003; Treib, 2003; Steunenberg, 2006) that the number of veto players affect implementation outcomes. Depending on the type of legal instrument chosen to transpose a directive, the numbers of ministries involved differs, as does the requirement of the parliament's approval, and so on and so forth. Legislative acts, for example, which rank highest in the hierarchy of legal instruments, are lengthy processes. Some studies argue that in some countries, parliament may be hesitant to cooperate with a legislative act if not consulted at an early stage (Krislov et al., 1986: 80). Since there is such variation, the speed of the national transposition processes can be affected in many ways. The first French case (case study 1) exemplifies the importance of the number of national transposition actors. Whereas all signs pointed to a swift and problem-free transposition, the large number of ministries directly involved in the ministerial order ultimately retarded the final adoption of the French transposing measure by several months.

Earlier public policy scholars, who wrote in the 1970s and 1980s, have shown that 'problems of coordination and communication are to be expected when the implementation of a statute involves the participation of several implementing agencies with varying degree of commitment to the achievement of statutory objectives' (Mazmanian, and Sabatier, 1981: 13). In addition, recent evaluations of national administrative models for implementing EU legislation (Kassim, 2005) argue that the number of veto players is a reoccurring but unavoidable (because legally enshrined) problem. Another unavoidable problem is this of 'Chinese walls' – a metaphor referring to the practice of making sure that preparation and transposition divisions of ministries and across ministries are kept apart so that information does not circulate freely and to prevent conflict of interests (From and Stava, 1993: 65; Ciavarini Azzi, 2000; Dimitrakopoulos, 2001: 447) – is a reoccurring but unavoidable (because legally enshrined) problem. More specific, in France, for example, although compulsory hearings and consultations of interest groups cannot change any text of the national legislation, they cause considerable delays. This is because these institutionalized meetings are very infrequent, and administrations may have to wait a long time before one actually occurs. For example, the special committee *Commission spéciale des installations nucléaires de base secrètes* and the *Agence française de la sécurité sanitaire des aliments* meet only once a year (Steunenberg and Voermans, 2005: 116). On average, delays caused by the infrequency of advisory committee meetings are between three and six months (Philip, 2004).

– *Occurance of national transposition package*

Member states often use one national implementing measure to transpose a handful of EU directives at the same time, in what is known as a national transposition package. Member states commonly use transposition packages to implement EU directives that cover similar policy issues to reduce redundancy and complexity. The package approach, however, affects the timeliness of the notification of national implementing measures to the Commission. Depending on the number of EU directives included in the package, and the parameters of their different deadlines, the package approach has either a significant delaying affect, or a significant accelerating affect.

This study qualified national transposition packages as a significant usually necessary condition for the fast transposition of the last directive in a package. Furthermore, two out of four of the case studies in this research illustrated the relevance of the package approach in affecting the timeliness of transposition. In the German case study (case study 3), the German ministry of transport transposed four European directives, whose transposition deadlines differed between 25 months, with one national instrument. In the end, the decision to apply a transposition package caused a considerable delay for the first measures in the package (almost 15 months), but had a speeding effect on the last directive in the package (about 1 month). The first French case study highlights the delaying effect of the first EU directive in the package (3 months delayed), and the accelerating effect of the last directive (8 months early).

But because of the characteristics of a national transposition package, particularly its size and the difference between deadlines, matter, we are not able to say, for example, that using one invariably produces late transposition of the directive with the earliest deadline. As a case in point, in the Spanish case study (case study 2), it was shown that although railway policymakers transposed three railway directives with one legal instrument, no effect whatsoever was found to affect the timeliness of transposition. This was because all three EU directives went into the package with the same transposition deadline.

From a broader point-of-view, however, the national package approach definitely distorts the regulatory framework in which businesses operate. According to the Commission's simplification policy (2005) that ensured that EU legislation is 'clear, understandable, up-to-date and user-friendly', national rules must also be addressed. In doing so, it is thereby important to acknowledge the distoring effect of national transposition packages for the timeliness of national transposition processes in particular and the regulatory environment which affects the competitiveness, growth and employment performances in general. Generating a high quality of regulatory environment with legal certainty for consumers and business requires simplification of national measures falling under the responsibility of the member states. The problem with national transposition packages is, however, that the number of directives included are applied arbitrarily. National transposition packages, in terms of a high quality of the regulatory environment, appear counterproductive.

– *Effects of external shocks*

Events that, quite suddenly, drastically change the external or internal environments affect the political, cultural, economic, and legal climates of member states. Over the last two decades, the relationship between crises and reform, in particular, has found its fervent advocates in economics (Drazen and Grilli, 1993) and political science literature (Almond, Flanagan and Mundt, 1973; van Waarden, 2006). For the purposes of this study, another important factor accelerating the national transposition process is transport-related accidents.

The accelerating effect of national transport-related accidents

In terms of national transposition processes, transport-related accidents occur in two dimensions: time and space. They occur before, during, or after a transposition process, and they occur either near or far from national soil. The timing of a transport-related accident is, of course, important. Events that occur during a transposition process invariably accelerate transposition times; critical junctures (Jones and Baumgartner, 2005) in which existing policies come under pressure may even 'jeopardize their self-evident legitimacy and de-institutionalize governance '(Boin, 't Hart, Stern and Sundelius, 2005: 122-123). But the more important variable of crises is where they occur. Transport-related accidents on national soil are usually necessary conditions for swift and problem-free transpositions. This is because such crises require immediate reactions from political actors in a particular member state. Windows of opportunity, such as these, must be taken (Keeler, 1993; Kingdon, 1995; Cortell and Peterson, 1999) to affect policy change; like general elections, crises make it possible for the government elites to reshuffle an action that would have not been politically feasible in normal times. If a crisis happens near national soil, it strongly accelerates transposition times. Even if a crisis occurred years ago and, was near national soil, it can and does have the effect of speeding up transposition. In combination with high political priority and an election set at the end of the transposition period, the combination of conditions represents a sufficient factor for timeliness.

Consider, for example, the case study of the German transposition of EU di rective 2002/59/EC. This directive was about a Community vessel traffic monitoring and information system. Two crises were linked to this transposition process. The first was an ecological disaster of Galacia, Spain that occurred during the transposition process. The second was also an ecological disaster, but it occurred much closer to Germany, in the North Sea, about four years before the transposition process of 2002/59/EC. Despite the facts that the Galacia accident attracted lots of German media attention and was so pertinent to directive 2002/59/EC, it had no effect on the timely completion of the transposition process. It was, instead, the 1998 Pallas accident in the North Sea that expedited Germany's transposition of EU directive 2002/59/EC. By all accounts, and despite a four year time-lag, the Pallas accident, so close to German soil, was still very present in administrators' minds. The accident was referred to by all of this study's German interviewees.

11.1.3 *To what extent will our findings on the national transposition processes of transport policy generalize to other EU policies?*

In the past, studies in the area of EU implementation have focused on environment and social policy. But, since I wanted both to broaden the implications of my research and to look at a somewhat ignored but theoretical interesting area, I opted to study transport policy. Besides being another area that represents the dominant regulatory nature of EU policies, the transport sector simply deserves more attention.

Little is known about EU transport policy. In political science and public administration edited volumes that cover a wide variety of EU policy processes, information about transport policy is poignantly amiss (Wallace, Wallace and Pollack, 2005). Therefore, this study started from the beginning. It explored the development of EU transport policy and the five transport sub-sectors, and this exploration, in turn, informed the case study selection and timeframe for this analysis. The uncovered five-fold characteristics of EU transport policy (recent, gradual, uneven, complex, and crisis-driven), then, guided the theoretical framework for apt transposition.

Furthermore, there is almost nothing exceptional in the transport case that would make the study's findings non-generalizable to other policy areas. The European-directive specific and national legal instrument specific variables all hold for the different domains of EU policy-making where we find a considerable number of directives (for an overview of EU legislative output see Alesina, Angeloni and Schuknecht, 2005: 298). Only regional aid does not dispose any directive, whereas the numbers of EU initiatives in all other EU policy areas range between 1 (international relations and foreign aid) to agriculture and fishery (484), sectoral business relations (650) and common market (890). Transport (121) claims the middle-field with environment (193) and with social policy (178). In terms of the crisis component, most policy areas are also endued with internal or external situational changes, a trick that 'creates in the minds of the incumbent decision-makers of a state a perceived threat from the external environment to the basic values to which to which a responsive decision is deemed necessary' (Brechner, 1977: 32). Money and fiscal policy are vulnerable to financial market crises, like we have experienced in East Asia in 1997-1998 and its disastrous consequences for Europe, crises, like those experienced in East Asia in 1997-1998 and its disastrous consequences for Europe. However, crises in, for example, the field of environment and consumers' protection (BSE, SARS...) are very much present in peoples' mind.

Lastly, from an empirical point of view, the Lisbon goals, drafted in 2000, were intended to make the EU 'the most competitive and dynamic knowledge-driven economy by 2010'. Transport policy may differ in economic, numeric, and organizational terms from other industrial sectors, but it is definitely crucial to understand in order to achieve the ambitious Lisbon goals on economic competitiveness and employment. If your transport system does not work you cannot move goods around the country/Union and you will not be economically viable. A fundamental catalyst for the fulfillment of these goals until 2010 is the timely transposition of EU directives – not only to meet the ambitious goals, but to appear credible. This study of the transport area does not cover the entire range of European policies. But, it does identify and stress those systematic aspects of regulatory policy that are heuristically significant in all EU policies.

11.2 Methodological contribution

In order to initiate a more valid and reliable account of transposition variations across member states in the EU, *this research combined two assets for comparative social research.* Both are methodological in nature. The first goal was to answer the research question about: determinants of transposition delay, the causal mechanisms lying beneath them and necessary and sufficient conditions for transposition delay. In order to increase the model's strength of inference and robustness, this study followed Lieberman's guide (2005) for carrying out a combined research design, which is often found in behavioral sciences (Tashakkori and Teddlie, 2003), but which has hardly been applied in EU implementation studies. While statistical analyses guided the case selection and provided direction for more focused case studies and comparisons, it was also used to provide, thereafter, an additional test of the adjusted theoretical model generated from small-n research. The second asset concerns data. In line with Denzin's (1978) term 'triangulation,' which involves combining data sources to study the same social phenomenon, this study relies on different sources of data and adds to existing data in the field (Gabel, Hix and Schneider, 2002). In the end, this book follows a truly mixed-method approach, incorporating multiple approaches in all stages of the study, namely: the research question, data collection and inference.

11.2.1 *'Dictatorship of the research question':*

In an ideal world, the paradigmatic position of the researcher would not determine what design will be used in a study. And, the selection of methods would not be made before the research question is formulated; a method would be chosen on the basis of it being the best way to answer the question. Tashakkori and Teddlie (1998) refer to the 'dictatorship of the research question,' which, however, requires scholars to use research tools for a variety of research questions, such as the one driving this study.

The study was driven by the three sub-questions: *what*, *how* and *to what extent*. The first research question of my study was *what determines transposition delays in member states?* To best address this question, the statistical analysis of the quantitative data analysis (ordered multinomial logistic regression) uncovered the effects of explanatory variables on the timeliness of the national transposition procedures of legal instruments. The second research question was *how do these determinants influence the timeliness of national transposition processes?* The third research question was about the relative significance of the single effects and combinations of them. These last two questions were mainly answered by the process-tracing efforts for four case studies and further tested by the middle-range-n fuzzy set technique.

This analysis presents an alternative way to understand the transposition problematic across EU member states by leaving aside the qualitative/quantitative divide in the field. Whereas scholars have applied either quantitative (Mbaye, 2001; Bursens, 2002; Giuliani, 2003; Mastenbroek, 2003; König, Luetgert and Mäder, 2005; Borghetto, Franchino and Giannetti, 2006; Perkins and Neumayer, 2007) or qualitative research tools to explain EU implementation outcomes (Knill and Lenschow, 1998; Haverland; 2000; Héritier et al., 2001; Falkner et al., 2005; Berglund, 2007), this study makes a call for combined designs. Starting with a regression- based method focused primarily on the problem of estimating the independent effect of each variable included in the analysis in the outcome I continued with process-tracing of four case studies – representing well-explained *and* deviant cases. Four comparative advantages make case studies almost 'a part of a social scientist's complete armamentarium' (Yin, 1993: xi), namely: (1) great potential for achieving high conceptual validity of dependent and independent variables; (2) strong procedures for fostering new hypotheses; (3) value as a useful means of closely examining the hypothesized role of causal mechanisms in the context of individual cases; and (4) capacity for addressing causal complexity. It is the case study based on earlier statistical findings that provides greater in-depth analysis, in which cases are more easily comparable, and causal mechanisms of the national transposition processes (microfoundations) are more clearly elucidated through process-tracing.

However, *the case study method also has its Achilles' heel*. Specifically, 'it suffers from the inability to support broad and well-bounded propositions, it tends to lack representativeness, and causal effects and probabilistic causal relations cannot be estimated' (Franchino, 2005: 250; George and Bennet, 2005; Gerring, 2004). *In order to examine the extent to which the previous findings were unique to the initial four cases, or relevant to a wider group of cases, therefore, I applied the diversity-oriented fuzzy set approach.* It helped shed additional light on the correlational and small-n analyses in this study. If we can observe a strong correlation in one set of data, then, it is far from certain that the same correlation will be observed in other data. Only if one assumes that regularities remain unchanged into infinity, the approach is a valid inference. Political priority, a variable derived from the case study analysis, has remained a significant variable explaining the timeliness of national transposition processes.

In addition, the fuzzy set technique offers some interesting alternative when one is confronted with coding problems linked with dichotomization. The conception of variables in terms of fuzzy set membership (Ragin, 2000) provides a way to operationalize and typologize phenomena that stick closer to theoretical discourse (Rhioux, 2006: 691). Indeed this study demonstrated how fuzzy set can be used to perform precise operationalizations of theoretical concepts such as timeliness. In line with the findings of Katz, vom Hau and Mahony (2005) it enriched the conclusions reached by prior analysis while focusing on necessity and sufficiency and combination of conditions.

However, fuzzy set should not be used in isolation. It is in combination with large-n and small-n studies that the fuzzy set research technique can resolve problems related to the quantitative and qualitative approaches, such as: autocorrelation, multicollinearity, selection bias, heteroscedasticity, and idiosyncrasy (Pennings, 2002). So, fuzzy set is a compatible technique and can be combined more systematically with other techniques. *Surprisingly, the fuzzy set methodology has not yet been widely addressed in EU research.*

To summarize, mixed strategy designs added 'breadth or depth to our analysis' (Fielding and Fielding, 1986: 33) by increasing 'scope, depth and consistency in methodological proceedings' (Flick, 1998: 230). Different vantage points, provided by the mixed method, allowed a fuller and more complete picture of the phenomenon concerned. It was, for example, not only the occurrence of national general elections, but also the reshuffling of government portfolios that hampered timely transposition. The identification of a correlation established that a relationship exists between general elections at the end of a national transposition process and the timeliness of the latter. But unless we understand the underlying mechanisms that caused it, we would have not known how the variable affects the other. In this respect, despite some limitations of the fuzzy set methodology (for references see Rhioux, 2006), the debate on implementation performance of member states in the EU profited from the capacity of fuzzy sets 'to capture the causal patterns behind complex and vague phenomena which remain largely invisible or are even misrepresented when conventional quantitative and qualitative approaches are used' (Pennings, 2002: 18).

Ultimately, this study is in line with Lieberman (2005) that the mixed-method approach is particularly well suited to cross-national analysis, where investigators tend to be interested not only in general patterns but also in the analysis of specific country cases. In this respect, the mixed-method design was further developed, especially by combining information from different data sources to understand the same phenomenon.

11.2.2 *'Who is afraid of cumulative data?'* [78]

As a relatively young polity, however, the EU has until recently offered only few ready-made empirical resources, such as extensive databases, available to scholars. It has been noted that, 'although the study of EU politics has developed considerably, we still lack scientific maturity in the key area of data accumulation and integration ... few research communities [in the many areas of EU research] have built a common data set that is sufficient to advance knowledge' (Gabel, Hix and Schneider, 2002: 482). Generally speaking, 'European integration studies have found it difficult to produce cumulative research' (Hooghe, 2001: 1).

This study is a good example of several pioneering projects across EU implementation studies that have begun to further develop the vastly untapped, but collectable or collected, EU data (Steunenberg and Rhinard, 2005; EUP special issues in 2005 and 2006). To address the concern of missing systematic collected data on EU politics, this study provided a collection of different data sources that accumulate knowledge about EU politics, in general, and national transposition processes across EU member states, in particular. The exercise is part of the second round of quantitative studies in the field, whose intention is to improve the quality of existing EU implementation data.

This study opted to focus on only recent cases of EU national implementation instruments in the area of transport. In doing so, it covered almost ten years (1995-2004) and nine member states, namely: France, Germany, Greece, Italy, Ireland, Spain, Sweden, the Netherlands, and the UK. Despite highly theoretically relevant for this study, about some of these states, little work had been done in implementation research before.

Furthermore, this study conducted data triangulation, which is the use of multiple cross-checked sources. For the statistical analysis, information about the EU transport directives was taken from the official legal EU databases – *Celex* and *Eurlex*. To compare and control for the quality of the existing EU data, each Transport Ministry in the nine Member States was contacted. From them, a full list of transport *acquis* from their national transposition databases was obtained. These lists dated back to the very first directive, which helped

---

78 Gabel, Hix and Schneider (2002)

me compile an almost complete data set. In order to translate the crisp scores of the dependent and independent variables into fuzzy set partial membership scores, information was again derived mainly from *Celex*, *Eurlex*, and national transposition databases. Also, information was added from official government websites of the selected five Member States, from the annual review of national politics by the *European Journal of Political Research*, and from five major national newspaper archives, namely: *The Guardian* (UK); *Le Monde* (France); *Frankfurter Allgemeine Zeitung* (Germany); *Corriere della Sera* (Italy); and *El País* (Spain). The data for process tracing included, in addition to aforementioned EU legal data bases, information from press accounts, European official documents, and interviews. Information about negotiation phases were found in *Prelex*. Information on the timing of national elections and the change of transport ministers were again found in the annual political data provided by the *European Journal of Political Research.* Information on national-level transport related accidents was studied through content analysis (Krippendorf, 2004) of newspapers. For cross-checking purposes and the procurement of additional data for these theoretical informed case studies, a total of thirty interviews in Brussels and in different member states were conducted between January 2003 and November 2006.

11.3 The outlook

As it stands, this study attempts to address some shortcomings in the existing transposition literature while representing another step in improving existing knowledge in the field of EU implementation studies. For future studies that build on its results and aim at understanding the transposition of EU legislation and Europeanization more generally, two elements in particular deserve attention. Based on the study's findings, the first element relates to the theoretical framework used to model national transposition processes; the second centers around issues of research design.

From a theoretical point-of-view, the EU implementation literature will benefit from attempts like this to theorize and research the role of domestic politics (Treib, 2003; Steunenberg, 2006; 2007) and administrations (Knill, 2001; Hille and Knill, 2006) on the process of implementation. A more theory-guided evaluation of the different stages of the implementation process will help further strengthen our understanding of EU implementation, in general, and its efficiency, efficacy and efficiency. Scholars (Falkner, Causse and Wiedermann, 2006) have shown that adapting to EU law willremain a EU-wide ambition, at least on the level of the statute books, including the new member states after the 2004 enlargement where the transposition of EU legislation remains dead letters instead of becoming living rights (Treib and Falkner, 2007). Whereas here the effect of domestic op position on timely transposition is mediated by a member state's culture of implementation, studies will further profit acknowledging that policy design as well as policy implementation related variables matter.

Inspired by the 1970s public policy implementation studies and in line with the recent implementation study by Falkner, Treib, Hartlapp and Leiber (2005) *this contribution argues that the link between the adoption phase and the subsequent implementation phase is crucial; i.e. that 'implementation should be part of design'* (Pressman and Wildavsky, 1973: 189). Explanations of implementation outcomes should consider, among other things, policy design related factors.

While, until recently, regulations and directives have been the dominant policy instruments in the EU, new modes of EU governance that are not based on legislation have increased in salience in European policy-making (Héritier, 2003; Caporaso and Wittenbrinck, 2006). The newly adopted open method of coordination, for example, which is applied in a number of EU policy fields (Borrás and Jacobsson, 2004), entails clear procedural mechanisms; it also includes a high-level of political participation, including the monitoring phases, and involves more mutual commitments and peer pressure mechanisms, where political priority palys an important role. Future studies comparing implementation patterns in *hard and soft law* traditions will need to engage in an intricate web of politics, economics and law. European Community law virtually cries out to be understood by means of interdisciplinary, contextual approach to law. *Explanatory factors will be by nature administrative, legally and political motivated.*

Last but not least, this study is somewhat forward-thinking in relation to the relatively young EU research community. From a methodological point-of-view, and in line with a relatively large number of studies in social and behavioral sciences in general (Tashakkori and Teddlie, 2003), this study has shown that the use of a mixed-method design (Lieberman, 2005) may improve results of simple mono-strand designs. In order to answer the initial questions about the timeliness of national transposition processes, this contribution subjected the theoretical framework to a battery of tests, including ordered multinomial logistic regression, process-tracing and fuzzy set analysis. In addition, it has sought to use as wide a variety of existing and new evidence as possible by accumulating existing data. It is important for the quality and scope of the implementation debate that not only the data, but also the methods that are used to analyze them, are as adequate. The results of the efforts are promising, and may strongly encourage EU scholars to consider moving beyond methodological dichotomies and leave some of the cut-and-dried opinions behind. *To date, little effort has been done to accomplish this. Particular attention may be paid to the fuzzy set methodology, a research technique that has been widely applied elsewhere, but may be still an underestimated treasure for EU studies.*

In any case, in terms of an ever important European project, and before we get lost in translation, it is time again to go full steam ahead in response to the challenges of EU law. After transposition, as generally known, is before transposition, with a European Commission having just issued 111 additional internal market directives in 2004 and 89 in 2005 [79] respectively.

79 I am greatful to Dimiter Toshkov who provided the data.

Samenvatting

Betere regelgeving kan niet worden bereikt zonder serieuze aandacht voor de omzetting van EU recht naar nationale wetgeving. Dit boek analyseert de punctualiteit van nationale transpositieprocessen en behandelt de volgende hoofdvraag: *Waarom missen lidstaten deadlines bij het omzetten van EU richtlijnen voor de interne markt?*

Het boek is op te splitsen in vier delen. Het eerste deel introduceert de lezer met hiaten in de bestaande EU implementatie literatuur, en met de belangrijkste kenmerken van het EU transportbeleid. Het tweede deel kenschetst de transportsector en legt daarmee de grond voor de toepassing van het actor-gericht theoretisch kader. Doel hiervan is om het verloop van transpositieprocessen te verklaren. Deel drie is gewijd aan de analyse van het onderzoek. Hierin wordt allereerst gepresenteerd hoe de kwaliteit van de bestaande EU data vergroot kan worden. Vervolgens wordt nauwgezet ingegaan op de problematiek rondom de implementatietekortkomingen. Met behulp van kwantitatieve en kwalitatieve data worden de in het theoretisch hoofdstuk geformuleerde verwachtingen met betrekking tot de punctualiteit van nationale transpositieprocessen getoetst. Een grote-n analyse wordt gevolgd door vier casestudies die de eerdere bevindingen verder uitwerken en een belangrijke missende factor aanwijzen. Vervolgens test de zogenaamde 'fuzzy set technique' de hypotheses die voortkomen uit het grote-n en kleine-n onderzoek. Deze techniek maakt het mogelijk om de relatieve significantie van enkele of een combinatie van omstandigheden beter te meten. Het vierde deel van deze studie vat de bevindingen samen en zoemt in op hun bijdrage aan de wetenschappelijke discussie en hun bredere implicaties voor betere regelgeving in de EU.

De vier genoemde delen worden in dit boek in elf afzonderlijke hoofdstukken besproken. Na een inleiding en eerste hoofdstuk, geeft hoofdstuk twee een kritische evaluatie van de bestaande literatuur die op het theoretische, methodologische en empirische vlak relevant is voor deze studie. Het legt de grote problematische kenmerken bloot van de literatuur over implementatie van EU regelgeving: *ad-hoc, weinig verklarende kracht bezittend, deterministisch, kortzichtig en bevooroordeeld.* In het bijzonder omarmt dit hoofdstuk de recente inspanningen van de zogenaamde 'derde golf' implementatiestudies. Deze stroming onderzoekt de rol van de binnenlandse politiek op implementatieprocessen om duidelijkere voorspellingen te kunnen genereren die empirisch getest kunnen worden. Deze studie bouwt op deze recente verbeteringen en voert deze door ten aanzien van de theoretische, empirische en methodologische tekortkomingen van de voorgaande EU-implementatiestudies.

Hoofdstuk drie richt zich vervolgens op de historische ontwikkeling van het EU transportbeleid. Na een bespreking van de politicologische literatuur op het gebied van EU transportbeleid presenteert dit hoofdstuk het institutionele landschap op EU-niveau met betrekking tot het transportbeleid. Het integratieproces op dit terrein kan gekarakteriseerd worden als *recent, geleidelijk, ongelijk, complex* en *crisisgedreven*. De inhoud van het huidige EU transportbeleid is het resultaat van (a) de verschillende uitbreidingsronden van de EU, (b) veranderingen in de benadering van de Commissie met betrekking tot transport, en (c) een aantal crises dat zich in de transportsector heeft voorgedaan.

Hoofdstuk vier ontwikkelt een actor-gedreven theoretisch kader voor de punctualiteit van nationale transpositieprocessen. Het presenteert een serie van testbare hypotheses, afgestemd op de transportsector, die echter kunnen worden gegeneraliseerd voor elke EU beleidssector. Transpositie is een zogenaamde onderhandelingsspel. *Wie* de implementatieonderhandeling beëindigt en *wanneer* hangt af van de verwachte beloning van de spelers. Met andere woorden, voor de actoren is de perceptie van de kosten/baten structuur met betrekking tot het wachten met de omzetting doorslaggevend. Terwijl de omvang van de baten positief gerelateerd is aan de renteverdeling en negatief gerelateerd is aan de tijd, wordt de omvang van de kosten bepaald door de spelers' kosten en tijd. Bovendien wegen verwachte toekomstige baten sterk mee in de beslissing van de speler of er vertraagd, gewacht, of uitgesteld wordt; met andere woorden: wachten in de hoop dat de ander een significante concessie doet. Aan de hand van deze 'war of attrition bargaining game'-logica komt in dit hoofdstuk eerst de manier waarop beleidsverandering tot stand komt aan bod. Daarna wordt ingegaan op de effecten van beleidsverandering. *Als aanvulling op de eerste twee delen van het theoretisch kader wordt in dit hoofdstuk de specifieke rol van transportgerelateerde incidenten in de omzettingsfase uitgelicht.*

Vervolgens presenteert hoofdstuk vijf een dataset van standaardvariabelen die essentieel zijn voor een deductieve, systematische, empirische, en analytische studie van de EU transpositieprestatie van de lidstaten. *Deze nieuwe, betrouwbaardere dataset omvat bijna tweederde van de volledige EU transport acquis van 1995 tot 2004.* Het bevat de kenmerken van elke EU richtlijn en van de nationale implementatie-instrumenten van negen lidstaten, te weten: *Frankrijk, Duitsland, Groot-Brittannië, Nederland, Griekenland, Spanje, Ierland, Zweden en Italië.* Eerst bespreekt dit hoofdstuk de keuzes voor het beleidsveld, de lidstaten en de tijdsperiode van het onderzoek. Vervolgens presenteert het de informatiebronnen en beoordeelt het in hoeverre de dataset compleet is. Hierbij wordt enige aandacht besteed aan de missende waarden.

Hoofdstuk zes biedt een eerste beschrijvende analyse van de nationale implementatie-instrumenten. *Het laat zien dat vooral Nederland, Frankrijk, Italië, Ierland, Griekenland en Duitsland errnstige transpositieproblemen hebben in de transportsector.* Gebaseerd op de informatie van 367 nationale implementatiemaatregelen laat dit hoofdstuk zien dat het EU transpositie deficit meer is dan alleen een statistische illusie. *Bijna 50 procent van de richtlijnen wordt niet op tijd omgezet en leidt tot een vertraging die kan oplopen tot tot bijna vijf jaar.* De variatie tussen landen is behoorlijk, het verschil tussen de achterblijver Nederland en de winnaar Zweden is aanzienlijk. Verder laten de verschillen in mediaan en het gemiddelde zien dat 70 procent van de vertraagde richtlijnen meer dan zes maanden te laat is. *Tot slot identificeert dit hoofdstuk drie groepen van uitkomsten: implementatie die op tijd is, implementatie die minder dan zes maanden te laat is, en implementatie die meer dan zes maanden te laat is.* Deze driedeling is voor de meer geavanceerde analyse belangrijk.

In hoofdstuk zeven worden de onafhankelijke variabelen geoperationaliseerd en worden de volgende onderzoeksmethoden gepresenteerd. Met een afhankelijke variabele die in een driedeling is gecodeerd (geen vertraging, korte- en een lange vertraging) wordt een 'ordered multinominal logistic regression'-analyse uitgevoerd. Hierdoor worden bestaande argumenten in de literatuur ter discussie gesteld of bevestigd. Wanneer de drie groepen van transpositie-uitkomsten worden vergeleken, wordt duidelijk dat *korte vertragingen verklaard kunnen worden door kenmerken van de individuele EU-richtlijn terwijl lange vertragingen verklaard worden door nationale factoren. De statistische resultaten ondersteunen duidelijk het centrale argument dat het Europese niveau, het nationale niveau, en crisisgerelateerde factoren samen verantwoordelijk zijn voor transpositievertragingen* en dat een actor-gecentreerd model enige verklarende kracht daarvoor geeft.

Er zijn duidelijke voordelen bij het gebruik van een grote-n studie in combinatie met een aanvullende casestudie als onderzoeksontwerp in EU implementatiestudies. Als voorbeeld van hoe een dergelijke uitdaging ondernomen kan worden houdt hoofdstuk acht zich bezig met de casusselectie, voordat het hier opvolgende casestudie hoofdstuk zal helpen om de bevindingen verder te verfijnen en voordat het enkele overgebleven beperkingen van de eerste resultaten zal behandelen. Eerst worden de selectiecriteria toegelicht. De geschiktheid van een casus hangt af van de mate waarin het statistische model toereikend is, hetgeen op zijn beurt weer afhangt van de berekende 'deviant residuals'. *In deze studie is gekozen voor het gebruik van een modeltestende en -verbeterende benadering.* Een 'meest gelijk danwel meest verschillend' ontwerp is richtinggevend voor de selectie van vier nationale implementatiemaatregelen: twee goed verklaarde (on-the-line) cases en twee afwijkende (off-the-line) casussen. De vier casussen omvatten drie landen en twee transport subsectors.

In hoofdstuk negen wordt dan een gecontroleerde casestudie analyse uitgevoerd. De structuur van de vier casussen wordt uitgetekend door de methode van process-tracing. De geselecteerde cassussen zijn: (a) het Franse implementatieproces van de richtlijn 98/55/EC van juli 1998 *met betrekking tot minimum vereisten voor de scheepvaart*, (b) het Spaanse transpositieproces van richtlijn 2001/14/EC *met betrekking tot de allocatie van de capaciteit van spoorweginfrastructuur*, (c) het Duitse transpositieproces van richtlijn 2002/59/EC *met betrekking tot het monitoring- en informatiesysteem voor het scheepvaartverkeer binnen de EU*, en (d) het Franse implementatieproces van richtlijn 2001/53/EC *over de marine-uitrusting*. Het bewijs uit deze casussen laat zien dat process-tracing een nuttig onderzoeksinstrument is en bijdraagt aan het meervoudige-methode ('mixed-method') onderzoeksontwerp van dit boek. De uitkomsten van deze methode bevestigen duidelijk de verwachtingen over de condities waaronder lidstaten de transpositiedeadlines missen. Het wijst ook op een factor die geen verklaringskracht heeft: *de mate van politieke prioriteit verbonden aan het specifieke transpositieproces.*

Omdat het problematisch is om voor 365 casussen de politieke prioriteit vast te stellen wordt een derde methode geïntroduceerd. Hoofdstuk tien completeert het gecombineerde 'mixed-method' ontwerp door een aanvullende test van de uitgebreide lijst van hypotheses, gegenereerd door middel van het kleine-n onderzoek, voor een 'middle range' set van data. Verder identificeert de 'fuzzy set technique' een set van voorwaarden die gewoonlijk voldoende, of noodzakelijk is om tijdig te kunnen implementeren. Deze techniek legt de beperkingen van eerdere analyses bloot. De 'calibrated data' van de uitkomsten en de causale factoren laten individueel zien dat de logica van 'partial membership' er beter in slaagt de diversiteit van de echte wereld te laten zien dan de gekunstelde onderzoeksdichotomieën van ja/nee opdrachten. *Het resultaat van vier omstandigheden die gewoonlijk noodzakelijk zijn, die in isolatie van alle andere factoren van invloed zijn en die aanwezig zijn in alle voorbeelden van uitkomsten, worden besproken.*

In hoofdstuk elf worden de bevindingen van het empirisch onderzoek samengebracht. De bevindingen van deze studie zijn voornamelijk tweeledig, namelijk: empirisch en methodologisch. Vanuit een empirisch gezichtspunt beargumenteert de schrijver dat de EU een implementatieprobleem heeft met meerdere facetten. Het blijkt dat bijna 70 procent van alle nationale implementatiemaatregelen voor het omzetten van het 2004 transport *acquis* problemen oplevert. Dit kan ofwel zijn doordat ze te laat omgezet worden waardoor een infringement procedure geriskeerd wordt, ofwel doordat ze te vroeg omgezet worden ('gold-plating'). Dit laatste kan negatieve gevolgen hebben voor de regelgeving omdat deze voor alle bedrijven en burgers in de EU gelijk zou moeten gelden.

Zeven drijvende factoren die cruciaal zijn voor de punctualiteit van nationale transpositieprocessen van EU wetgeving worden geïdentificeerd. Ze worden onderverdeeld in drie brede groepen: beleidsontwerp gerelateerd (op niveau van de EU), beleidsimplementatie gerelateerd (op het nationale niveau), en crisisgerelateerde factoren. Het blijkt dat deze zeven factoren verschillende effecten hebben op de lengte van het implementatieproces. Wanneer een onderscheid tussen op tijd, een korte en een lange vertraging gehandhaafd wordt, blijkt dat de kenmerken van de richtlijnen verantwoordelijk zijn voor korte vertragingen. Langdurige vertragingen (van meer dan zes maanden) zijn het resultaat van factoren op het nationale niveau. Verder zijn ook de timing van nationale verkiezingen in een lidstaat en crises gerelateerd aan de beleidssector vertragend of accelereren ze juist het transpositieproces omdat de politieke prioriteit die aan de transpositie wordt verbonden een significante voorwaarde is voor punctualiteit.

Vanuit een methodologisch gezichtspunt wordt geopperd in deze studie dat het, ondanks epistemologische onvolkomenheden, mogelijk is om correlaties, casestudie en de 'fuzzy set technique' te gebruiken. Juist omdat deze technieken gezamenlijk nog niet eerder gebruikt zijn in EU studies, kunnen ze de kennis over implementatie van EU wetgeving verrijken. Terwijl de regressieanalyse duidelijkheid verschaft over de effecten van een oorzaak en de casestudies over de oorzaken van de effecten, staat de 'fuzzy set' methode toe dat er gevraagd kan worden onder welke omstandigheden bepaalde causale factoren voldoende of noodzakelijk zijn voor een bepaalde uitkomst. *Kortom, de 'mixed-method' benadering in het algemeen, en de 'fuzzy set technique' in het bijzonder blijken voor EU implementatiestudies 'diamonds in the rough'.*

Appendices

Annex 1: EU transport transposition data set 1995-2004.

Directives	Title	Publication in Official Journal	Date of transposition deadline
2002/0059	Suivi du trafic des navires	5.8.02	5.2.04
2002/0084	Sécurité martitime/prévention pollution	29.11.02	23.11.03
2000/0056	Permis de conduire	21.9.00	30.9.03
2002/0030	Restrictions exploitation aéroports	28.3.02	28.9.03
2002/0006	Formalités déclaratives des navires	9.3.02	9.9.03
2001/0096	Chargement/déchargement vraquiers	16.1.02	4.8.03
2001/0105	Inspection et visite des navires	22.1.02	22.7.03
2001/0106	Contrôle par l'Etat du port	22.1.02	22.7.03
2001/0016	Interopérabilité ferroviaire conventionnel	20.4.01	20.4.03
2002/0075	Equipements marins	23.9.02	23.3.03
2001/0012	Modif.91/440/CE dévelopt chemins de fer	15.3.01	15.3.03
2001/0013	Modif.95/18/CE licences	15.3.01	15.3.03
2001/0014	Capacités d'infrastructure ferroviaire	15.3.01	15.3.03
2001/0011	Contrôle tech. Véhicules utilitaires	17.2.01	9.3.03
2002/0035	Sécurité navires de pêche + 24m	27.4.02	1.1.03
2002/0050	Equipement sous pression	7.6.02	1.1.03
2000/0059	Installations portuaires - déchets	28.12.00	28.12.02
2001/0007	Transp. march. dangéreuses route	1.2.01	31.12.02
2001/0006	Transp. march. dangéreuses par fer	1.2.01	31.12.02
2002/0025	Modif.98/18/CE sécurité navires	15.4.02	15.10.02
2000/0030	Contrôle tech. Véhicule utilitaires	10.8.00	10.8.02
2001/0009	Contrôle tech. Véhicules utilitaires	17.2.01	9.3.02
2001/0053	Equipements marins	28.7.01	17.2.02
2001/0026	Transp. march. dangéreuses route	23.6.01	23.12.01
2001/0002	Equipements sous pression	10.1.01	1.7.01
1999/0036	Equipements sous pression	1.6.99	1.7.01
2000/0062	Transp. march. dangéreuses par fer	1.11.00	1.5.01
2000/0061	Transp. march. dangéreuses route	1.11.00	1.5.01
1999/0097	Contrôle par l'Etat du port	23.12.99	14.12.00
1999/0035	Visite sécurité transbordeurs	1.6.99	1.12.00
1999/0052	Contrôle technique	5.6.99	1.10.00
2000/0018	Conseillers sécurité march. dang.	19.5.00	19.8.00
1999/0019	Sécurité navires de pêche + 24 m	27.3.99	31.5.00
1996/0035	Conseillers sécurité march. dang.	19.6.96	31.12.99
1998/0074	C.mini.Navires March. Dangereuses	13.10.98	2.11.99

Directives	Title	Publication in Official Journal	Date of transposition deadline
1998/0076	Accès prof. Transp. par route	14.10.98	1.10.99
1999/0028	Modification annexe dir.92/14/EC	6.5.99	1.9.99
1999/0048	Transp.march. dangereuses par fer	5.7.99	1.7.99
1999/0047	Transp.march. dangereuses route	5.7.99	1.7.99
1998/0035	Formation des gens de mer	25.5.98	25.5.99
1998/0085	Equipements marins	25.11.98	30.4.99
1996/0048	Interopérabilité ferroviaire TGV	17.9.96	8.4.99
1998/0020	Limitation exploit. des avions	7.4.98	28.2.99
1998/0055	C.mini.navires march. dangereuses	1.8.98	31.12.98
1997/0070	Sécurité navires de pêche + 24m	9.2.98	31.12.98
1998/0042	Contrôle par l'Etat du port (PSC)	27.6.98	30.9.98
1997/0058	Inspection et visites des navires	7.10.97	30.9.98
1998/0025	Contrôle par l'Etat du port (PSC)	7.5.98	1.7.98
1998/0018	Sécurité navires à passagers	15.5.98	1.7.98
1996/0098	Equipements marins	17.2.97	30.6.98
1996/0050	Certif. conduite navigation int.	17.9.96	7.4.98
1996/0096	Contrôle technique	17.2.97	9.3.98
1997/0026	Permis de conduire	7.6.97	1.1.98
1997/0015	Normes Eurocontrol	10.4.97	1.12.97
1996/0067	Assistance en escale	25.10.96	25.10.97
1997/0034	C.mini.navires march. dangereuses	17.6.97	30.9.97
1996/0053	Dimensions max. véhicules routiers	17.9.96	16.9.97
1996/0039	C.mini.navires march. dangereuses	7.8.96	7.8.97
1995/0018	Licences entreprises ferroviaires	27.6.95	27.6.97
1996/0040	Carte d'identité insp. PSC	7.8.96	1.2.97
1996/0075	Modalités d'affrètement nav.int.	27.11.96	1.1.97
1995/0050	Transp.march. dangereuses route	17.10.95	1.1.97
1996/0087	Transp.march.dangereuses par fer	24.12.96	31.12.96
1996/0086	Transp.march. dangereuses route	24.12.96	31.12.96
1996/0049	Transp.march.dangereuses par fer	17.9.96	31.12.96
1996/0047	Permis de conduire	17.9.96	30.6.96
1995/0021	Contrôle par l'Etat du port	7.7.95	30.6.96

Source : European Commission (DG Transport)

Annex 2: Table of correlations.

	Discretion rate	Transposition time set in the directive	Number of veto players	First directive in national transposition package	Last directive in national transposition package	Start of transposition in election year	End of transposition in election year	Transport related accidents
Discretion rate	1.000							
Transposition time set in the directive	0.167	1.000						
Number of veto players	0.141	0.141	1.000					
First directive in national transposition package	0.000	-0.036	0.005	1.000				
Last directive in national transposition package	-0.089	0.034	-0.053	-0.102	1.000			
Start of transposition in election year	-0.080	0.054	-0.057	-0.155	0.099	1.000		
End of transposition in election year	-0.014	-0.159	0.093	0.123	-0.138	-0.083	1.000	
Transport related accidents	0.054	0.123	-0.027	-0.037	0.039	0.100	-0.052	1.000

References

Abbati, C. degli (1987) *Transport and European Integration*, Luxembourg: EC Publications Office.

Achen, C. H. and D. Snidal (1989) 'Rational Deterrence Theory and Comparative Case Studies', *World Politics* 41(2): 167-168.

Adamsky, D. (2005) 'Disregarding the bear: How US intelligence failed to estimate the soviet intervention in the Egyptian-Israeli war of attrition?', *Journal of Strategic Studies* 28(5): 803-831.

Alesina, A., I. Angeloni and L. Schuknecht (2005) 'What does the European Union do?', *Public Choice* 123: 275-319.

Alesina, A. and A. Drazen (1991) 'Why are Stabilizations Delayed?', *American Economic Review* 81: 1170-88.

Allio, L. and M. H. Fandel (2006) *'Making Europe work: improving the transposition, implementation and enforcement of EU legislation'*, EPC working paper no. 25

Almond, G. A., S. Flanagan and R. Mundt (1973) *Crisis, Choice and Change: Historical studies of political development*, Boston: Little Brown.

Ambler, T., F. Chittenden and M. Obodovski (2005) *How much regulation is gold plate? A study of UK elaboration of EU directives*, London: British Chambers of Commerce.

Anderson, K. and M. Kaeding (2006) 'Belgium, the Netherlands and Luxembourg: Increasingly Cautious Europeans', in Eleanor E. Zeff and Ellen B. Pirro (eds) The European Union and the Member States, London: Lynne Rienner Publishers, pp. 107-128.

Armstrong, K. and S. Bulmer (1998) *The Governance of the Single Market*, Manchester: Manchester University Press.

Aspinwall, M. (1995) *Moveable Feast*, Aldershot: Avebury.

Aspinwall, M. (1999) 'Planes, trains and automobiles: transport governance in the EU', in: Beate Kohler-Koch and Rainer Eising (eds.), *The transformation of Governance in the EU*, London: Routledge.

Aspinwall, M. D. and G. Schneider (2000) 'Same Menu, Separate Tables: The Institutionalist Turn in Political Science and the Study of European Integration', *European Journal of Political Research* 38: 1-36.

Banister, D., K. Dreborg, L. Hedberg, S. Hunhammar, P. Steen and J. Akerman (2000) 'Transport Policy Scenarios for the EU: 2020 Images of the Future', *Innovation: The European Journal of Social Sciences* 13(1): 27-45.

Bardach, E. (1977) *The Implementation Game: what happens after a bill becomes a law*, Cambridge: MIT Press.

Barroso, J. M. 'Delivering quality in European regulation', speech delivered at the European Parliament plenary on 4 April 2006.

Baur, J. (2004) 'Europäische Verkehrspolitik. Zu Lande, zu Wasser und in der Luft', *Osteuropa* 54(5-6): 387-396.

Beach, D. (2005) 'Why governments comply: an integrative implementation model that bridges the gap between instrumental and normative models of implementation', *Journal of European Public Policy* 12 (1): 113-42.

Bekkers, V., J. Bonnes, A. De Moor van Vugt, P. Schoneveld and W. Voermans (1995) in: Spyros A. Pappas (ed.), *National administrative procedures for the preparation and implementation of community decisions*, Maastricht: European Institute of Public Administration, pp. 397-477.

Bellis, R. (2003) *Improving implementation of EU legislation*, Foreign and Commonwealth Office, UK: London.

Berglund, S., I. Gange and F. van Waarden (2006) 'Mass Production of Law. Routinization in Transposition of European Directives. A Sociological- institutional account', *Journal of European Public Policy* 13(5): 692-716.

Berglund, S. (2007) Three paths to delay: A case study analysis of the transposition of public utilities directives, Paper presented at the EUSA 10th Biennial International Conference, 17-19 May, Montreal, Canada.

Berman, P. (1978) 'The study of macro- and micro-implementation', *Public Policy* 26(2): 157-184.

Boin, A., P. 't Hart, E. Stern and B. Sundelius (2005) *The Politics of Crisis Management. Public Leadership under Pressure*, Cambridge: Cambridge University Press.

Börzel, T. A. (2001) 'Non-compliance in the European Union: pathology or statistical artifact?', *Journal of European Public Policy* 8(5): 803-824.

Börzel, T. A. (2003) *Environmental leaders and laggards in Europe: Why there is (not) a 'Southern Problem'*, Aldershot, UK: Ashgate.

Börzel, T. A. and T. Risse (2003) 'Conceptualising the domestic impact of Europe', in: K. Featherstone and C. Radaelli (eds.), *The Politics of Europeanization*, Oxford: Oxford University Press, pp. 57-80.

Börzel, T. A., T. Hoffmann and M. Dudziak (2005) *'Who's afraid of the ECJ? Member states, court referrals, and (non-) compliance'*, Paper presented at the 33rd Joint Sessions of Workshops, Granada, Spain.

Bolden, T. and R. Harman (2002) 'Realizing the new opportunity for railways', *Public Money and Management* 22(2): 61-66.

Bomberg, E. and A. Stubb (2003) *The European Union: How Does it Work?*, Oxford: Oxford University Press.

Borghetto, E., F. Franchino and D. Giannetti (2006) 'Complying with the transposition deadlines of EU directives. Evidence from Italy', *Rivista Italiana di Politiche Pubbliche* 1: 7-38.

Borooah, V. K. (2002) *Logit and Probit. Ordered and multinomial models*, London: Sage Publications.

Borrás, S. and K. Jacobsson (2004) The open method of co-ordination and new governance patterns in the EU, *Journal of European Public Policy* 11(2): 185-208.

Bovens, M. and Yesilkagit (2004) *'The impact of European legislation on national legislation in the Netherlands'*, USBO working paper, Utrecht.

Box-Steffensmeier, J. and S. J. Bradford (1997) 'Time is of the essence: Event history models in Political Science', *American Journal of Political Science* 41 (4): 1414-61.

Box-Steffensmeier, J. M., D. Reiter and C. Zorn (2003) 'Nonproportional Hazards and Event History Analysis in International Relations', *Journal of Conflict Resolution* 47 (1): 33-53.

Box-Steffensmeier, Janet and S. J. Bradford (2004) *Event History Modeling. A Guide for Social Scientists*, Cambridge: Cambridge University Press.

Brady, H. E. And D. Collier (2004) *Rethinking social inquiry: deverse tools, shared standards*, Lanham, MD: Rowman & Littlefield.

Braumoeller, B. F. and G. Goertz (2000) 'The methodology of necessary conditions', *American Journal of Political Science* 44(4): 844-858.

Brecher, M. (1977) 'Toward a theorie of international crisis behavior: A preliminary report', *International Studies Quarterly*, 21(1):39 – 74.

Buller and Gambler (2002) 'Conceptualising Europeanisation', *Public Policy and Administration* 17(2): 4-24.

Búrca, de G. (1992) 'Giving Effect to European Community Directives', *The Modern Law Review* 55(2): 215- 240.

Bursens, P. (2002) 'Why Denmark and Belgium have different implementation records: On transposition laggards and leaders in the EU', *Scandinavian Political Studies* 25(2):173-95.

Button, K. (1984) *Road haulage Licensing and EC Transport Policy*, Aldershot: Gower.

Button, K., K. Haynes and R. Stough (1998) *Flying into the future: Air transport policy in the European Union*, Northampton: E. Elgar.

Caporaso, J. A. and J. Wittenbrinck (2006) 'The new modes of governance and political authority in Europe', *Journal of European Public Policy* 13(4): 471-480.

Carré, M. (2000) 'Debt stabilization with a deadline', *European Economic Review* 44: 71-90.

Casella, A. and B. Eichengreen (1994) *'Can foreign aid accelerate stabilization?'*, Working paper no. 4694. NBER, Cambridge, MA.

Checkel, J. T. (2003) ''Going Native' in Europe? Theorizing Social Interaction in European Institutions', *Comparative Political Studies*, 36(1-2): 209-231.

Checkel, J. (2005) *It's the process stupid! Process tracing in the study of European and International Politics.* Arena working paper No. 26, http://www.arena.uio.no.

Ciavarini Azzi, G. (2000) 'The slow march of European legislation: The implementation of directives.' In: Karl-Heinz Neunreither and Anje Wiener (eds.), *European Integration after Amsterdam: Institutional dynamics and prospects for democracy,* Oxford: Oxford University Press, pp. 52-67.

Cini, M. (2003) *European Union Politics*, Oxford: Oxford University Press.

Collier, P., A. Hoeffler and M. Söderbom (2004) 'On the duration of civil war', *Journal of Peace Research* 41(3): 253-274.

Collier, P., H. E. Brady and J. Seawright (2004) 'Source of Leverage in Causal Inference: Toward an Alternative View of Methodology', in: H. E. Brady and D. Collier (eds.) *Rethinking Social Inquiry: Diverse Tools, Shared Standards*, Berkeley, CA: Rowman& Littlefield and Berkeley Public Policy Press.

Conant, L. (2002) *Justice contained. Law and Politics in the European Union,* New York: Cornell University Press.

Cortell, A. P. and S. Peterson (1999) 'Altered states: Explaining domestic institutional change', *British Journal of Political Science* 29: 177-203.

Council of the European Union (2006) *A strategic review of Better Regulation in the European Union*, COM (2006) 690 final.

Cress, D. M. and D. A. Snow (2000) 'The Outcomes of Homeless Mobilization: The Influence of Organization, Disruption, Political Mediation and Framing', *American Journal of Sociology* 105 (4): 1063-1104.

Curtin, D. (1990) 'Directives: The effectiveness of judicial protection of individual rights', *Common Market Law Review* 27: 709- 739.

Davidson Review (2006) *Implementation of EU legislation*, London: Better Regulation Executive Cabinet Office.

Demmke, C. (2001) *'Towards effective environmental regulation: innovative approaches in implementing and enforcing European environmental law and policy'*, Harvard Jean Monnet Working Paper 5/01, Cambridge, MA: Havard Law School.

Denzin, N. K. (1978) The logic of naturalistic inquiry. In N. K. Denzin (ed), *Sociological methods: A sourcebook.* New York: McGraw-Hill.

Deutsch, K. W., S. A. Burrell, R. A. Kann (1957) *Political community and the North Atlantic area: international organization in the light of historical experience,* Princeton: Princeton University Press.

Dienel, H.-L. and P. Lyth (1998) *Flying the Flag, European commercial Air Transport since 1945,* Basingstoke: Macmillan.

Dimitrakopoulos, D. G. (2001a) 'Learning and steering: Changing implementation patterns and the Greek central government', *Journal of European Public Policy* 8(4): 604-22.

Dimitrakopoulos, D. G. (2001b) 'The Transposition of EU Law: 'Post-decisional politics and institutional autonomy', *European Law Journal* 7(4): 442-458.

Dimitrakopoulos, D. G. (2005) 'Norms, interests and institutional change', *Political Studies* 53(4): 676-693.

Dimitrova, A. and B. Steunenberg (2000) 'The search for convergence of national policies in the European Union: an impossible quest?', *European Union Politics* 1: 201-26.

Dimitrova, A. and M. Rhinard (2005) 'The power of norms in the transposition of EU directives', *European Integration online Papers.*

Dinan, D. (1999) *Ever Closer Union. An Introduction to European Integration*, London: Routledge.

Di Pietrantonio, L. and J. Pelkmans (2004) *The Economics of EU Railway Reform,* Bruges European Economic Policy Briefings No 8, Bruges: College of Europe.

Dobbin, F. (1993) 'What do markets have in common? Toward a fast train policy in the European Community.', in Kjell Eliassen and Svein Andersen (eds) *Making Policy in Europe: The Europeification of national policy-making,* London: Sage, pp. 69-91.

Dobbin, F. (2001) 'Rail and Transport Policy: *National Paradigms and Supranational Structures', in S. Andersen and K. Eliassen (eds), Making Policy in Europe,* London: Sage.

Dowding, K. (2000) 'Institutionalist research on the European Union: A critical review', *European Union Politics* 1(1): 125-44.

Drazen, A. and V. Grilli (1993) 'The Benefit of Crises for Economic Reforms', *The American Economic* Review 83 (3): 598-607.
Duina, F. (1997) 'Explaining legal implementation in the European Union', *International Journal of the Sociology of Law* 25: 155-79.
Duina, F. and F. Blithe (1999) 'Nation-states and common markets: the institutional conditions for acceptance', *Review of International Political Economy* 6(4): 494-530.
Eichener, V. (1995) 'European Health and Safety Regulation: No "Race to the Bottom"', in: B. Unger and F. v. Waarden (eds). *Convergence or Diversity? Internationalization and Economic Policy Response*, Aldershot: Avebury.
Eijlander, P. and W. Voermans (2000) *Wetgevingsleer.* Den Haag: Boom Juridische Uitgevers.
El País, (2004) 'Fomento aplaza un ano la entrada en vigor de la ley que abrirá el ferrocarril a la competencia', by Galindo, C. and R. Munoz , p.60.
Erdmenger, J. (1983) *The European Community Transport Policy*, Aldershot: Gower.
European Commission, Annual Reports on Commission Monitoring of the Application of Community Law, (1984-2003): COM(84)181 final, COM(85)149 final, COM(86) 204 final, COM(87) 250 final, COM(88) 424 final, COM(89) 411 final, COM(90) 288 final, COM(91) 321 final, COM(92) 136 final, COM(93) 320 final, COM(94) 500 final, COM(95) 500 final, COM(96)600final, COM(97) 299 final, COM(98) 317 final, COM(99) 301 final, COM(2000) 92 final, COM(2001) 309 final, COM(2002) 324.
European Commission (2000) *Statistical eye on Europe. Eurostat yearbook. Data 1988-1998*, Luxembourg: European Commission.
European Commission (2001) *European Transport Policy for 2010: time to decide*, Brussels: DG Transport.
European Commission (2002) *Bettering monitoring of the application of community law*, COM (2002) 725 final.
European Commission (2002) *Panorama of transport. Statistical overview of transport in the European Union. Data 1970 -2000*, Luxembourg: European Commission.
European Commission (2002) *EU Intermodal Freight Transport. Key Statistical Data 1992-1999*, Luxembourg: European Commission.
European Commission (2002) *EU Energy and Transport Figures. Statistical pocketbook 2002*, Luxembourg: European Commission.
European Commission (2003) *The Internal Market Strategy – Priorities 2003-2006*, COM (2003) 238 final.
European Commission (2003) *Revitalising Europe's Railways. Towards an integrated European railway area*, Luxembourg: Office for Official Publications of the European Communities.
European Commission (2003) *Panorama of transport. Statistical overview of transport in the European Union. Data 1970-2000*, Luxembourg: Office for Official Publications of the European Communities.
European Commission (2004) *General Report on the Activities of the European Union*, Luxembourg: Office for Official Publications of the European Communities.
European Commission (2005) *Communication from the Commission to the Council and the European Parliament. Better Regulation for Growth and Jobs in the European Union*, Brussels.
European Commission (2005) *Lisbon Action Plan Incorporating EU Lisbon Programme and Recommendations for Actions To Member States for Inclusion in Their National Lisbon Programmes*, COM(2005) 24, SEC (2005) 192.
European Commission (2005) *Communication 'Implementing the Community Lisbon programme: A strategy for the simplification of the regulatory environment*, COM (2005) 535 final.
European Commission (2006) *Internal Market Scoreboard*, Brussels: Internal Market and Services DG.
Falkner, G., M. Hartlapp, S. Leiber and O. Treib (2004) 'Non-Compliance with EU directives in the Member States: Opposition through the Backdoor?', *West European Politics* 27(3): 452-473.
Falkner, G., O. Treib, M. Hartlapp and S. Leiber. (2005) *Complying with Europe? The Impact of EU Minimum Harmonisation and Soft Law in the Member States*, Cambridge: Cambridge University Press.
Falkner, G., E. Causse and C. Wiedermann (2006) *'Post-Accession Compliance in Central and Eastern Europe: Transposition and Application after the Age of Carrots and Sticks'*, Paper presented at the eps-net plenary conference, 16-17 June 2006, Budapest, Hungary.

Falkner, G., M. Hartlapp and O. Treib (2007) Worlds of Compliance: Why leading approaches to European Union implementation are only 'sometimes-true stories', *European Journal of Political Research* 46(3): 395- 416.

Farrell, H. and A. Héritier (2003) 'Formal and informal institutions under codecision: Continuous constitution building in Europe', *Governance* 16(4): 577-600.

Fearon, James D. (1998). 'Bargaining, Enforcement, and International Cooperation', *International Organization* 52 (2): 269-305.

Fearon, J.D. (2004) 'Why do some civil wars last so much longer than others?', *Journal of Peace Research* 41(3): 275-302.

Featherstone, K. and C. Radaelli (2003) *The Politics of Europeanization*, Oxford: Oxford University Press.

Fielding, N. G. and J. L. Fielding (1986) *Linking data. Qualitative Research Methods*. London: Sage.

Fischer, J., A. Kaiser and I. Rohlfing (2006) 'The push and pull of resignations in Germany, 1969-2005', *Electoral studies* 29(4): 709-735.

Flick, U. (1998) *An introduction to qualitative research*. Thousand Oaks, CA: Sage.

Franchino, F. (2004) 'Delegating Powers in the European Community', *British Journal of Political Science* 34: 269-293.

Franchino, F. (2005) 'A formal model of delegation in the European Union', *Journal of Theoretical Politics* 17(2): 217-247.

Franchino, F. (2005) 'The study of EU public policy – Results of a survey', *European Union Politics* 6 (2): 243-252.

From, J. and Stava, P. (1993) 'Implementation of Community Law: the last stronghold of national control', in: S.S. Andersen and K.A. Eliassen (eds), *Making Policy in Europe: The Europeification of National Policy Making*, London: Sage, pp. 55-67.

Gabel, M., S. Hix and G. Schneider (2002) 'Who is afraid of cumulative research? Improving Data on EU politics', *European Union Politics* 3(4): 481-500.

Gallagher, M., M. Laver and P. Mair (2001) *Representative governments in Modern Europe*, Boston: Mc Graw-Hill.

George, A. L. and A. Bennett (2005) *Case Studies and Theory development in the Social Sciences*, London: MIT Press.

George, S. and I. Bache (2001) *Politics in the European Union*, Oxford: Oxford University Press.

Gerring, J. (2004) 'What is a case study and what is it good for?', *American Political Science Review* 98 (2): 341-54.

Cil Ibánez, A. J. (1999) *The administrative supervision and enforcement of EC law: powers, procedures and limits*, Oxford: Hart.

Giorgi, Liana and Michael Schmidt (2003) 'European Transport Policy – a historical and forward looking perspective', *Working paper of the interdisciplinary centre for comparative research in the social sciences (IFS-ICCR-CIR)*, Vienna, Austria.

Giuliani, Marco (2003) 'Europeanization in Comparative Perspective: Institutional Fit and National Adaptation', in: Kevin Featherstone and Claudio Radaelli (eds.), *The Politics of Europeanization*, Oxford: Oxford University Press, pp. 134-155.

Giuliani, M. (2005) '*EU policies and domestic compliance: between International relations, Implementation and Europeanization*', Working Paper no. 5, Unità di Ricerca sulla Governance Europea (URGE), Fondazione Collegio Carlo Alberto, Moncalieri.

Giuliani, M. (2006) '*Dov'è il problema? L'Italia e il recepimento della normativa comunitaria*,' Unità di Ricerca sulla Governance Europea (URGE), Fondazione Collegio Carlo Alberto, Moncalieri. Goertz, G. (2002) 'Cause, Correlation, and Necessary Conditions', in: G. Goertz and H. Starr (eds.) *Necessary Conditions: Theory, methodology, and Application*, New York: Rowman and Littlefield, pp. 47-64.

Goertz, G. (2002) 'The Substantive Importance of Necessary Condition Hypotheses', in Gary Goertz and Harvey Starr (eds.) Necessary Conditions: Theory, methodology, and Application, New York: Rowman and Littlefield, pp. 65-94.

Goertz, G. and J. S. Levy (forthcoming) *Causal explanations, necessary conditions, and case studies: World War II and the end of the Cold War*.

Goertz, G. and H. Starr (2002) *Necessary Conditions: Theory, methodology, and Application*, New York: Rowman and Littlefield.

Goldman, K. (2005) 'Appropriateness and consequences: The Logic of Neo-Institutionalism', *Governance* 18(1): 35-52.
Golub, J. (1999) 'In the Shadow of the Vote? Decision Making in the European Community', *International Organization* 53 (4): 733-764.
Gomez, C. (2005) 'Los trenes privados brillan por su ausenscia', *El País* 11 December, p. 5.
Graziano, P. and M. Vink (2006) *Europeanization. New Research Agendas*, London: Palgrave Macmillan.
Greaves, Rosa (2000) *EC Transport Law*, London: Longman.
Green Cowles, M., J. Caporaso and T. Risse (eds.) (2001) *Transforming Europe: Europeanization and Domestic Change*, Ithaca and London: Cornell University Press.
Guardian (2000a) '*Paying up for dirty tankers*', Tuesday November 21, 2000 by Jonathan Wills.
Guardian (2000b) '*Tighten shipping controls, EU told*', Thursday November 21, 2000 by Paul Webster in Paris.
Haas, E. B. (1958) *The Uniting of Europe: Political, social and economic forces 1950-1957*, London: Stevens and Sons.
Haas, P.M. (2000) 'Choosing to comply: Theorizing from international relations and comparative politics', in: D. Shelton (ed.) *Commitment and compliance. The role of non-binding norms in the international legal system*, Oxford: Oxford University Press, pp. 43-64.
Häge, F. (2005) 'Constructivism, Fuzzy Sets and (Very) Small N: Revisiting the Conditions for Communicative Actions', *www.compass.org/Haege2005.pdf*.
Häge, F. and M. Kaeding (2007) Reconsidering the European Parliament's Legislative Influence: Formal vs. Informal Procedures', *Journal of European Integration* 29(3): 341- 361.
Haggard, S. (1990) *Pathways from the periphery: The Politics of Growth in the Newly Industrializing Countries*, Ithaca, NY: Cornell University Press.
Hendricks, K., A. 'Weiss and C. Wilson (1988) The War of attrition in continuous time with complete information', *International Economic Review* 29(4): 663-680.
Haverland, M. (2000) 'National adaptation to European integration: the importance of institutional veto points', *Journal of Public Policy* 20 (1): 83-103.
Haverland, Markus. (2001). 'The impact of the European Union on national environmental policies: The state of the art,', in: K. Featherstone and C. Radaelli (eds) *The politics of Europeanisation: Theory and analysis*, Oxford: Oxford University Press, pp. 203-224.
Haverland, M. (2006) 'Does the EU Cause Domestic Developments? Improving Case Selection in Europeanisation Research', *West European Politics* 29(1): 134-146.
Haverland, M. and M. Romeijn (2007) 'Do member states make European policies work? Analyzing the EU transposition deficit', *Public Administration* (forthcoming).
Héritier, A. (1997) 'Market-making policy in Europe: its impact on member state policies. The case of road haulage in Britain, the Netherlands, Germany and Italy', *Journal of European Public Policy* 4(4): 539-55.
Héritier, A. (2002) 'Public-interest services revisited', *Journal of European Public Policy* 9(6): 995-1019.
Héritier, A. (2003) 'New Modes of Governance in Europe: Increasing Political Capacity and Policy Effectiveness?', in: T. Börzel and R. Cichowski (eds.), *The State of the European Union. Law, politics and society*, Oxford, New York: Oxford University Press, pp. 105-126.
Héritier, A., D. Kerwer, C. Knill, D. Lehmkuhl, M. Teutsch, and A-C. Douillet, (2001), *Differential Europe: New Opportunities and Restrictions for Policymaking in the Member States*, Lanham, MD: Rowman and Littlefield.
Hille, P. and C. Knill (2006) 'It's the Bureaucracy, Stupid'. The implementation of the Acquis Communeautaire in EU Candidate Countries, 1999-2003', *European Union Politics* 7(4): 531-552.
Hirshman, A. (1985) 'Reflections on the Latin American Experience', in: Leon Lindberg and Chalres Maier (eds.) *The Politics of Inflation and Economic Stagnation: Theoretical approaches and International studies*, Washington, DC: Brookings Institution, pp. 53-57.
Hix, S. (2005) *The Political System of the European Union*, London: Routledge.
Hofmann, S. (1966) 'Obstinate or Obsolete? The Fate of the Nation State and the Case of Western Europe', *Daedalus* 95(4): 862-915.
Hood, C. (1983) *The tools of government*, London: Macmillan.

Hooghe, L. (2001) *The European Commission and the integration of Europe*, Cambridge: Cambridge University Press.
Hosmer, D. W, Jr., and S. Lemeshow (1999) *Applied Survival Analysis*. New York: John Wiley & Sons.
House of Commons (2006) *Lost in translation? Responding to the challenges of European law. Twenty-seventh report of session 2005-06*, London: The Stationery Office.
Hudson, G. (2005) *On the Trail of National Implementation measures*, Focus: University of Bradford, July / August 2005.
Jones, B. D. and F. R. Baumgartner (2005) *The politics of attention: how government prioritizes problems*, Chicago: Chicago University Press.
Jonsson, C. and J. Tallberg (1998) 'Compliance and post-agreement bargaining', *European Journal of International Relations* 4 (4): 371-408.
Jupille, J. (2005) *'A thousand flowers blooming? Methdological Practices in European Union Studies'*, EPS Newsletter Spring / Summer, pp. 2-6.
Jupille, J., and J.A. Caporaso (1999) 'Institutionalism and the European Union: Beyond International Relations and Comparative Politics', *Annual Review of Political Science* 2: 429- 444.
Kaeding, M. (2007) 'Administrative Convergence Actually – An Assessment of the European Commission's Best Practices for Transposition of EU Legislation in France, Germany, Italy, Sweden and Greece', *Journal of European Integration* 29(4): 425- 445.
Kaeding, M. (2006) 'Determinants of transposition delay in the European Union. The member state perspective,' *Journal of Public Policy* 26(3): 229-253.
Kaeding, M. and T. Selck (2005) 'Mapping out Political Europe: Coalition Patterns in EU Decision-Making', *International Political Science* Review 26: 271-290.
Kassim, H. (2005) 'The Europeanization of Member States Institutions', in: S. Bulmer and C. Lequesne (eds.) *The Member States of the European Union*, Oxford: Oxford University Press, pp. 285-316.
Kassim, H. , G. Peters and V. Wright (2000) *The national coordination of EU policy: the domestic level*, Oxford: Oxford University Press.
Katz, Aaron, Mattias vom Hau and James Mahoney (2005) 'Explaining the Great Reversal in Spanish America. Fuzzy Set Analysis versus Regression Analysis', *Sociological Methods and Research* 33(4): 539-573.
Keeler, J. T. S. (1993) 'Opening the window for reform: Mandates, crises and extraordinary policy making', *Comparative Political Studies* 25: 433-86.
Kernohan, D. (2005) 'Integrating Europe's Transport System. Practical Proposals for the Mid-Term Review of the Transport White Paper', Brussels: *CEPS Working Paper*.
Kersbergen, v. K., Lauwers (2005) *'The Social Construction of Rational Choice? A critical look at the research agenda of policy implementation and transposition in the EU'*, Paper presented at the workshop 'European integration, domestic institutions and policy-making', Politicologenetmaal, Antwerp 19-20 May 2005.
Kerwer, D. and M. Teutsch (2001) 'Transport Policy in the European Union', in A. Héritier et al. (eds.), *Differential Europe, The European Union Impact on National Policymaking*. Lanham, Md: Rowman & Littlefield, pp.23-56.
King, G., R. O. Keohane and S. Verba (1994) *Designing Social Inquiry: Scientific Inference in Qualitative Research*, Princeton: Princeton University Press.
Kingdon, J. W. (1995) *Agendas, Alternatives, and Public Policies*, New York: HarperCollins.
Knill, C. (2001) *The Europeanization of National Administrations: Patterns of Institutional Change and Persistence*, Cambridge: Cambridge University Press.
Knill, C. and Lehmkuhl, D. (2000) 'An Alternative Route of European Integration: The Community's Railways Policy', *West European Politics* 23(1): 65-88.
Knill, C., and A. Lenschow (1998) 'Coping with Europe: the Impact of British and German Administrations on the Implementation of EU Environmental Policy', *Journal of European Public Policy* 5: 595 -615.
Kok, W. (2004) *Facing the challenge. The Lisbon Strategy for growth and employment*, Luxembourg: European Commission.
König, T., B. Luetgert and L. Mäder (2005) *'Troubles with Timeliness: Explaining Trends in Transposition Delay'*, Paper presented at the 33rd Joint Sessions of Workshop in Granada, Spain.

Krippendorf, K. (2004) *Content Analysis. An Introduction to Its Methodology,* Thousand Oakes: Sage Publications.
Krislov, S., C. Ehlermann and J. Weiler (1986) 'The political organs and the decision-making process in the United States and the European Community', in: M. Cappelletti, M. Seccombe and J. Weiler (eds.), *Integration through Law: Eruope and the American Federal Experiece* (Volume 1, book 2), Berlin: Walter de Gruyter, pp. 3-110.
Kvist, J. (1999) 'Welfare reform in the Nordic countries in the 1990s. Using fuzzy set theory to assess conformity to ideal types', *Journal of European Social Policy* 9(3): 231-252.
Kvist, J. (2004) 'Does EU enlargement lead to a race to the bottom? Strategic interaction among EU member states', *Journal of European Social Policy* 14 (3): 301-318.
Kvist, J. (2006) 'Diversity, ideal types and fuzzy sets in comparative welfare state research', in: B. Rihoux and H. Grimm (eds.) *Innovative Comparative Methods for Policy Analysis: Beyond the quantitative-qualitative divide,* New York: Springer, pp. 167-184.
Ladrech, R. (1994) 'Europeanization of Domestic Politics and Institutions: The Case of France', *Journal of Common Market Studies* 32(1): 69-88.
Lampinen, R. and P. Uusikyla. (1998) 'Implementation Deficit – Why Member States do not Comply with EU directives?', *Scandinavian Political Studies* 21(3): 231-251.
Laver, M. and K. A. Shepsle (1994) *Cabinet Ministers and Parliamentary Government*, Cambridge: Cambridge University Press.
Laver, M. and K.A. Shepsle (1996) *Making and Breaking Governments,* Cambridge: Cambridge University Press.
Lawton, T. C (1999) 'Governing the Skies: Conditions for the Europeanisation of Airline Policy', *Journal of Public Policy* 19: 91-112.
Levy, J. S. (2002) 'The role of necessary conditions in the outbreak of World War I', in: G. Goertz and H. Starr (eds.) *Necessary Conditions: Theory, methodology, and Application,* New York: Rowman and Littlefield, pp. 41-70.
Lewis, I., J. Semeijn and D.B. Vellenga. (2001) 'Issues and initiatives surrounding rail freight transportation in Europe', *Transportation Journal* 41 (2-3): 23-31.
Lieberman, E. S. (2005) 'Nested Analysis as a Mixed-Method Strategy for Comparative Research', *American Political Science Review* 99(3): 435-452.
Lieberson, S. (1992) 'Small n's and big conclusions: An examination of the reasoning in comparative studies based on a small number of cases', in: C.C. Ragin and H. Becher (eds) *What is a case? Exploring the Foundation of Social Inquiry,* Cambridge: Cambridge University Press, pp. 105-128.
Lindberg, L. N. (1963) *The Political Dynamics of Economic Integration.* Oxford: Oxford University Press.
Linos, K. (2007) How Can International Organizations Shape National Welfare States? Evidence From Compliance With European Union Directives, *Comparative Political Studies* 40 (5): 547-570.
Long, J. S. (1997) *Regression models for categorical and limited dependent variables, vol. 7 of Advanced Quantitative Techniques in the Social Sciences,* Thousand Oaks, CA: Sage Publications.
Long, J. and J. Freese (2003) *Regression Models for categorical dependent variables using Stata,*Texas: Stata Press.
Lowi, T. J. (1964) 'American Business, Public Policy, Case-Studies, and Political Theory', *World Politics* 16: 677-715.
Mahoney, J. (2000) 'Path Dependence in Historical Sociology', *Theory and Society* 29: 507- 548.
Mahoney, J. (2003) 'Long-Run Development and the Legacy of Colonialism in Spanish America', *American Journal of Sociology* 108 (1): 50-106.
Mair, P. (2004) 'The Europeanization Dimension', *Journal of European Public Policy* 11 (2): 337-348.
Majone, G. (1991) 'Cross-National Sources of Regulatory Policy-making in Europe and the United States', *Journal of Public Policy* 11(1): 79-106.
Majone, G. (1994) 'The Rise of the Regulatory State in Europe', *West European Politics* 17(3): 78-102.
Majone, G. (1996) *Regulating Europe,* London: Routledge.

Mandrup, T. Raudi and E. Pennings (2002) *Het wetgevingsprocess in Denemarken*, Den Haag: Ministerie van Justitie, Kenniscentrum Wetgeving.
Marks, G., L. Hooghe and K. Blank (1996) 'European Integration from the 1980s: state-centric versus multi-level-governance', *Journal of Common Market Studies* 34(3).
Martin, L. W. (2004) 'The Government Agenda in Parliament', *American Journal of Political* 48 (3): 445-461.
Martin, L. W. and G. Vanberg (2004) 'Policing the Bargain: Coalition Government and Parliamentary Scrutiny', *American Journal of Political Science* 48(1): 13-27.
Martin, L.W. and G. Vanberg (2005) 'Coalition Policymaking and Legislative Review', *American Political Science Review* 99(1): 93-106.
Mastenbroek, E. (2003) 'Surviving the deadline: Transposition of EU directives in the Netherlands', *European Union Politics* 4(4): 371-355.
Mastenbroek, E. (2005) 'EU Compliance: Still a 'black hole'?', *Journal of European Public Policy* 12(6): 1103-1120.
Mastenbroek, E. (2007) *The politics of compliance. Explaining the transposition of EC directives in the Netherlands,* Wageningen: Ponsen&Looijen.
Mastenbroek, E., and M. van Keulen (2006) 'Beyond the goodness of fit. A preference-based account of Europeanization', in: M. Haverland and R. Holzhacker (eds.), *European research reloaded: Cooperation and integration among Europeanized states.* Kluwer: Deventer, pp.19-42.
Mastenbroek, E. and M. Kaeding (2006) 'Europeanization beyond the goodness of fit: Domestic Politics in the forefront', *Comparative European Politics* 4: 331-354.
Mazmanian, D. and P. Sabatier (1981) 'The implementation of Public Policy: A Framework of Analysis', in: D. Mazmanian and P. Sabatier (eds.), *Effective Policy Implementation,* Lexington: Lexington Books.
Mbaye, H. A. D. (2001) 'Why National States Comply with Supranational Law', *European Union Politics* 2(3): 259-281.
McCormick, J. (2005) *Understanding the European Union,* London: Palgrave Macmillan.
McCreevy (2005) *The Internal Market Strategy Implementation – Scoreboard Press Conference on the Internal Market Strategy Implementation Scoreboard*, Brussels, 23 January 2005.
Mendriou, M. (1996) 'Non-compliance and the European Commission's role in integration', *Journal of European Public Policy* 3(1): 1-22.
Metcalfe, J. S. (1994) 'Evolutionary Economics and technology policy', *The Economic Journal* 104: 931-944.
Mitrany, D. (1966) *A Working Peace System*, Chicago: University of Chicago Press.
Moravcsik, A. (1991) 'Negotiating the Single European Act: National Interests and Conventional Statecraft in the European Community', *International Organization* 45(1): 19-56.
Moravcsik, A. (1998) *The Choice for Europe: Social Purpose and State Power from Messina to Maastricht,* London: Cornell University Press.
Müller, W. C. and K. Strom (2004) *Coalition Governments in Western Europe,* Oxford: Oxford University Press.
Nash, C. and T. Sansom (2001) 'Pricing European transport systems – Recent developments and evidence from case studies', *Journal of Transport Economics and Policy* 35: 363-380.
Nicolaides, P. and H. Oberg (2006) *The Compliance Problem in the European Union,* EIPASCOPE 2006/1.
Niemann, A. (2004) 'Between Communicative Action and Strategic Action: the 133 Committee and the negotiations of the WTO Basic Telecommunications Services Agreement', *Journal of European Public Policy* 11(3): 379-408.
Nugent, N. (1999) *The Government and Politics of the European Union,* London: Routledge.
Nugent, N. (2003) *The Government and Politics of the European Union*, Durham: Duke University Press.
Nyikos, S. A. and M. A. Pollack (2003) *'Researching the European Union: Qualitative and Quantitative Approaches'*, Paper presented at the EUSA conference 2003.
Olsen, J. (2002) 'The Many Faces of Europeanization', *Journal of Common Market Studies*, 40. 921-952.

O'Reilly, D. and A. Stone Sweet (1998) 'The Liberalization and Re-Regulation of Air Transport', *Journal of European Public Policy* 5(3): 447-66.
Ostner, I. and J. Lewis (1995) 'Gender and the Evolution of European Social Policy', in: S. Leibfried and P. Pierson (eds), *European social policy: Between fragmentation and integration*, Washington DC: Brookings Institution.
Pahre, R. (2005) 'Formal Theory and Case-Study Methods in EU Studies', *European Union Politics* 6 (1): 113-146.
Paixao, A. C. and P. B. Marlow (2001) 'A review of the European Union shipping policy', *Maritime Policy & Management* 28(2): 187-198.
Pallis, A. (2002) *The Common EU Maritime Transport Policy*, Aldershot: Ashgate.
Pappas, S. A. and P. Arpino (1995) *National administrative procedures for the preparation and implementation of community decisions*, Maastricht: Institut europeen d'administration publique.
Pelkmans, J. (2001) *European integration: Methods and economic analysis*, London: Prentice Hall.
Pennings, P. (2002) *'The diversity of welfare state reforms explored with fuzzy sets,'*, Paper presented at the joint sessions of workshops of the ECPR in Torino, Italy, 22-27 March 2002.
Pennings, P. (2003) 'Beyond dichotomous explanations: Explaining constitutional control of the executive with fuzzy-sets', *European Journal of Political Research* 42: 541-567.
Perkins, R. and E. Neumayer (2007) Do Membership Benefits Buy Regulatory Compliance? An Empirical Analysis of EU Directives, 1978- 99, *European Union Politics* 8(2): 180- 206.
Philip, C. (2004) *La transposition des directives européennes*, Paris: Assemblée Nationale, 1 July 2004 (Rapport d'information Assemblée Nationale no. 1709).
Pierson, P. (2004) *Politics in Time : History, Institutions, and Social Analysis*, Princeton : Princeton University Press.
Plaza Martin, C. (1994) 'Furthering the effectiveness of EC directives and the judicial protection of individual rights thereunder', *International and comparative law quarterly* 43(1): 26-54.
Pollack, M. A. (2001) 'International Relations and European Integration', *Journal of Common Market Studies* 39(2): 211-244.
Ponsati, C. (1995) 'The deadline effect: A theoretical note', *Economics Letters* 48: 281-285.
Ponti, M., M. A. Cappiello (2000) 'Road Transport', in: G. Galli and J. Pelkmans (eds.) *Regulatory Reform and Competitiveness in Europe*, 2, Brussels: CEPS publication, pp. 228-261.
Prechal, S. (1995) *Directives in European Community Law. A study of directives and their enforcement in national courts*, Oxford: Oxford University Press.
Pressman, J. L. and A. Wildavsky (1973) *Implementation. How Great Expectations In Washington Are Dashed in Oakland; or, Why It's Amazing That Federal Programs Work At All*, Los Angeles: University of California Press.
Przeworski, A. and H. Teune (1970) *The Logic of Comparative Social Inquiry*, New York: Wiley.
Radaelli, C. M. (2007) *Towards Better Research on Better Regulation*, Paper delivered to the Advanced Colloquium on Better Regulation Centre for Regulatory Governance, University of Exeter, 25-26 January 2007.
Ragin, C.C. (1987) *The comparative method: Moving beyond qualitative and quantitative strategies*, Berkeley: University of California Press.
Ragin, C.C. (2000) *Fuzzy-set social science*, Chicago: University of Chicago Press.
Ragin, C.C. and P. Pennings (2005) 'Fuzzy Sets and Social Research', *Sociological Methods and Research* 33(4): 423-430.
Raiffa, H., J. Richardson and D. Metcalfe (2002) *Negotiation analysis: the science and art of collaborative decision-making*, Cambridge: Havard University Press.
Rehbinder, E. and R. Stewart (1984) *Environmental Protection Policy: Integration through Law. Europe and the American Federal Experience*, Vol. 2. Berlin: de Gruyter.
Renda, A. (2006) *Impact Assessment in the EU. The State of the Art and the Art of the State*, Brussels: CEPS Publication.
Rhioux, B. (2006) 'Two methodological worlds apart? Praises and critiques from a European comparativist', *Political Analysis* 14(3): 332-355.
Rhioux, B. (2006) 'Qualitative Comparative Analysis (QCA) and Related Systematic Comparative Methods. Recent Advances and Remaining Challenges for Social Science Research', *International Sociology* 31(5): 679-706.

Rihoux, B. and H. Grimm (2006) *Innovative Comparative Methods for Policy Analysis: Beyond the quantitative-qualitative divide,* New York: Springer.

Richardson, J., G. Gustafson and G. Jordan (1982) 'The concept of policy style', in: J. Richardson (ed.) *Policy styles in Western Europe,* London: George Allen& Unwin, pp. 1-16.

Risse, T. (2001) 'A European Identity? Europeanization and the Evolution of Nation-State Identities.', in: M. Green Cowles, J. Caporaso and T. Risse (eds) *Europeanization and Domestic Change. Transforming Europe,* Ithaca: Cornell University Press, pp: 198-216.

Risse, T. (2003) 'Social Constructivism and European Integration', in: T. Diez and A. Wiener (eds.), *European Integration Theory,* Oxford: Oxford University Press.

Rodrik, D. (1994) 'Comment', in: Williamson, J. (ed.) *The Political Economy of Policy Reform,* Institute for International Economics, Washington, DC, pp: 212-215.

Rohlfing, I. (2005) '*What you see (possibly) isn't what you get- a two-step procedure for nesting case studies in regression analysis*', Paper presented at the Annual Meeting of the American Political Science Association, September 1-4, 2005.

Rosamond, B. (2000) *Theories of European Integration,* London: Palgrave.

Ross, J. F. L (1998) *Linking Euorpe: Transport Policies and Politics in the European Union,* Westport, CT: Praeger.

Rubinstein, A. (1982) 'Perfect equilibrium in a bargaining model', *Econometrica* 50 (1): 97-109.

Sachs, J. (1994) 'Life in the economic emergency room', in: Williamson, J. (ed) *The Political Economy of Policy Reform,* Institute for International Economics, Washington, D.C., pp: 503-523.

Sandholtz, W. and A. Stone Sweet (1997) 'European Integration and Supranational Governance', *Journal of European Public Policy* 4(3): 297-317.

Sbragia, A. (2001) 'Italy Pays for Europe: Political Leadership, Political Choice, and Institutional Adaptation', in: M. Green Cowles, J. Caporaso and T. Risse (eds) *Europeanization and Domestic Change. Transforming Europe,* Ithaca: Cornell University Press, pp: 79-96.

Scharpf, F.W. (1996) 'Negative and positive integration in the political economy of European welfare states.', in: G. Marks, F. W. Scharpf, P. C. Schmitter, and W. Streeck (eds) *Governance in the European Union,* London: Sage.

Scheerlinck, I. L.M.A. Hens and R. S'Jegers (1998) 'On the road to transport liberalization? Belgian road hauliers' policy preferences', *Journal of Transport Economics and Policy* 32: 365-381.

Schimmelfennig, F. (2000) 'International Socialization in the New Europe: Rational Action in an Institutional Envrionment', *European Journal of International Relations* 6 (1): 109-139.

Schmidt, M. and L. Giorgi (2001) 'Successes, Failures and Prospects for the Common Transport Policy', *Innovation* 14 (4): 293-313.

Schmidt, M. and L. Giorgi (2003) 'Institutional development and the Accession Process: The Case of Transport', *ICCR IFS CIR working paper.*

Schroeder, P. (2002) 'Necessary Conditions and World War I as an unavoidable war', in G. Goertz and H. Starr (eds.) *Necessary Conditions: Theory, methodology, and Application,* New York: Rowman and Littlefield, pp. 123-161.

Schulz, H. and T. König. (2000) 'Institutional reform and decision-making efficiency in the European Union', *American Journal of Political Science* 44(4): 653-666.

Shepsle, K. A. and M. S. Boncheck (1997) *Analyzing Politics. Rationality, Behavior, and Institutions,* London: W. W. Norton & Company.

Shughart II, W. F. and L. Razzolini (2004) *The Elgar Companion to Public Choice,* Cheltenham: Edward Elgar.

Siedentopf, H. and J. Ziller (1988) *Making European policies work: the implementation of Community legislation in the member states,* London: Sage Publications.

Smith, J. M. (1974) 'The theory of games and evolution in animal conflict', *Journal of Theoretical Biology* 47: 209-221.

Smith, A and A.C. Stam (2004) 'Bargaining and the nature of war', *Journal of Conflict Resolution* 48 (6): 783-813.

Smithson, M. and J. Verkuilen (2006) *Fuzzy Set Theory. Applications in the Social Science,* London: Sage.

Snyder, F. (1993) 'The effectiveness of European Community Law: Institutions, processes, tools and techniques', *The Modern Law Review* 56(1): 19-54.

Spinelli, A. (1972) 'The Growth of the European Movement since the Second World War', in: M. Hodges (ed.), *European integration*, Harmondsworth: Penguin.
Spongenberg, H. (2006) 'Brussels to launch 50 energy law cases', *EUobserver* 3.4.2006, http://euobserver.com/9/21291.
Stata (2001) *Stata Statistics, Graphics, Data Management References*, Texas: Stata Press.
Stephen, D. (2004) 'Regulation by Brussels? The Myths and the Challenges', *European Movement Policy Paper* 2, London.
Steunenberg, B. (2006) 'Turning swift policymaking into deadlock and delay: National policy coordination and the transposition of EU directives', *European Union Politics* 7: 293-319.
Steunenberg, B. (2007) 'A Policy Solution to the European Union's Transposition Puzzle: Interaction of Interests in Different Domestic Arenas', *West European Politics* 30(1): 23-49.
Steunenberg, B. and M. Rhinard (2005) 'Hare or Turtle? Member States catching up with the transposition of EU directives', Leiden University Working paper.
Steunenberg, B. and W. Voermans (2005) *De omzetting van Europese richtlijnen: Instrumenten, technieken en processen in zes lidstaten vergleken*, WODC: Leiden Universiteit. [The transposition of EU directives: Instruments, techniques and processes in six member states.]
Steunenberg, B. and M. Kaeding (2007) When time goes bye. Explaining the transposition of maritime directives. Leiden University working paper.
Stevens, H. (1997) '*Liberalisation of Air Transport in Europe*', Working Paper at the European Institute, London School of Economics and Political Science.
Stevens, H. (2004) *Transport Policy in the European Union*, London: Palgrave, Macmillan.
Strom, K., W.C. Müller and T. Bergman (2003) *Delegation and Accountability in Parliamentary Democracies*, Oxford: Oxford University Press.
Sverdrup, U. (2002) 'An institutional perspective on treaty reform: contextualizing the Amsterdam and Nice Treaties', *Journal of European Public Policy* 9 (1): 20-140.
Sverdrup, U. (2004) Compliance and conflict resolution in the European Union – Nordic exceptionalism', *Scandinavian Political Studies* 27(1): 23-43.
Sverdrup, U. (2005) 'Implementation and European integration: A review essay', *Arena working paper* 25, October 2005, http://www.arena.uio.no.
Tallberg, J. (2002) 'Paths to compliance: Enforcement, management and the European Union', *International Organization* 56 (3): 609-43.
Tashakkori, A. and C. Teddlie (2003) *Handbook of mixed methods in social and behavioural research*, London: Sage.
Tashakkori, A. and C. Teddlie (1998) *Handbook of mixed methods in social and behavioural research*, London: Sage.
Taylor, P. (1982) 'Intergovernmentalism in the European Communities in the 1970s: Patterns and Perspectives', *International Organization* 36(4): 741-66.
Teutsch, M. (2001) 'Regulatory Reforms in the German Transport Sector: How to Overcome Multiple Veto Points', in A. Héritier, D. Kerwer, C. Knill, D. Lehmkuhl, M. Teutsch, and A.C. Douillet, (eds.) *Differential Europe: New Opportunities and Restrictions for Policymaking in the Member States*, Lanham, MD: Rowman and Littlefield, pp: 133-172.
Thomson, R., R. Torenvlied and J. Arregui (2005) '*Executive discretion and the paradox of compliance in the European Union*', Paper presented at the ECPR Joint Sessions, Granada, 14-19 April, 2005.
Thomson, R. , F. N. Stokman, C. H. Achen and T. König (2006) *The European Union Decides*, Cambridge: Cambridge University Press.
Tinbergen, J. (1965) *International Economic Integration*, Amsterdam: Elsevier.
Tomz, M., J. Wittenberg and G. King (2001) '*Clarify: Software for Interpeting and Presenting Statistical Results*', typescript (http://GKing.Harvard.edu).
Toshkov, D. (2007) In Search of the Worlds of Compliance: Culture and Transposition Performance in the European Union, *Journal of European Public Policy* (forthcoming).
Treib, O. (2003) 'Die Umsetzung von EU-Richtlinien im Zeichen der Parteipolitik: Eine akteurzentrierte Antwort auf die Misfit-These', *Politische Vierteljahresschrift* 44(4): 506-528.
Treib, O. (2003) '*EU governance, misfit and the partisan logic of domestic adaptation: an actor-centered perspective on the transposition of EU directives*', Paper presented at the EUSA 8th International Biennial Conference, Nashville, Tennesse, 27-29 March 2003.

Treib, O. (2006) Implementing and complying with EU governance outputs, *Living Reviews in European Governance 1*, CONNEX and NEWGOV.
Treib, O. and G. Falkner (2007) Making Dead Letters Live: Strategies to Improve the Effectiveness of EU Legislation in Central and Eastern Europe, Paper presented at the EUSA 10th Biennial International Conference, 17-19 May 2007, Montreal, Canada.
Tsebelis, G. (2001) *Veto Players Data,* URL (accessed 04.07.2004) http://www.polisci.ucla.edu/tsebelis/.
Tsebelis, G. (2002) *Veto players: How political institutions work,* Princeton: Princeton University Press.
Tullock, G. (1967) *Towards a mathematics of politics,* Ann Abor: Michigan University Press.
Verkuilen, J. (2005) 'Assigning Membership in a Fuzzy Set Analysis', *Sociological Methods and Research* 33(4): 462-496.
Versluis, E. (2004) 'Explaining Variations in Implementation of EU Directives', *European Integration online Papers,* Vol. 8, N° 19, http://eiop.or.at/eiop/texte/2004-019a.htm
Vink, M. (2003) 'What is Europeanization? And Other Questions on a New Research Agenda', *European Political Science,* 3:1: 63-74.
Vogel, D. (1986) *National Styles of Regulation. Environment Policy in United Kingdom and the United States,* Ithaca/London: Cornell University Press.
Waarden v., F. (2006) 'Taste, Traditions, Transactions and Trust: The Public and Private Regulation of Food', in: C. Ansell and D. Vogel (eds.) *'What's the Beef?' The contested governance of European Food Safety,* Cambridge: MIT Press, pp. 35-59.
Wallace, H. and W. Wallace (2000) *Policy-making in the European Union,* Oxford: Oxford University Press.
Wallace, H., W. Wallace and M. Pollack (2005) *Policy-making in the European Union,* Oxford: Oxford University Press.
Weatcroft, S. and G. Lipman (1986) *Air Transport in a Competitive European Market,* London: The Economist Publications Ltd.
Wecheln von, H. (1999) *Lokale Wirkungen und geänderte Politik. Der PALLAS- Unfall.* SDN Magazin.
Wessels, W., A. Maurer and J. Mittag. (2003*) Fifteen into One. The European Union and its member states,* Manchester: Manchester University Press.
Whitelegg, J. (1988) *Transport Policy in the EEC,* London: Routledge.
WMU (2006) 'International Maritime Legislation – the EU and enforcing resolutions', *Journal of Maritime Affairs.*
Yin, R. K. (1993) *Applications of case study research,* London: Sage.
Zeff, E. E. and E. B. Pirro (2001) *The European Union and the member states: cooperation, coordination, and compromise,* Boulder: Lynne Riener.
Zeff, E. E. and E. B. Pirro (2006) Road Safety: A Lesson in the Complexities of EU policy-making, EUSA Public Interest Section Essay, Fall 2006.
Zeff, E. e. and E. B. Pirro (2007) EU transportation policy. The challenge of Europeanization, Paper presented at the EUSA 10th Biennial International Conference, 17-19 May 2007, Montreal, Canada.

Interview partners

Interview partners (1998/55/EC and 2001/14/EC):

Olga Lefèvre, MTETM/DGMT/MMD, Ministry of Transport, Paris, 19.12.2005.

Sergio Cavalho, Directorate General for Energy and Transport, European Commission, 20/21 October 2005, Brussels.

Angel Cuesta Muñoz, Director de Asuntos Europeos, Administrador de infraestructuras ferroviarias (ADIF), 12 December 2005, Madrid.

Rafael Garcia Alcolea, Vocal Asesor, Dirección General de Ferrocarriles, Ministerio de Fomento, 12 December 2005, Madrid.

Jan Scherp, Rail Transport and Interoperability Unit, Directorate General for Energy and Transport, European Commission, 20 October 2005, Brussels.

Joaquin Jiménez Otero, Director Corporativo de Relaciones Internacionales, Administrador de infraestructuras ferroviarias (ADIF), 12 December 2005, Madrid.

Santiago Badillo Diaz, Jefe de Organismos Internacionales, Administrador de infraestructuras ferroviarias (ADIF), 12 December 2005, Madrid.

Interview partners (2001/53/EC and 2002/59/EC):

James Wood, Assistant to the Director, Bureau of the Executive Director, European Maritime Safety Agency (EMSA), Brussels, 1.11.2005.

Francisco Broissin Capo, Project Officer, Marine Equipment, European Maritime Safety Agency (EMSA), Brussels, 1.11.2005.

Joseph Benoît, Marine Equipment Certification Manager, Marine Division Technical Management, Bureau Veritas, Paris, 14.11.2005.

Sophie Sanquer, SM2 division: regulation and ship safety office, Directorate of Maritime Affairs, Maritime safety Department, Paris, 14.11.2005.

Beate Beckmann, Internationale und EU-Seeverkehrspolitik, Recht des Seeverkehrs, Bundesministerium für Verkehr, Bau- und Stadtentwicklung, Bonn, 6.12.2005.

Peter Escherich, Referat LS 23, Maritime Sicherheit, Seeleute, Bundesministerium für Verkehr, Bau – und Stadtentwicklung, Bonn, 6.12.2005.

Sergio Cavalho, Directorate General for Energy and Transport, European Commission, 20/21 October 2005, Brussels.

Alexandro Martínez– Godin, European Commission, DG Transport TREN A 4. Marché intérieur, service public, concurrence et droits des usagers, 1.12.2002-30.11.2006.

Author and subject index

Curriculum vitae

Michael Kaeding was born on 19 June 1977 in Wuppertal (Germany) where he received his *Abitur* at the *St. Anna Schule* in 1996. From 1997 to 2002, he studied Public Policy and Management at the University of Konstanz, Moscow State University (Russia) and *Università degli Studi di Pavia* (Italy). In October 2002, he graduated with a master thesis on rapporteurship assignments in the European Parliament. From December 2002 to November 2006, he worked as a Ph.D. fellow in a NWO-funded research project on 'Analyzing EU Policies: The Transposition of Directives ' at the Department of Public Administration of Leiden University in the Netherlands. He followed post-graduate training at the ECPR Summer School in Data Analysis and Social Sciences in Essex, the Oslo Summer School at ARENA, the Copenhagen Business School and the Netherlands Institute of Government. From December 2006 to September 2007, he was a Postdoc in the GAK-financed project *'Hervorming Sociale Zekerheid'* at the Leiden Department of Tax Law and Economics. His publications include articles for *European Union Politics, Journal of Public Policy, Journal of European Public Policy, Journal of Common Market Studies, Comparative European Politics, French Politics, Journal of European Integration, European Law Journal, Journal of Legislative Studies* and *International Political Science Review*. He gained teaching experience at the University of Konstanz (Germany), Leiden University (the Netherlands), the University of Victoria (Canada) and the University of Grenoble (France). Work experience includes the Delegation of the European Commission to the U.S. (Political Section and Press & Public Affairs), the Secretariat General of the Council of the European Union (DGC III Transport) and the Brussels-based Centre for European Policy Studies (CEPS). Currently Michael Kaeding is a Lecturer at the EU Decision-Making Unit of the European Institute for Public Administration (EIPA) in Maastricht, the Netherlands.

In de boekenreeks van het E.M. Meijers Instituut voor Rechtswetenschappelijk Onderzoek van de Faculteit der Rechtsgeleerdheid, Universiteit Leiden, zijn in 2006 en 2007 verschenen:

MI-100 J.H. Nieuwenhuis & C.J.J.M. Stolker (red.), *Vooruit met het recht. Wat geldt in de rechtswetenschap als vooruitgang?*, Den Haag: Boom Juridische uitgevers 2006, ISBN 90 5454 741 3

MI-104 E.C.C. Punselie, *Voor een pleegkind met recht een toekomst*, (diss. Leiden), Deventer: Kluwer 2006, ISBN 90 13 03328 8

MI-105 A. Hendriks, *In beginsel. De gezondheidsrechtelijke beginselen uitgediept*, (oratie Leiden), Leiden: NJCM-boekerij 2006, ISBN 90 6750 046 1

MI-106 T. Barkhuysen, *Eenheid en coherentie van rechtsbescherming in de veellagige Europese rechtsorde*, (oratie Leiden), Deventer: Kluwer 2006, ISBN 90 1303 568 X

MI-107 N.J.H. Huls & Z.D. Laclé, *Meer macht voor de consument?*, Deventer: Kluwer 2006, ISBN 90 5454 697 2

MI-108 W. Zwalve, *Simplex et perpetuum. Beschouwingen over eigendom en tijd*, Den Haag: Boom Juridische uitgevers 2006, ISBN 90 54547 12 X

MI-109 T.J. de Graaf, *Exoneraties in (ICT-)contracten tussen professionele partijen*, Deventer: Kluwer 2006, ISBN 90 1303 660 0

MI-110 N. Jungmann, *De Wsnp: bedoelde en onbedoelde effecten op het minnelijk traject*, Amsterdam: Amsterdam University Press 2006, ISBN 90 8728 004 1

MI-111 R. van Alebeek, *The Immunity of States and their Officials in the Light of International Criminal Law and International Human Rights Law*, (diss. Leiden) 2006

MI-112 J.H. Gerards, *Belangenafweging bij rechterlijke toetsing aan fundamentele rechten* (oratie Leiden), Deventer: Kluwer 2006, ISBN 90 13 03837 9

MI-113 W. Huisman, L.M. Moerings en G. Suurmond (red.), *Veiligheid en recht. Nieuwe doelwitten en strategieën*, Boom Juridische uitgevers 2006, ISBN 90 5454 732 4

MI-114 A.C. Rijkers & H. Vording (red.), *Vijf jaar Wet IB 2001*, Deventer: Kluwer 2006, ISBN 90 13 03851 4

MI-115 T. Barkhuysen, W. den Ouden & Y.E. Schuurmans (red.), *Het model Tak: Verhoogde rechtsbescherming in het bestuursrecht?*, Alphen aan den Rijn: Kluwer 2006, ISBN 90 1303 852 2

MI-116 Y.E. Schuurmans (red.), *Bewijzen en beslissen*, Deventer: Kluwer 2006, ISBN 90 1303 756-9

MI-117 H.J.Th.M. van Roosmalen, *Overheidsaansprakelijkheid in Engeland en Nederland*, (diss. Leiden), Den Haag: Sdu 2007, ISBN 978 90 12 11846 0

MI-118 R.W.J. Crommelin, *Het aanvullen van de rechtsgronden*, (diss. Leiden), Alphen aan den Rijn: Kluwer 2007, ISBN 978 90 13 04635 9

MI-119 L.A.R. Siemerink, *De overeenkomst van Internet Service Providers met consumenten*, (diss. Leiden), Deventer: Kluwer 2007, ISBN 90 13 04357 7

MI-120 I.S.J. Houben, K.J.O. Jansen, P. Memelink, J.H. Nieuwenhuis & L. Reurich (red.), *Europees contractenrecht. Techniek en moraal*, Deventer: Kluwer 2007, ISBN 90 13 04036 5

MI-121 S. Hillebrink, *Political Decolonization and Self-Determination. The Case of the Netherlands Antilles and Aruba*, (diss. Leiden) 2007, ISBN 978 90 9021470 2

MI-122 B.W. Schermer, *Software agents, surveillance, and the right to privacy: a legislative framework for agent-enabled surveillance*, (diss. Leiden) 2007, Leiden: Leiden University Press 2007, ISBN 978 90 8728 021 5

MI-123 C.G. Breedveld-de Voogd, *Vorm, vrijheid en gebondenheid bij de koop van een woning*, (diss. Leiden), Den Haag: Boom Juridische uitgevers 2007, ISBN 978 90 5454 412 8

MI-124 T. Barkhuysen, W. den Ouden & T. Steyger (red.), *Europees recht effectueren. Algemeen bestuursrecht als instrument voor de effectieve uitvoering van EG-recht*, Deventer: Kluwer 2007, ISBN 978 90 13046 28 1

MI-125 A.C. Beunen, *Protection for databases, The European Database Directive and its effects in the Netherlands, France and the United Kingdom*, (diss. Leiden), Nijmegen: Wolf Legal Publishers 2007, ISBN 978 90 5850 267 4

MI-126 Z. Deen-Racsmány, *Active Personality and Non-extradition of Nationals in International Criminal Law at the Dawn of the Twenty-first Century: Adapting Key Functions of Nationality to the Requirements of International Criminal Justice,* (diss. Leiden), Leiden: Leiden University Press

MI-127 C.P.L. van Woensel, MERK, GOD EN VERBOD, Oneigenlijk gebruik en monopolisering van tekens met een grote symbolische waarde, (diss. Leiden), Amstelveen: Uitgeverij deLex BV 2007, ISBN 978 90 8692 010 5

MI-128 J.A.J. Peter, Levering van roerende zaken, (diss. Leiden), Deventer: Kluwer 2007, ISBN 978 90 13043 81 5

MI-129 A.C. Hendriks & H.-M.Th.D. ten Napel (red.), *Volksgezondheid in een veellagige rechtsorde. Eenheid en verscheidenheid van norm en praktijk,* Alphen a/d Rijn: Kluwer 2007, ISBN 978 90 13 04720 2

MI-130 H.R. Kranenborg, *Toegang tot documenten en bescherming van persoonsgegevens in de Europese Unie. Over de openbaarheid van persoonsgegevens,* (diss. Leiden), Deventer: Kluwer 2007, ISBN 978-90-13-04886-5

Zie voor de volledige lijst van publicaties: www.law.leidenuniv.nl/onderzoek

Printed in Dunstable, United Kingdom

91343646R00138